Ayurveda
The Science of
Self-healing

Ayurveda
The Science of Self-healing

Vaishali Verma

ABD PUBLISHERS
Jaipur ■ New Delhi

ABD PUBLISHERS

Regd. Off. "Bony Residency", Gate No. 2
Opp. Tilak Public School, Vishweswariya Nagar,
Gopalpura Road, Jaipur - 302018, India
Ph: 0141 - 2761280, Telefax: 2761381
Email: abdpublishersjpr@gmail.com

Delhi Office: 102, 1st Floor, Satyam House,
4327/3, Ansari Road, Darya Ganj,
New Delhi - 110002, India
Ph: 011-45652440

visit us: www.oxfordbookcompany.com

Distributed By
KEYA INTERNATIONAL PRESS LLP
E-mail: keyainternationalpressllp@gmail.com

Published in India, 2025

ISBN : 978-81-19343-20-1

Typeset by Shivangi Computer, Jaipur

Printed and bound in India by Thomson Press Ltd.,
New Delhi

Contents

Preface

Ayurveda, or Ayurvedic medicine, is a traditional medical system that uses a holistic approach to improve physical and mental health. It originated in India in the 2nd century BC and is still widely used there. Ayurvedic medicine focuses on restoring the balance between a person's mind, body, spirit, and environment. Treatment involves a personalized plan that includes diet, movement, massage, herbs, and other therapies. The word "Ayurveda" is derived from the Sanskrit word *Ayu* (life) and *Veda* (knowledge or science). Ayurveda centers around the idea that imbalance leads to illness. These elements combine to form three energy types in the human body: Pitta dosha (air and space), Vata dosha (water and fire), and Kapha dosha (earth and water). Together, these Tridoshas help regulate how the body functions. In Ayurveda, the body is comprised of seven types of tissues known as Sapta Dhatus.

Tri Malas and Agni are other important elements in Ayurveda. Tri Malas involves three types of waste products: sweat, urine, and feces. Agni represents the biological fire that helps carry out metabolic processes. Imbalances in either Tri Malas or Agni can lead to a variety of conditions including digestive issues and skin irritation. Each dosha is associated with specific physical qualities, personality traits, and emotional strengths and weaknesses. Every person has a combination of all three doshas, but one or two doshas are usually dominant. Vata dosha consists of the elements air and space (also called ether). Vata qualities include cold, light, dry, subtle, and rough. People with strong vata tend to be creative, lighthearted, energetic, and flexible decision-makers. They often have a more delicate build and speak more quickly than other doshas. Pitta dosha consists of the elements fire and water. Pitta qualities include hot, liquid, sharp, and pungent. People with strong pitta tend to be strong-willed, direct, and fierce with opponents. They often have a medium, more muscular build. Pitta involves processes responsible for metabolism, digestion, vision, and temperature regulation. Kapha dosha consists of the elements water and earth. Kapha qualities include soft, cold, stable, and heavy. People with strong kapha tend to be calm, loving, and caring. They often have a strong build and move more slowly than other doshas. Kapha involves joint lubrication, processes for storage and stability, and maintenance and growth of body structures. Ayurveda believes that diet affects your genetic constitution (Prakriti) and supports healing processes. Diet also affects the three doshas. Ayurvedic medicine includes following a diet that helps bring your predominant dosha into greater balance with your other doshas. For example, Vata is light, rough, and cold. Eating heavy, smooth, and warm foods can help bring a Vata person into greater balance. In the United States, Ayurveda is considered a complementary or alternative health approach. It might offer some benefits, but more research is needed to determine its effectiveness for specific conditions, as well as the safety of products that might contain potentially toxic ingredients.

This comprehensive book clearly explains the principles and practical applications of Ayurveda, the oldest healing system in the world. The book will be useful for all those interested in Ayurveda and its self healing applications.

— ***Vaishali Verma***

Chapter 1

History and Philosophy of Ayurveda

Introduction

Ayurveda, or Ayurvedic medicine, is a traditional medical system that uses a holistic approach to improve physical and mental health. It originated in India in the 2nd century BC and is still widely used there. Ayurvedic medicine focuses on restoring the balance between a person's mind, body, spirit, and environment. Treatment involves a personalized plan that includes diet, movement, massage, herbs, and other therapies. In the United States, Ayurveda is considered a complementary or alternative health approach. It might offer some benefits, but more research is needed to determine its effectiveness for specific conditions, as well as the safety of products that might contain potentially toxic ingredients.

Principles of Ayurveda

The word "Ayurveda" is derived from the Sanskrit word Ayu (life) and Veda (knowledge or science). Ayurveda centers around the idea that imbalance leads to illness.

According to Ayurveda, the universe is made of five elements:

- Jala (water)
- Vayu (air)
- Prithvi (earth)
- Aakash (space)
- Teja (fire)

These elements combine to form three energy types in the human body: Pitta dosha (air and space), Vata dosha (water and fire), and

Kapha dosha (earth and water). Together, these Tridoshas help regulate how the body functions.

In Ayurveda, the body is comprised of seven types of tissues known as Sapta Dhatus. These include:

- Rakta Dhatu (blood tissue)
- Rasa (plasma)
- Meda (adipose or fat tissue)
- Mamsa (muscular tissue)
- Majja (bone marrow)
- Shukra (reproductive tissue)
- Asthi (bone tissue)

Tri Malas and Agni are other important elements in Ayurveda. Tri Malas involves three types of waste products: sweat, urine, and feces. Agni represents the biological fire that helps carry out metabolic processes. Imbalances in either Tri Malas or Agni can lead to a variety of conditions including digestive issues and skin irritation.

The Three Doshas: Each dosha is associated with specific physical qualities, personality traits, and emotional strengths and weaknesses. Every person has a combination of all three doshas, but one or two doshas are usually dominant.

Vata Dosha: Vata dosha consists of the elements air and space (also called ether). Vata qualities include cold, light, dry, subtle, and rough. People with strong vata tend to be creative, lighthearted, energetic, and flexible decision-makers. They often have a more delicate build and speak more quickly than other doshas.

Vata involves processes that are responsible for cell signaling and division, electrolyte imbalance, waste elimination, movement, and cognition.

Pitta Dosha: Pitta dosha consists of the elements fire and water. Pitta qualities include hot, liquid, sharp, and pungent. People with strong pitta tend to be strong-willed, direct, and fierce with opponents. They often have a medium, more muscular build.

Pitta involves processes responsible for metabolism, digestion, vision, and temperature regulation.

Kapha Dosha: Kapha dosha consists of the elements water and earth. Kapha qualities include soft, cold, stable, and heavy. People with strong kapha tend to be calm, loving, and caring. They often have a strong build and move more slowly than other doshas.

Kapha involves joint lubrication, processes for storage and stability, and maintenance and growth of body structures.

Ayurvedic Diet: Ayurveda believes that diet affects your genetic constitution (Prakriti) and supports healing processes. Diet also affects the three doshas.

Ayurvedic medicine includes following a diet that helps bring your predominant dosha into greater balance with your other doshas. For example, Vata is light, rough, and cold. Eating heavy, smooth, and warm foods can help bring a Vata person into greater balance.

Here are some diet recommendations based on predominant doshas:

- Vata: Eat foods that are fresh, warm, and heavy with sweet, sour, or salty tastes. Avoid bitter and astringent foods that leave a drying sensation in your mouth, like apples or unripe bananas. Too much fasting leads to greater Vata imbalance.
- Pitta: Eat foods that are hot, less oily, and light. Avoid sour or salty foods, as well as canned foods, vegetable oils, instant foods, coffee, and vinegar. A mostly vegetarian diet helps balance Pitta.
- Kapha: Eat warm and light foods with a bitter or astringent taste. Avoid sweet, sour, or salty foods, as well as frozen foods and cold water. A lower-carbohydrate and lower-fat diet supports Kapha.

The 12 Best Herbs and Spices for Better Health

Ayurvedic Treatment: Ayurveda focuses on personalized treatments to prevent illness and disease, as well as reduce symptoms. Ayurvedic practitioners will ask questions about your diet, lifestyle, medical history, environmental conditions, dosha characteristics, and general health status to help determine whether you're experiencing any imbalances or possible symptoms. They will then suggest a treatment approach that aligns with your health condition and imbalances.

Ayurvedic medicine includes Panchakarma, a treatment method that cleanses and rejuvenates the body and promotes longevity. The steps include:

1. Preparing the body for the treatment
2. Main treatment
3. Procedures to return the body to its normal state

Ayurvedic treatment options include herbs, dietary changes, detoxification, Ayurvedic massage (which uses warm herbal oils), meditation, and yoga.

Does Ayurveda Work: Several clinical trials and systematic reviews suggest that Ayurveda can be effective, particularly the herbs and supplements used in treatment.

For example, one clinical trial of 440 people with knee osteoarthritis found that Ayurvedic preparations of plant extracts reduced pain and improved function as well as the non-steroidal anti-inflammatory (NSAID) drug Celebrex (celecoxib). Ayurvedic herbs such as black cumin, garlic, and guggul have been reported to moderately improve hypercholesterolemia (high cholesterol).

Research often focuses on particular elements of Ayurveda, like specific herbs, yoga, or massage. Other potential benefits of Ayurvedic medicine include:

- Reducing raised cortisol levels, which is one of the effects of stress
- Supporting a healthy immune system
- Improving cognitive function

Improving sleep quality and efficiency: Ayurveda still lacks sufficient scientific evidence. There's also great variability within Ayurveda-for example, in the components and dosage of different preparations.

Larger, more rigorous studies that monitor participants for longer periods of time could help determine potential benefits of Ayurvedic treatment approaches for different conditions.

Possible Risks and Side Effects: Ayurveda is most often well tolerated. However, there are some potential risks.

Some herbs can lead to gastrointestinal side effects such as:

- Diarrhea
- Constipation
- Nausea
- Vomiting
- Heartburn

More severe side effects include:

- Ulcer (painful sore on the lining of the stomach or lower intestine)

- Kidney disease
- Bradycardia (low heart rate)
- Hypotension (low blood pressure)
- Infertility

Some commonly used herbs are contraindicated for certain conditions. For example, curcumin (turmeric) slows blood clotting, so it can worsen some bleeding conditions.

More research is needed to determine the safety of Ayurvedic treatments during pregnancy and breastfeeding, as well as for children. The origin of the product is not always clear, and some products might be harmful.

Drug Interactions: Herbs used in Ayurveda might interact with medications. Here are a few herbs commonly used in Ayurveda and possible interactions:

- Ashwagandha: Diabetes medications, immunosuppressants (medications that reduce your body's immune response), anticonvulsants (anti-seizure medications), and thyroid hormone medications
- Ginger: Anticoagulants (blood thinners) like aspirin, Coumadin (warfarin), and heparin (brand names include Lovenoz and Fragmin)
- Holy basil: Thyroid hormone medications, anticoagulation drugs, and antiplatelet drugs (medications that prevent blood clots)

Always consult with a licensed healthcare provider before taking any Ayurvedic herbs.

Heavy Metal Poisoning: Some Ayurvedic supplements contain heavy metals like lead, mercury, or arsenic. One meta-review of 220 case reports and series found that most participants had elevated levels of heavy metals. Many people had levels of heavy metals above the permissible limit per the Food and Agriculture Organization/ World Health Organization (FAO/WHO).

Another small study of people who use Ayurvedic supplements found elevated blood levels of lead in 40% of participants. About 25% of the preparations exceeded the recommended maximum level of lead and about 50% exceeded the recommended maximum level of mercury.

Other Considerations: Ayurvedic practice or study has no significant regulation in the United States. Practitioners are not required to have licenses.

Like other supplements, Ayurvedic preparations are not regulated by the Federal Drug Administration (FDA) The effects of these products vary from person to person and depend on many variables, including type, dosage, frequency of use, and interactions with current medications. Always speak with a licensed healthcare provider or pharmacist before starting any supplements, especially if you're pregnant, have a medical condition, or are taking any medications.

A Quick Review: Ayurveda is one of the oldest medical systems. It originated in India and is still widely used there. Ayurvedic medicine focuses on holistic approaches that promote health by balancing the body, mind, and spirit.Ayurvedic treatment involves dietary changes, herbs, massage, yoga, and meditation. These treatment components have many potential benefits.

However, more research is needed to determine how Ayurveda might affect specific symptoms and conditions. Possible risks include side effects of herbs, drug interactions, and heavy metal poisoning. It's important to talk to your healthcare provider before trying Ayurveda.

Ayurveda And The Western Mind

According to Indian thoughts, manas (mind) is one of the major operational concepts in the process of learning and the cause of bandha (entanglement/attachement). Manas has dimension which is anu (beyond atom in its minutest aspect), and is capable of remaining atindriya (beyond sensory perception). An attempt has been made to focus on various aspects like concept of atma, evolution and constituents of man, location of manas, dimension and qualities of manas and process of Jnanotpatti etc.

Sitting amidst a mountain of wealth and prosperity man lives a life of worry, anxiety and discontentment, which is a sad paradox. This state can be overcome by understanding manas which is mainly responsible for pleasure-pain perceptions. Therefore, ayurveda, the ancient wisdom of life, which aims at the blissful state of man, lays emphasis on the need of overcoming the impediments like, Kama (desire) and Krodha (anger) which are reflected in the form of psychological, social and physical illnesses, and prescribes methods to ward them off effectively. Charaka defines ayu (life) as the combined state of shareea (body), indriya (senses), satwa (psyche) and atma (soul). The first two are grosser entities and easy to understand. The latter two are subtler and beyond sensory experience, hence difficult to understand. The need for understanding manas assumes greater importance for it is the yoking principle between shareera and atma.

Atma in Ayurveda

Being an evolute of Vedas, it is natural that ayurveda has accepted some of the imoprtant philosophical postulates like the theory of punarjanma (rebirth), karmaphala (results of actions from one birth to another), karanashareera (body of causality), sookshma shareera (subtle or etheral body), to mention a few, in order to solve the problems of chikitsapurusha (treatable man) and bestow him the blissful state. It is said that after ones death the results of the right or wrong acts of the individual are carried along with sookshma shareera, causing birth in the womb of different species. Atma (jeevatma) is given greater importance while explaining punarjanma since all the other concepts are ultimately linked with it. Atma is called 'kharta' (doer) and 'bhokta' (experiencer). Icha, dwesha, sukha (pleasure), duhkha (pain), prayatna (initiation), dhriti (control), chetana (life), buddhi (decision), smriti (memory) ahankara (ego) are some of the attributes of atma. Among these, icha (desire), dwesha (hatred), prayatna (effort) and budhi (decision) denote 'kartrtwa' and sukha and duhkha denote 'bhoktrtwa' of atma. But the fact is that manas is always associated with atma and only during this association atma will be either karta or bhokta or both. In other words, atma will be the 'knower' and manas will be the 'doer' representing atma. Atma is said to exert its influence in the emergence of ayu (life span), manas (psyche), indriya (senses), prana (inspiration), apana (exopiration), prerana (induction), akrta (shape), swara (voice), varna (complexion), sukha (pleasure), duhkha (pain), icha (desire) dwesha (hatred), chetana (consciousness), dhriti, budhi, smriti (memory), ahankara (ego) etc., of the foetus in embryonic state itself [6]. Thus the knowledge about atma is essential for a better understabnding of chikitsapurusha.

Evolution and Constitutents of Man

The theory of creation of universe described in ayurveda is a postulate based on the sankhya, vaiseshika and other ancient philosophical schools. As it appears, the evolutionary scheme is not necessarily chronological in the stricter sense and the order put forth is mainly for transactional convenience, since the evolutionary process transcends time limitations. It is also said that each of the evolutes will possess the basic characteristics of the priciples from which it originates. According to Sushruta who closely follows the sankhya view of '25 principles of evolution,' avyakta (unmanifest) is the first priciple in the process of chetanasrsti (animate creation). Mahan (magnum) is the second evolute generated from avyakts. From mahan, ahankara (I ness) is evolved . This ahankara is of three types viz., satwika (neutral or pure) or vaikarika ahankara, rajasa (passionate) or taijasa ahankara and tamasa (inert) or bhootadi ahankara. Vaikarika ahankara with the aid of taijasa ahankara produces the five buddhendriyas, five karmendriyas and manas. Similarly, bhootadi ahankara with aid of taijasa ahankara gives rise to the five tanmatras which in turn produce the five bhootas. When purusha, the 25th principle joins them, chetana srsti takes place. These 25 principles have been categortised into 4 categories viz., prakrty, prakrtivikrti, vikrty and naprakriti navikrti. Avyakta is termed as moola prakrti (primordial principle). Mahan, ahankara and the panchatanmatras are called as sapta prakrtivikrtis.

The five jnanendriyas, five karmendriyas and manas are known as shodashavikrtis. The twentyfifth principle viz., purusha is termed as naprakrti-navikrti. Among them, moolaprakrti and the seven prakrtivikrtis are collectively termed as astaprakrtis. Charaka considered only 24 of the above 25 principles of evolution by merging purusha (the 25th principle according to Sushruta) with avyakta. He also calls purusha as kshetrajna, the remaining 23 principles as kshetra, mahat as buddhi and the astaprakrtis as dhatuprakrtis. According to Charaka avyakta or purusha is the first principle. From avyakta, mahan (buddhi) is evolved and from mahan, ahankara is evolved. From ahankara the 5 khadeeni, 5 arthas and ekadashendriyas viz., 5 -jnanendriyas, 5 karmendriyas and manas are evolved. However, Charaka does not consider the 3 types of ahankara put forth by Sushruta.Although he considers first Khadeeni and then the arthas in the chronology of evolution Chakrapani the commentator opines that the 5 Khadeeni should be understood as the 5 sookshmabhootas or tanmatras. Thus both Sushruta and Charaka consider the astaprakrtis and the evolutes of ahankara, alike. Further, commenting on the 5 arthas Chakrapani suggests that the five arthas should be understood as 5 bhootas since the subtler gunas (arthas) viz., shabda, sparsha, roopa, rasa and gandha can not be understood without the grosser gunas or principles viz, akasha, vayu, agni, jala and prithwi. This also appears logical since it is natural for grosser principles to evolve from the subtler ones and not the vice-versa and our process of understanding is also from grosser to sublter aspects. Even in the process of pralaya (dissolution) of the srsti it is said that the vyakta (grosser) principles will convulge into the avyakta (subtle) state. Chakrapani also clarifies that this view by stating that the panchabhootas, punchatanmatras, ahankara, mahan and atma merge into one another in an ascending sequence in the process of dissolution. Further, it would also be logical to consider that both tanmatras and ekadashendriyas coalesce with ahankara together since both are derived from it is simultaneously.

Charaka terms the state of congolmeration of the 24 principles as 'chaturvimshatika purusha'. Man is also said to be the product of the six elements viz, atma, and the Panchabhootas (elements) and hence termed 'shatdhatu purusha'. Some opine that man is constituted of atma alone and they call man, 'ekadhatu' or 'chetana dhatupurusha'. Thus, 3 kinds of Purusha are explained in the ayurvedic works. However, the concept of shatdhatu purusha is the one which is ultimately accepted by Charaka. The concepts of Chaturvimshatika purusha and ekadhatu purusha could also be explained under shatadhatu purusha concept as follows: (a) Avyakta, buddhi, mahat, ahankara and manas are included under chetana (atma). The remaining aspects viz, the 10 indriyas, 5 tanmatras, and panchabhootas are inclucded under khadayah. Thus the concept of chaturvimshatika purusha is explained under shatadhatu purusha. (b) Since chetana is already considered in explaining the concept of shatdhatu purusha the concept of chetana purusha can as well be understood under shatadhatu purusha. Thus, these three views though appear divergent from one another, are synonymous with each other when critically examined. Purushavichaya ie., Eco-self or universe- individual theory of ayurveda presented by Charaka illustrates the inseparable relationship between man and his environment and their mutual interactions.

A knowledge of this universe-individual relationship is essential in understanding the true nature of man.

Manas and Panchabhootas

There are two divergent views about the nature of manas in relation to the panchabhootas (five elements). Some scholars opine that manas is panchabhautika while some argue that it is non panchabhautika or non-physical. Both quote textual references in favour of their views. But if the texts are critically examined it would be possible to conclude that there are no strong points to claim that 'manas is panchabhautika'. However, it is a fact that oushadha, ahara and vihara, influence manas in its well-being, creativity, causation of its imbalance and finally in the treatment of manas vikaras. Therefore, consideration of panchabhootas would be essential at the stage of preservation and promotion as well as prevention and cure of manasika vikaras from the viewpoint of an ayurvedic physician.

Concept of life and health in relation to manas: Ayu (life) is defined as the combined state of shareera, indriya, satwa and atma. Here satwa refers to manas. It is classified as hitayu (good life) as well as ahitayu (bad life) and sukhayu (happy life) and asukhayu (unhappy life). The life of such a man is called sukhayu who is not afflicted with either bodily or mental ailments, who is endowed with youth, strength, virility, reputation, enterprise and boldness, who is wealthly and prosperous, and who can plan as he likes. A life contrary to this is deemed asukhayu. The life of that man is said to be hitayu, who is a well wisher of all creatures, who does not covet other's goods, who is honest and peace loving, who acts with deliberation, is not negligent, is devoted to the 3 ends namely dharma (righteousness) artha (wealth) and kama (desires) without letting anyone come into conflict with the other two, who revers elders, who is scholarly, scientific and of retiring disposition, of well curbed passion, desires, anger, envy, pride and conceit, constantly given to charitable acts, devoted always to austerity, knowledge and quietitude, endowed with spiritual insight, contemplative of the good in this world and the next, and endowed with memory and understanding.

That life which is of the opposite nature to this, is said to be ahitayu. Manas is considered as the factor responsible for yoking atma with shareera and indriya. The concept of ayu is based on the state of manas for, manas is chiefly responsible for perceiving sukha, dukha, hita, ahita etc., in relation to life. Briefly speaking, sukhayu and asukhayu refer to the individual's physical well or ill being while hitayu and ahitayu refer to the social and spiritual well or ill being of an individual. In other words, sukhayu and asukhayu refer to mind body relationship whle hitayu and ahitayu refer to the psychosocial and psychospiritual relationship as ayurveda gives equal importance to the welfare of manas here and hereafter. Thus the importance of manas is understood in relation to life. Let us now examine the relationship of manas with health. A person is said to be healthy when the doshas and bodily elements are balanced and harmonious, when the digestion is normal, when the excretion of waste products is unimpaired and when he is endowed with tranquility and clarity of soul, mind and senses. Lucid descriptions are available in the texts to illustrate that the 3 doshas, the 7 bodily elements digestive activities, the excretory function and the indriyas are liable to be impaired by manas even when they are normal. This demonstrates the importance of manas in calling a person swastha or healthy. Therefore, an accurate knowledge of manas will be the base in order to understand even the fundamentals like what is life, and health. In other words, without the knowledge of manas, nothing can be rightly percieved of pursued. This makes the study of manas all the more important.

Definition and synonyms of manas: According to Charaka, that entity by which contemplation and understanding are made possible is known as manas. Citta, cetus, cetana, hrdaya, hrit, swanta, manasam, mana, satwa are its synonyms. Citta, cetus and cetana denote the origin of perception, hrit and hrdaya indicate the sensory attraction and sensory control.

Location of Manas

1. Although there are five sense organs with the corresponding objects of theirs, there is only one faculty viz, th.
2. The place between shiras (head) and talu (hard palate) is said to be the seat of manas according to Bhelasamh.
3. Like Charaka, Bhela also considers that citta which is the cause of all activities, feeling and judgement, is loc. According to Sushruta when manas is tired and clouded with inaction, karmatma withdraws from vishayas (subjects) and this results in the man getting sleep. According to Astangasangraha also, heart is the seat of satwa.
4. While describing the functions of some of the different moities of the tridoshas viz., pranavayu, udanavayu, v.

It is interesting to note that even at the time of Charaka, head was considered as one of the three major marmas (vital spots) of the body where in the senses, and the vital centres of living being are situated. Causation of mental dearrangement due to head injury was also known at the time. By going through these textual descriptions, it is possible to crystallise the ayurvedic aproach on the functions of manas vedic approach on the functions of manas into two categories viz.,

(1) activities related to indriyas and

(2) activities related to the emotions.

The activities of the indriyas are related with brain while the activities of the emotions are connected with heart.

Dimensions and Qualities of Manas

1. Manas is said to be constitued of 3 operational qualities viz., satwa or kalyanabhaga, rajas or roshabhaga. These are understood by the role they play in the emergence of the three response patterns. Satwa is indicated by self-control, knowledge, discriminative ability, power of exposition etc. Rajas is indicated by violence, despotic envy, authoritativeness, self-adoration etc. Tamas is indicated by dullness, non-action, sleep etc. These three qualities act as the functional dimensions of manas.
2. Satwa rajas and tamas by virtue of their influence give rise to seven types of satwika, six types of rajasa.
3. Buddhi, smrti and dhrti are recognised as intrinsic dimensions of manas. The word manas when used in general sense, refers to the totality of 'knowing' or 'doing' and indicates buddhi, smrti and dhrti as well. Manas as a specific term refers only to its intial contact with the vishaya (object), in other words 'perception' in the process of doing or knowing. In a given kriya (act or process), manas (general) is called smrti at the level of recall, buddhi at the level of decision and dhrti in the moderation of the act throughout. Manas has been attributed with two intrinsic qualities viz., anutwa and ekatwa meaning its dimension which is beyond atom in its manifest aspect and oneness. These denote the asarvagata, asarvavyapaka and ekadesheeya nature of manas in contrast to those of atma. Manas and atma being eternally coexistent, participate in all acts of man. Manas is also said to possess the capacity to carry the psychic imprints of the previous birth to the present one.

Action of manas and jnanotpatti: Indriyabhigraha (controlling the senses), swanigraha (selfcontrol), ooha (guess), and vichara (discriminative ability) are the actions of manas.

Indriyabhigraha refers to the proper functioning of jnanedriya and karmendriya in the absence of any defects in the indriyas (ceebral organic factors-central) or Indriyadhisthanas (sensory and motor organs-peripheral) which impeded the functions of indriyas apart from disordered manas. Manonigraha refers to mental control which is the ability to concentrate on something and stick to the given task or chosen course of action without being unduly interrupted by the distracting stimuli from outside. Ooha refers to the subject's ability to guess different possibilaties when he comes across a familiar situation. Vichara refers to the ability to discriminate between right and wrong, possible and impossible, acceptable and unacceptable etc.,

Following the actions of manas, buddhi decides which is good or right, what is to be done etc., in a given act. The objects of manas are those which are chintya (thought about), vicharaya (discriminated from), oohya (speculated upon), dhyeya (aimed at) and sankalpya (decided upon). Manas is indicaed by the presence of cognition as well as the absence of cognition. Knowledge occurs when the sequential relationship of indriyartha (sensory objects), indriya (senses), and manas including atma (soul) is established. Thus, in the foregoing pages certain conceptual details pertaining to manas as described in ayurveda (keeping chikitsa-purusha in view) are presented.

Ayurveda and the Mind-Body Connection

Have you ever wondered just how much impact your state of mind has on your health? This has long been debated, and is somewhat difficult to study empirically. But the short answer, at least according to Ayurveda, is that the mind has a very powerful influence on our overall health and well-being.

Ayurveda defines health not only as an absence of disease, but as a completely holistic level of vitality throughout all facets of our lives. As a result, the Ayurvedic approach to treating any single aspect of our health begins with taking into account the whole of who we are-body, mind, and spirit.

Similarly, the Ayurvedic tradition recognizes that any of these three aspects of self-body, mind, or spirit-can either support or undermine our well-being, making the mind one of three equally influential players in our overall health.

Ayurveda considers even minor disturbances in the mind to be deeply influential, with the potential to compromise the quality of our lives, and to cause any number of diseases-physical and otherwise.

Thankfully, Ayurveda also provides us with a very elegant and insightful perspective on the mind, and on the art of fostering its health-a thriving state of mental, emotional, and even spiritual well-being. With this goal in mind, Ayurveda offers a number of practical and powerfully effective tools for balancing common disturbances of the mental and emotional realm.

Whether you are interested in fine-tuning the habits of your mind, strengthening your mental acuity, or simply cultivating a more calm and peaceful emotional state, you've come to the right place. We will begin by exploring the Ayurvedic perspective on the mind and conclude with links to several useful resources geared toward supporting you in cultivating vibrant mental and emotional health.

The Big Picture: According to Ayurveda, the body is a crystallization of the mind.

So just as impaired agni and indigestion are at the root of all diseases, the mind also plays a critical role in our overall health. In fact, mental ama (toxins) and unresolved emotions can lead to disease in very concrete ways.

For example, unresolved anger can accumulate in the liver and impair its functioning, unprocessed grief can disturb the lungs, and chronic anxiety can upset the health of the colon. Beyond these, there are countless other ways that imbalances in the mind can manifest as physical disease.

When it comes down to it, the mind is incredibly influential and has a very direct and potent impact on our overall health and well-being-making the channel of the mind genuinely worthy of our sincere care and attention.

Ultimately, our focused efforts to support the channel of the mind can't help but ripple out to positively impact every cell, tissue, and subtle pathway throughout our mind-body ecology.

The Channel of the Mind

According to Ayurveda, substances and energies move throughout the body via distinct channels-both physical and energetic-known as srotamsi. Remarkably, one of the primary channels named in the Ayurvedic tradition is the channel of the mind, known in Sanskrit as mano vaha srotas.

The fact that there is a channel of the mind at all tells us how important a role the mind plays in our overall health and longevity. And the more we explore the particulars of this channel, the more we will see how significant and influential it actually is.

But before we delve into the Ayurvedic perspective, let's examine our own personal and cultural preconceptions for a moment. Briefly reflect on this idea of "mind." What are your natural associations with it? And where in the body do you imagine the mind resides?

Here in the West, most of us think immediately of the head. Our culture tends to associate the mind with the brain itself, and so we are naturally inclined to envision the "mind" residing within the confines of the cranium. But in no way does Ayurveda subscribe to these same limitations.

Instead, the Ayurvedic tradition defines the mind far more broadly. Ayurveda's map of the mind quite elegantly reveals its significance in the broader landscape of who we are-both in terms of its level of importance, and also in terms of its vast field of influence on our overall mind-body ecology.

Ayurveda's Map of the Mind

For each of the major srotamsi, Ayurveda describes a root (mula), a pathway through the body (marga), and an opening (mukha). These aspects of each channel serve to orient us to its prominent locations in the body, illuminate important influences upon it, and inform our approach when it comes time to restore balance.

The Root of the Mind: In general, the root of each channel is seen as the developmental center, or point of origin, for that particular srotas. As such, it tends to hold a unique significance for the channel system as a whole. Think back to where you first imagined the mind might be located in the body-very likely the brain. Now, consider this: according to Ayurveda, mano vaha stortas is rooted-not in the brain-but in the heart. Let me say that one more time. The channel of the mind is rooted in the heart.

It is also located in the ten great vessels, but we'll get to that in a moment. So as soon as we begin to explore the channel system of the mind, Ayurveda asks us to get out of our heads and step into our hearts. This is incredibly significant because the Vedic sciences of Ayurveda, Yoga, and Tantra all view the heart as a critically important energetic hub in the body-a meaningful intersection of a diverse range of physical and energetic pathways.

Picture a wagon wheel with the heart at the center, each spoke representing a different system, channel, or substance that either originates from, resides within, or passes through the heart.

For example, of the thirteen srotamsi present in both men and women, three of them are rooted in the heart. This is notable because it is actually rather unusual for the physical location of distinct channels to overlap at all. Incidentally, the three channels rooted there also happen to permeate the entire physical body-which is also rare. So we are beginning to get a sense of the heart as the powerhouse organ and energy center that it is. The heart is intimately connected to every cell and tissue throughout the body, three different times, through three distinct channels. No other organ in the Ayurvedic srotamsi shares that level of integration with the entire body.

The heart center is also said to be the very seat of our emotional experience, home to our purest form of self. And of course, the heart chakra (anahata chakra) is associated with our capacity for unconditional love. As the root of the mind, all of these energies that are associated with the heart take on a newfound significance. In truth, Ayurveda invites us to adopt a fundamentally expanded view of the mind as a whole-one that includes the heart and its connection to the entire body.

The Ten Great Vessels

The fact that the mind is also rooted in the ten great vessels (an important set of subtle energetic pathways that inform the subtle body) is a testament to the profound level of influence that subtle energies have upon the mind. While this is a vast and meaningful topic, we will keep our exploration brief.

For now, it is important to understand that of the ten great vessels, the three that are considered most influential are the solar, lunar, and central channels-ida, pingala, and sushumna.

These nadis, or subtle energy channels, travel from the base of the spine to the crown of the head, intersecting at each of the seven chakras, and are said to carry the flow of prana, or life force. These subtle channels establish an important relationship between prana, the subtle body, the heart, and the mind.

Interestingly, when we practice pranayama (yogic breathing exercises), ida, pingala, and sushumna are among those pathways that are most profoundly activated, cleansed, and balanced. This is why pranayama so powerfully supports our psycho-spiritual health.

As we can see, mano vaha srotas extends far beyond the boundaries of the brain and the rational mind. In fact, as we continue to explore the Ayurvedic map of the mind, this channel's immense field of influence only expands further.

The Pathway of the Mind: According to Ayurveda, the pathway, or physical location, of mano vaha srotas is the entire body, making it the most overtly all-encompassing srotas of them all. The mind quite literally affects and is affected by every cell and tissue throughout the body-meaning that there is a direct and undeniable relationship between the mind and our overall health and vitality.

And this field of influence travels in both directions. In other words, while the mind certainly influences physical matter, our physical health also affects our state of mind. In this way, our every experience has the potential to either support or disturb our overall state of balance-in both the body and the mind.

Doorways to the Mind: The channel system of the mind also has a number of important openings (mukhas) to the exterior of the body. These doorways significantly influence the channel of the mind, and, when necessary, can be used strategically to help restore balance to mano vaha srotas.

First among these openings are the five sense organs-the eyes, ears, nose, tongue, and skin.

When it comes to our mental and psycho-spiritual health, the sense organs-as well as the sensory input they receive on a daily basis-play a major role.

For better or worse, we tend to align energetically with the qualities of our day-to-day sensory experience. For instance, if we are exposed to a great deal of trauma, our systems develop a natural and familiar association with that energetic pattern-and begin to anticipate its recurrence.

On the other hand, if we are routinely surrounded by loving, inspiring relationships, our systems naturally tend to orient toward hope and possibility.

Of course, each of us has a unique degree of sensitivity to these influences. For some, simply watching or listening to a disturbing news broadcast can cause a noticeable shift in the tendencies of the mind. Others are less sensitive and may not notice much of a shift at all when exposed to the same sensory input.

But for all of us, changing the overall quality of our sensory experience can radically alter our state of mind. If we are serious about inviting vibrant health and balance into the channel of the mind, the quality of our sensory input is a vitally important consideration.

Another important doorway to the mind is found in the marmani-a set of precise energy points on the surface of the skin that are connected to deeper, more subtle energetic pathways throughout the body.

Each marma point offers a powerful access point for shifting the energy within the channel of the mind and working with these points can be an effective means of restoring balance to mano vaha srotas.

Sattva, Rajas, and Tamas

Ayurveda names three maha gunas (universal attributes or qualities of consciousness)-sattva, rajas, and tamas-that are especially pertinent to this conversation. Though these qualities are very subtle, they are present in our food, our experiences, and our overall state of consciousness.

Together, sattva, rajas, and tamas are said to give rise to all phenomena in nature, and they have a profound influence on the subtle body and the mind.

- Sattva engenders equilibrium, clarity, light, intelligence, compassion, insight, and wisdom.
- Rajas ignites kinetic energy, movement, passion, and the ability to act.
- Tamas is responsible for inertia, darkness, heaviness, slowness, sleep, and decay.

Over the course of our lives, there is a natural place for all three of these energies. For example, tamas supports restful sleep, rajas engenders decisiveness and excitement in our lives, and sattva supports clarity of mind.

But when it comes to our evolving psycho-spiritual health, the Vedic sciences reflect a clear preference for sattva, because it is directly aligned with the qualities of liberation and enlightenment. Conversely, most mental imbalances can be attributed to an imbalance in rajas or tamas-usually an excess in one or both of these energies.

Mental Constitution: Just as each of us is born with a unique ratio of vata, pitta, and kapha in our constitution, we are also born with a distinctive proportion of sattva, rajas, and tamas.

The relationship between the three becomes an individual baseline for what Ayurveda calls manas prakriti-the mental constitution.

This reflects our capacity, with practice, to develop more sattvic states of consciousness throughout our lives.

Of course, manas prakriti can also change for the worse, especially if we consistently make poor lifestyle choices and surround ourselves with negativity. This is where Ayurveda's map of the mind becomes an incredibly useful tool. It helps us to see where to direct our attention in order to support the evolution of consciousness-to encourage thriving mental and emotional health.

As we have already discovered, some of the most effective tools in this realm include welcoming the heart center into the conversation, monitoring the quality of the sensory input we receive daily, being mindful of the quality of our relationships, working with the marma points, and engaging with practices that help to activate and balance the subtle pathways of the mind-pranayama, yoga, meditation, and prayer.

The Five Elements and Man

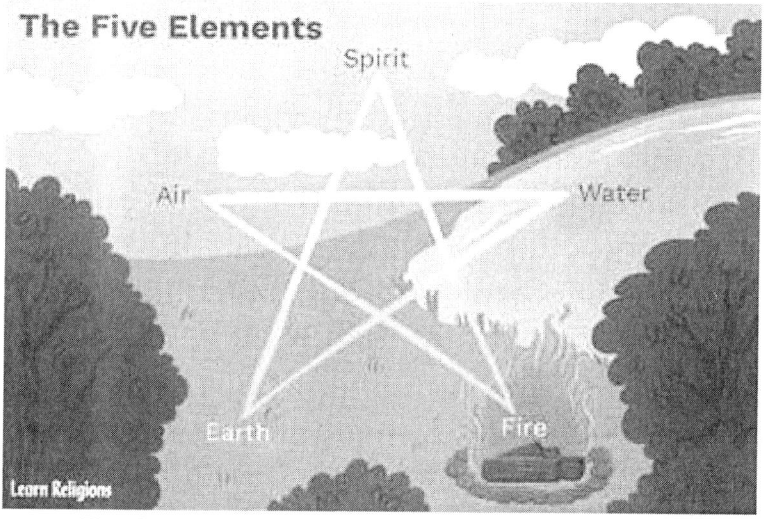

Figure: *The Greeks proposed the existence of five basic elements. Of these, four were the physical elements-fire, air, water, and earth-of which the entire world is composed. Alchemists eventually associated four triangular symbols to represent these elements.*

The fifth element, which goes by a variety of names, is more rarefied than the four physical elements. Some call it Spirit. Others call it Aether or Quintessence (literally "the fifth element" in Latin).

In traditional Western occult theory, the elements are hierarchical: Spirit, fire, air, water, and earth-with the first elements being more spiritual and perfect and the last elements being more material and base. Some modern systems, such as Wicca, view the elements as equal.

Before we examine the elements themselves, it is important to understand the qualities, orientations, and correspondences that are associated with the elements. Each element is connected with aspects in each of these, and it helps correlate their relationship to one another.

Elemental Qualities

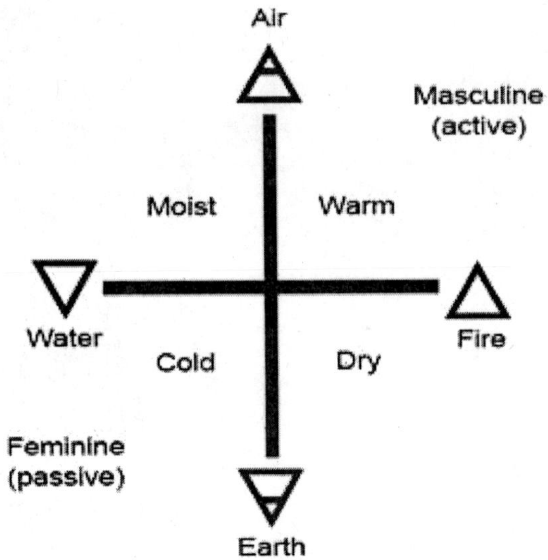

Figure: *In classical elemental systems, each element has two qualities, and it shares each quality with one other element.*

Warm/Cold: Each element is either warm or cold, and this corresponds with a male or female gender. This is a strongly dichotomous system, where male qualities are things like light, warmth, and activity, and female qualities are dark, cold, passive, and receptive.

The orientation of the triangle is determined by warmth or coldness, male or female. Male, warm elements point upward, ascending toward the spiritual realm. Female, cold elements point downward, descending into the earth.

Moist/Dry: The second pair of qualities is moistness or dryness. Unlike the warm and cold qualities, moist and dry qualities do not immediately correspond to other concepts.

Opposing Elements: Because each element shares one of its qualities with one other element, that leaves one element completely unrelated.

For example, air is moist like water and warm like fire, but it has nothing in common with earth. These opposing elements are on opposite sides of the diagram and are distinguished by the presence or absence of the crossbar within the triangle:

- Air and earth are opposites and have the crossbar
- Water and fire are also opposites and lack the crossbar.

Hierarchy of Elements: There is traditionally a hierarchy of elements, although some modern schools of thought have abandoned this system. The lower elements in the hierarchy are more material and physical, with the higher elements becoming more spiritual, more rarefied, and less physical.

That hierarchy can be traced through this diagram. Earth is the lowest, most material element. Circling clockwise from earth you get water, and then air and then fire, which is the least material of the elements.

Elemental Pentagram

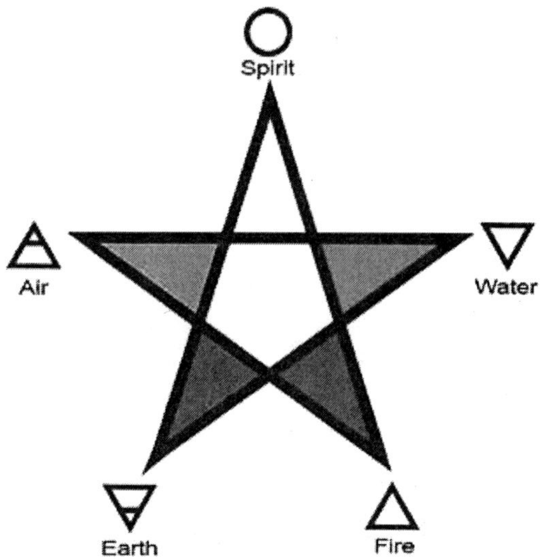

Figure: *The pentagram has represented many diverse meanings over the centuries. Since at least the Renaissance, one of its associations is with the five elements.*

Arrangement: Traditionally, there is a hierarchy among the elements ranging from the most spiritual and rarefied to the least spiritual and most material. This hierarchy determines the placement of elements around the pentagram.

Starting with spirit, the highest element, we descend to fire, then follow the lines of the pentagram over to air, across to water, and down to earth, the lowest and most material of the elements. The final line between earth and spirit completes the geometric shape.

Orientation: The issue of a pentagram being point-up or point-down only gained relevance in the 19th-century and has everything to do with the arrangement of elements. A point-up pentagram came to symbolize spirit ruling over the four physical elements, while a point-down pentagram symbolized spirit being subsumed by matter or descending into matter.

Since then, some have simplified those associations to represent good and evil. This is generally not the position of those who commonly work with point-down pentagrams, and is often not the position of those associating themselves with point-up pentagrams either.

Colours: The colours used here are those associated with each element by the Golden Dawn. These associations are commonly borrowed by other groups as well.

Elemental Correspondences

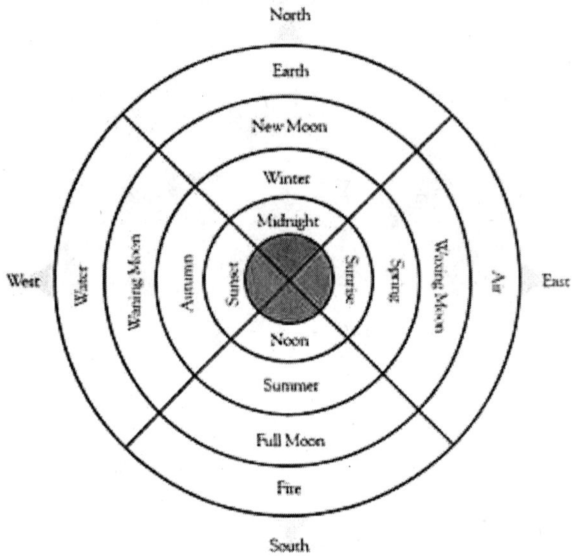

Figure: *Ceremonial occult systems traditionally depend on systems of correspondences: collections of items that are all associated in some way with the desired goal. While the types of correspondences are nearly endless, associations between elements, seasons, time of day, elements, moon phases, and directions have become fairly standardized in the West. These are frequently the basis for additional correspondences.*

The Golden Dawn's Elemental/Directional Correspondences

The Hermetic Order of the Golden Dawn codified some of these correspondences in the 19th-century. Most notable here are the cardinal directions. The Golden Dawn originated in England, and the directional/ elemental correspondences reflect a European perspective. To the south are the warmer climates, and thus is associated with fire. The

Atlantic Ocean lies to the west. The north is cold and formidable, a land of the earth but sometimes not a lot else.

Occultists practicing in America or elsewhere sometimes do not find these correspondences to work.

Daily, Monthly, and Yearly Cycles

Cycles are important facets of many occult systems. Looking at daily, monthly, and yearly natural cycles, we find periods of growth and dying, of fullness and barrenness.

- Fire is the element of fullness and life, and it is closely associated with the Sun. Therefore, it's unsurprising that noon and summer would be associated with fire. By that same logic, the full moon should also be in the same category.
- Earth is in the opposite direction as fire and therefore corresponds with midnight, winter, and the new moon. While these things might represent barrenness, more often they are representative of potential and transformation; the point where the old gives way to the new; the empty fertility readies to feed new creations.
- Air is the element of new beginnings, youth, increase, and creativity. As such, it is associated with spring, the waxing moon, and sunrise. Things are growing warmer and brighter, while plants and animals give birth to a new generation.
- Water is the element of emotion and wisdom, particularly the wisdom of age. It represents a time past the peak of livelihood, moving toward the end of the cycle.

Fire

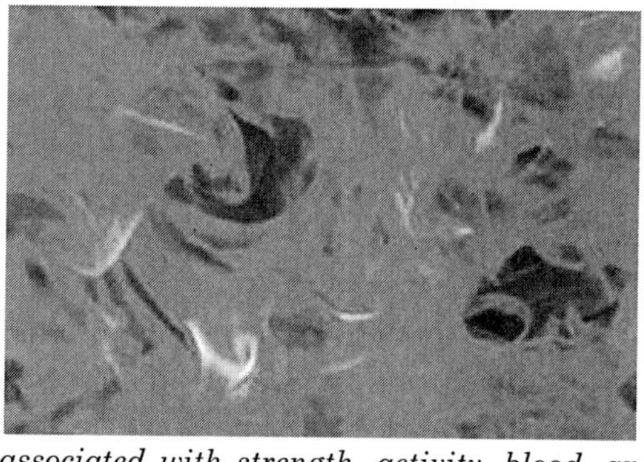

Figure: *Fire is associated with strength, activity, blood, and life-force. It is also seen as highly purifying and protective, consuming impurities and driving back the darkness.*

Fire is traditionally seen as the most rarefied and spiritual of the physical elements because of its masculine properties (which were superior to female properties). It also lacks physical existence, produces light, and has a transformative power when it comes in contact with more physical material.

- Qualities: Warm, Dry
- Gender: Masculine (active)
- Elemental: Salamander (Here referring to a mythological lizard creature which could burst into flames)
- Golden Dawn Direction: South
- Golden Dawn Colour: Red
- Magical Tool: Sword, athame, dagger, sometimes wand
- Planets: Sol (Sun), Mars
- Zodiac signs: Aries, Leo, Sagittarius
- Season: Summer
- Time of Day: Noon

Air

Figure: *Air is the element of intelligence, creativity, and beginnings. Largely intangible and without permanent form, air is an active, masculine element, superior to the more material elements of water and earth.*

- Qualities: Warm, Moist
- Gender: Masculine (active)
- Elemental: Sylphs (Invisible beings)

- Golden Dawn Direction: East
- Golden Dawn Colour: Yellow
- Magical Tool: Wand, sometimes sword, dagger or athame
- Planets: Jupiter
- Zodiac Signs: Gemini, Libra, Aquarius
- Season: Spring
- Time of Day: Morning, Sunrise

Water

Figure: *Water is the element of emotion and the unconscious, as opposed to the conscious intellectualism of air.*

Water is one of two elements that have a physical existence that can interact with all of the physical senses. Water is still considered less material (and thus superior) to earth because it possesses more motion and activity than earth.

- Qualities: Cold, Moist
- Gender: Feminine (passive)
- Elemental: Undines (water-based nymphs)
- Golden Dawn Direction: West
- Golden Dawn Colour: Blue
- Magical Tool: Cup
- Planets: Moon, Venus
- Zodiac Signs: Cancer, Scorpio, Pisces
- Season: Fall
- Time of Day: Sunset

Earth

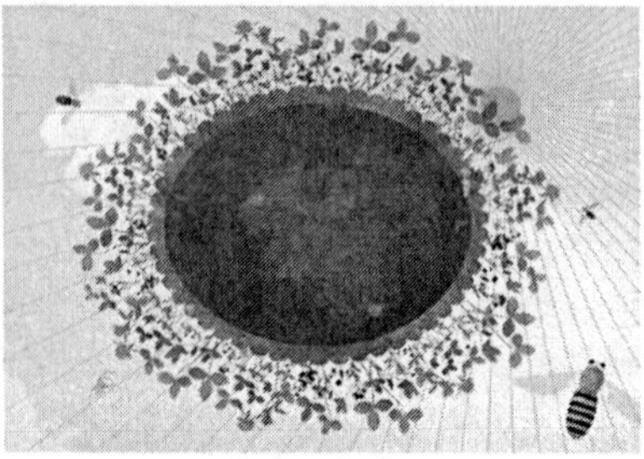

Figure: *Earth is the element of stability, groundedness, fertility, materiality, potential, and stillness. Earth can also be an element of beginnings and endings, or death and rebirth, as life comes from the ground and then decomposes back into the earth after death.*

Qualities: Cold, Dry

Gender: Feminine (passive)

Elemental: Gnomes

Golden Dawn Direction: North

Golden Dawn Colour: Green

Magical Tool: Pentacle

Planets: Saturn

Zodiac Signs: Taurus, Virgo, Capricorn

Season: Winter

Time of Day: Midnight

Spirit

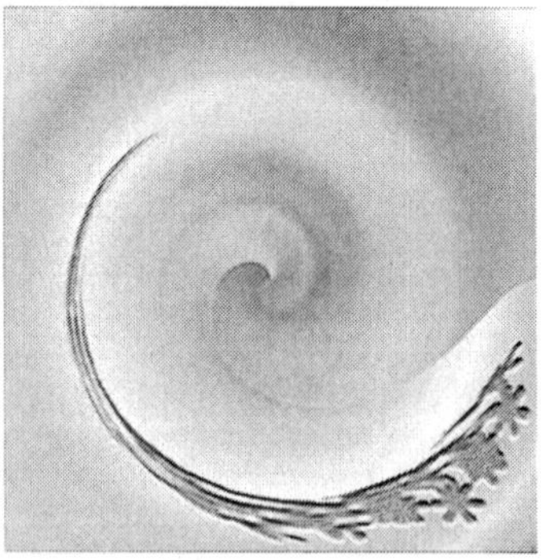

Figure: *The element of spirit does not have the same arrangements of correspondences as the physical elements since spirit is not physical. Various systems may associate planets, tools, and so forth to it, but such correspondences are far less standardized than those of the other four elements.*

The element of spirit goes by several names. The most common are spirit, ether or aether, and quintessence, which is Latin for "fifth element."There is also no standard symbol for spirit, although circles are common. Eight-spoked wheels and spirals are also sometimes used to represent spirit.Spirit is a bridge between the physical and the spiritual. In cosmological models, the spirit is the transitory material between the physical and celestial realms. Within the microcosm, the spirit is the bridge between body and soul.

- Golden Dawn Direction: Above, Below, Within
- Golden Dawn Colour: Violet, Orange, White

Man As Microcosm

One of the basic tenets of Ayurveda is that man is a microcosm of the very world that he inhabits. This implies explicitly that whatever man is made up of, the world too is made up of those same things or elements, but of different combinations and degrees. The microcosm-macrocosm analogy (or, equivalently, macrocosm-microcosm analogy) refers to a historical view which posited a structural similarity between the human being (the microcosm, i.e., the small order or the small universe) and the cosmos as a whole (the macrocosm, i.e., the great order or the great universe). Given this fundamental analogy, truths about the nature of the cosmos as a whole may be inferred from truths about human nature, and vice versa.

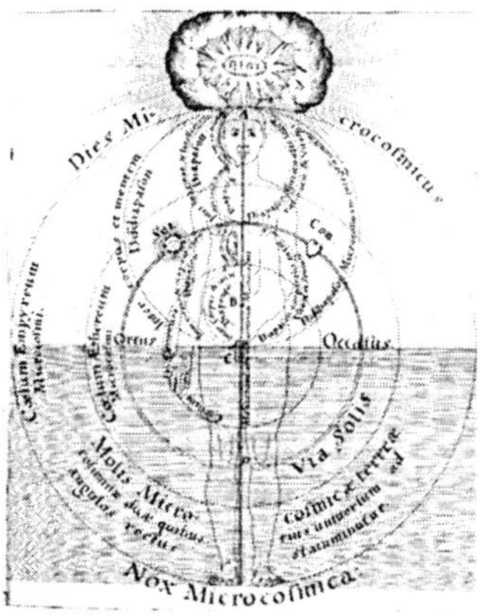

Figure: *Illustration of the analogy between the human body and a geocentric cosmos: the head is analogous to the cœlum empyreum, closest to the divine light of God; the chest to the cœlum æthereum, occupied by the classical planets (wherein the heart is analogous to the sun); the abdomen to the cœlum elementare; the legs to the dark earthy mass (molis terreœ) which supports this universe.*

One important corollary of this view is that the cosmos as a whole may be considered to be alive, and thus to have a mind or soul (the world soul), a position advanced by Plato in his Timaeus. Moreover, this cosmic mind or soul was often thought to be divine, most notably by the Stoics and those who were influenced by them, such as the authors of the Hermetica. Hence, it was sometimes inferred that the human mind or soul was divine in nature as well.

Apart from this important psychological and noetic (i.e., related to the mind) application, the analogy was also applied to human physiology. For example, the cosmological functions of the seven classical planets were sometimes taken to be analogous to the physiological functions of human organs, such as the heart, the spleen, the liver, the stomach, etc.

The view itself is ancient, and may be found in many philosophical systems world-wide, such as for example in ancient Mesopotamia, in ancient Iran, or in ancient Chinese philosophy. However, the terms microcosm and macrocosm refer more specifically to the analogy as it was developed in ancient Greek philosophy and its medieval and early modern descendants.

In contemporary usage, the terms microcosm and macrocosm are also employed to refer to any smaller system that is representative of a larger one, and vice versa.

The study of personality has fascinated psychologists since a long time. Personality as an area of study has grown so much that a wealth of literature is available. On the other hand, the socio-ethnic dynamics of human race in the emerging global village context provoking psychologists to develop a personality theory which can treat certain basic components of personality as invariants, so that irrespective of culture, race, and nativity could still be able to study personality which will have universal applicability and relevance, is still far away.

In the above emerging backdrop, "Ayurveda" has perhaps an important role to play as it can enable providing a theoretical and empirical base of personality traits and types. These Ayurvedic concepts are applicable to all human beings irrespective of caste, colour, sex or race. Therefore, it is interesting to build on the Ayurvedic knowledge which has already given us so much since time immemorial, and validate some of these issues related to personality from psychological perspective. There are already certain efforts in understanding Sattva, Rajas, and Tamas Gunas. It can be furthered so that a comprehensive personality picture can be generated, which can have implications for health, career, education and many other dimensions of life.

The Manifestation of the Five Proto-elements in Man: One of the basic tenets of Ayurveda is that man is a microcosm of the very world that he inhabits. This implies explicitly that whatever man is made up of, the world too is made up of those same things or elements, but of different combinations and degrees. Here, by elements is meant the five Mahabhutas-that is, Akasa, Vayu, Tejas, Ap and Prithvi. The earth and man are made up of these five elements. In fact, Ayurveda postulates that all living beings on the earth, including the non-living too, are made up of these same five elements in varying degrees, specific to each form, matter and species, and according to a predetermined ratio that cannot be changed. These five elements combine with each other to form the three humors of Vata, Pitta and Kapha (also called as the Tridoshas in unison) which is the cornerstone of Ayurvedic philosophy.

If changes do occur, then this leads to an imbalance in the organism, or a modified version of the organism is formed, the survival of which will depend upon its ability to adapt to its environment. Ayurvedic principles are drawn heavily from Samkhyan Philosophy.

"In Ayurveda, the three Doshas are considered to be universal principles that function in all aspects of material creation, including the mineral, plant, and animal kingdoms, the time of day, the seasons of the year, even the planets and galaxies. In this way, the human physiology is inexorably connected to the whole of existence. The Doshas have been correlated with systems theory in the field of physics, providing a sound theoretical basis for this Ayurvedic concept, and research utilizing a bio-statistical approach to quantify the Doshas reveals a sound empirical basis as well. A pilot study revealed the possibility of utilizing Prakriti to correlate phenotypes with genotypes in the human population, which could have wide-ranging implications for health care".

The five elements combine to form the Tridoshas in biodiversity

"According to Ayurveda, the universe evolved out of the 'un-manifested' (Avyakta), which implies Prakriti (primordial matter) and Purusa (primordial consciousness). Mahan (intellect) then evolves from Avyakta, and Ahamkara (ego) follows. Ego has three different qualities (Gunas): Sattva (the pure), Rajas (the dynamic), and Tamas (the inert). Sattva and Rajas together then produce eleven Indriyas (sense and motor organs known as Jnanendriyas and Karmendriyas) and Manas. The Gunas, Tamas and Rajas combine to produce five Tanmatras (energy quanta), which in their turn produce the five Mahabhutas (elements in the ancient sense, sometimes also called proto-elements). From these Mahabhutas the entire material world is made up... Living beings consist of the Mahabhutas as well as the Indriyas".

Dash, in his book Fundamentals of Ayurvedic Medicine (pg. 16, 17), has explained the inter-relatedness of man with the environment and how the Pancha Mahabhutas have evolved in man to form the different body organs and organ systems. He says, "...man has five senses and through these senses he perceives the external world in five different ways. The sense organs are the ears, the skin, the eyes, the tongue and the nose.

Through these sense organs, the external object is not only perceived, but also absorbed into the human body in the form of energy. These five types of senses are the basis on which the entire universe is divided, grouped or classified in five different ways, and they are known as five Mahabhutas.... According to Ayurveda, the body of the individual is composed of five Mahabhutas. Similarly, other things of the world are also composed of five Mahabhutas. In the human body these five Mahabhutas are explained in terms of Doshas, Dhatus and Malas..."

The play of the five proto-elements or the Pancha Mahabhutas is not restricted to the physical body only. It finds expression in the mind too, which also is purported to be made up of the five elements. Frawley in his book Ayurveda and the Mind is of the opinion that the mind transcends all the five gross elements because through the mind we can perceive all the elements and their inter-relationships. He further says that all the forms of earth, water, fire, air and ether can be observed, imagined and contemplated on. "Yet the elements do provide a key to how the mind works. Though the elements in the mind are more subtle than those in the body, they retain the same basic attributes and actions. We can understand the mental elements through the analogy of the physical".

Charaka Samhita expresses this idea in verses 46-47 (as stated in Mental Health in Ayurveda) as follows: "Mind, Soul and the Body-these three constitute a tripod, upon the meaningful combination of which the world is sustained. They constitute the substratum for everything, which is endowed with life. This (combination of the above three) is Purusha who is sentient and who is the subject matter for this science. It is for this that Ayurveda has been brought to light". Verse 1-55 also states: "The body and the mind are the abodes of diseases as well as health. Proper body-mind interaction is the cause for happiness".

The Senses

A sense is a biological system used by an organism for sensation, the process of gathering information about the world through the detection of stimuli. Although in some cultures five human senses were traditionally identified as such (namely sight, smell, touch, taste, and hearing), many more are now recognized. Senses used by non-human organisms are even greater in variety and number. During sensation, sense organs collect various stimuli (such as a sound or smell) for transduction, meaning transformation into a form that can be understood by the brain. Sensation and perception are fundamental to nearly every aspect of an organism's cognition, behaviour and thought.

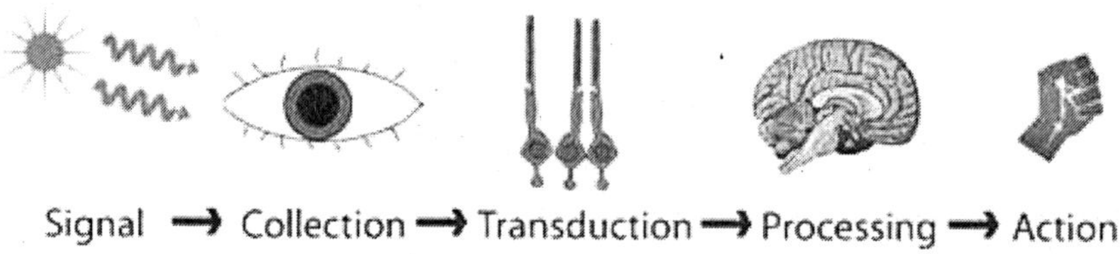

Figure: *Sensation consists of signal collection and transduction.*

In organisms, a sensory organ consists of a group of interrelated sensory cells that respond to a specific type of physical stimulus. Via cranial and spinal nerves (nerves of the Central and Peripheral nervous systems that relay sensory information to and from the brain and body), the different types of sensory receptor cells (such as mechanoreceptors, photoreceptors, chemoreceptors, thermoreceptors) in sensory organs transduct sensory information from these organs towards the central nervous system, finally arriving at the sensory cortices in the brain, where sensory signals are processed and interpreted (perceived).

Sensory systems, or senses, are often divided into external (exteroception) and internal (interoception) sensory systems. Human external senses are based on the sensory organs of the eyes, ears, skin, nose, mouth and the vestibular system. Internal sensation detects stimuli from internal organs and tissues. Internal senses possessed by humans include spatial orientation, proprioception (body position) and nociception (pain). Further internal senses lead to signals such as hunger, thirst, suffocation, and nausea, or different involuntary behaviours, such as vomiting.

Some animals are able to detect electrical and magnetic fields, air moisture, or polarized light, while others sense and perceive through alternative systems, such as echolocation. Sensory modalities or sub modalities are different ways sensory information is encoded or transduced. Multimodality integrates different senses into one unified perceptual experience.

For example, information from one sense has the potential to influence how information from another is perceived. Sensation and perception are studied by a variety of related fields, most notably psychophysics, neurobiology, cognitive psychology, and cognitive science.

Panchendriyas

Panchendriyas are the sense organs of the human body in Hinduism, consisting of mind and action, each consisting of five subtypes. Five buddhi-indriyas or Jnanendriyas ("mental or senses") and five Karmendriyas ("sense organs that deal with bodily functions").

Five Gyanendriyas

Gyanendriya is the organ of perception, the faculty of perceiving through the senses. The first five of the seventeen elements of the subtle body are the "organs of perception" or "sense organs". According to Hinduism and Vaishnavism there are five gyanendriya or "sense organs" - ears, skin, eyes, tongue and nose.The organs of sense

1. The eye - the organ of sight having visible formes as its object.
2. The ear - the organ of hearing, having sound as its object.
3. The nose - the organ of smelling, having smell (odors) as its object.
4. The tongue - the organ of tasting, having flavors as its object.
5. The skin - the organ of feeling, having touch (contact) as its object.

Five Karmendriyas: Karmendriya is an Indian philosophical concept. Karmendriya is the "organ of action" according to Hinduism and Jainism. Karmendriyas are five, and they are: hasta, pada, bak, anus, upastha. In Jainism these are the senses used by the experiencing soul to perform actions.

The Human Constitution

Figure: *The body is made of five elements, space, air, fire water and earth. Physiologically, these elements function as three bio-dynamic forces, called vata, pitta and kapha. These are called variously dhatus, substances, dosha, or prakriti, our natural constitution.*

When you are sitting by a stream of gushing water, absorbed in it, it can be hard to realize this simple fact of life-we are that.

We are made up of water and the other five elements that exist in nature. This understanding forms the baseline of Ayurveda, a 5000-year-old science of wellness and longevity; a science so precise that when your pulse is examined by an Ayurveda doctor, he/she can tell you not just about the imbalances at the root of existing diseases but can share in elaborate detail specific qualities about your body type, behaviour, and conditions you may be predisposed to.

The science of Ayurveda is all about creating balance-balance between the body, mind, and spirit, and balance between the tridosha (three doshas) that take from the five elements in nature. It does this by first identifying the prakruti or nature of an individual. Secondly, it examines the existing dosha imbalances.

Lastly, Ayurveda provides a roadmap to an individual to live a healthy, perfectly balanced life using specific herbs, holistic cleanses and detox treatments, personalized diet that is aligned with one's unique dosha constitution.

Your Ayurvedic body type, or constitution, is at the heart of Ayurveda's approach to well-being. Knowing your constitution allows you to maximize your quality of life, health, and happiness by following the recommendations for food and lifestyle for each constitution.

Ayurveda is a personalized school of medicine where there is no one size fits all when it comes to wellness and treatments. Ayurveda uses an ancient and time tested tool for diagnosis of imbalances in the body called the Nadi Pariksha, or pulse diagnosis.

An Ayurvedic pulse diagnosis with an expert is the best way to recognize one's constitution. It can help determine what your dosha dominance is and what are the current vikritis, or dosha imbalances. Pulse diagnosis in Ayurveda is different and runs much deeper than the Western method of pulse examination. In Ayurveda, it includes examination of an individual's state of body, mind, and spirit as a whole. It meaningfully examines not just the pulse rate, rhythm, and volume but also observes the flow, amplitude, force, and consistency. It is based on the knowledge that symptoms manifest in the pulse before they manifest in the affected part of the body and that severe aggravation of doshas leads to illnesses in the body. For example, the effect of an imbalance in your blood can be detected much earlier in your pulse.

The interplay and architecture of genetic, epigenetic, and environment-induced changes in the DNA sequences contribute to large phenotypic variations. The post-human genome era, embarked on several major international projects and subsequently their databases such as Human Genome Project, Genome Wide Association Studies, human ENCODE consortium, dbSNPs, dbCNVs, HapMap have all contributed significantly to the understanding of the position, degree, nature, and structure of DNA and its contributions to number of phenotypes as well as diseases. The variation in anatomical, physiological, immunological, psychological, disease susceptibility, disease prognosis, and response to treatment, forms the basic principles of personalized medicine. These variations are diverse and efforts are being made to classify humans based on geographical origin, ethnicity, race, and other factors.

Ayurveda, Unani (Graeco-Arabic medicinal system), Sasang constitution (Korean medicinal system), and Chinese medicinal system are well known branches of traditional knowledge, which intend to classify individuals based on body temperament by deciphering specific phenotypic characters for health management. Ayurveda, an Indian traditional system of medicine considers every individual as unique and the treatment is based on the defined constitution types. A basic feature of the theory and practice of Ayurveda is the classification of human beings into three doshas (vata, pitta, and kapha) and their mixed constitutional types called prakriti. The prakriti or the Ayurvedic constitutional type of an individual is fixed at conception and is articulated through physical, psychological, immunological, and behavioural traits as described elaborately in original ayurvedic texts written by Charaka and Susruta. Further, prakriti also influences the manifestation and course of diseases in an individual and importantly, an individual's response to treatment. Therefore the determination of constitution type or prakriti of a subject or patient is very important in the practice of Ayurveda.

Several biochemical, genetic, and molecular studies have been performed to relate various features of an individual to prakriti. Initial study by Patwardhan et al. demonstrated a correlation between HLA-DRB1 types with the specific prakriti. Subsequently, Prasher et al. reported biochemical profiles, hematological parameters, and gene expression patterns among vata, pitta, and kapha subjects relating them to inflammatory or cardiovascular diseases. Frequency of association among CYP2C19 genotypes in a prakriti specific fashion was also reported. Similarly expression of EGLN1 gene and the association of rs479200 (C/T) and rs480902 (T/C) in high-altitude adaptation in relation to prakriti was reported. Prakriti determination is traditionally a qualitative, subjective exercise carried out by vaidya. Since it is experience and skill based, inter-observer variations will be inherent. A quantitative tool, such as software, could eliminate much of the subjectivity such that it could be reiteratively tested, modified, and adopted to provide similar prakriti determination. Therefore, considering the immense potential, an interdisciplinary approach to interrogate Ayurvedic principles in the context of contemporary medicine is essential.

Traditionally, the prakriti assessment is carried out by the ayurvedic physician on the basis of his knowledge and experience and is therefore subject to inter-observer variations. The quantitative approach to the qualitative assessment of prakriti for the practice of personalized medicine both by ayurvedic physician and contemporary science is essential and attempts are made based on the use of psychometric scaling; however, these lack the physiological and anatomical features in scaling different prakriti types.

Chapter 2

Basic Principles Diagnostic Techniques

Introduction

The five main types of diagnostic methods in Ayurveda, according to Madhava, involve an examination of Purvarupa (prodromal symptoms), Rupa (manifested symptoms) and Samprapti (pathogenesis), and the conduct of Upasaya (therapeutic tests), and Ashtavidha Pareeksha (physical examination).

Purvarupa (prodromal symptoms) is a reference to the early signs of a disease, which eventually lead up to the full-fledged symptoms of the illness appearing in patients.

Rupa (manifested symptoms) is the set of problems and ailments that the patient brings to the notice of the vaidyan who then uses touch and percussion to judge the state of the individual's health.

Samprapti (pathogenesis) traces the onset of symptoms in the patient all the way from the Nidana stage, i.e., the personal and family medical history of the patient. Here, the status of metabolism, age and overall physical and mental condition of the patient play a crucial role in the diagnosis.

Upasaya (therapeutic tests) are the herbal remedies and lifestyle tips that work against the disease and its further propagation.

Ashtavidha Pareeksha (physical examination) is the special stage where a thorough examination takes place.

The physician inspects the Nadi (pulse), the Jihva (tongue), the Sabda (voice), the Sparsa (touch), the Drik (eyes), the Akruti (appearance), the Mutra (urine), and the Mala (faeces)of the patient.

Understanding Tridosha

The concept of the Tridoshas is unique to medical science. Ayurveda considers the body to be made up of tissues (dhatus), waste products (malas), and doshas (Energetic Forces).

Tridoshas (Vata, Pitta and Kapha) assist in the creation of various tissues of the body and to remove any unnecessary waste products from the body. It is also the Tridoshas that influence all movements, all transformations, all sensory functions, and many of the other activities in the human body and mind.

The Doshas are dynamic energies that constantly change in response to our actions, thoughts, emotions, the foods we eat, the seasons, and any other sensory inputs that feed our mind and body. That's why in Ayurveda we advise to make lifestyle and dietary decisions that foster balance within our Doshas.

When we live against our intrinsic natures and support unhealthy patterns that lead to physical and mental imbalances.

Vata dosha: The word vata means to blow or move like the wind.

Vata derives from the elements of Space and Air and translates as "wind" or "that which moves things."

It is the energy of movement and the force governing all biological activity. Vata is often called the "King of the Doshas," since it governs the body's greater life force and gives motion to Pitta and Kapha.

- Just as the wind in balance provides movement and expression to the natural world, the balanced Vata individual is active, creative, and gifted with a natural ability to express and communicate.
- When the wind in a Vata type rages like a hurricane, negative qualities quickly overshadow these positive attributes.
- Common signs of Vata imbalance include anxiety and bodily disorders related to dryness, such as dry skin and constipation.

Qualities of Vata: The qualities of Vata are dry, rough, light, cold, mobile and having ability to penetrate fine particles.

1. Prana: relates to chest and respiration.
2. Udana: concerns the upper gut. This responsible in emesis and other motility disorders of upper gut. Also responsible for the voice.
3. Samana: refers to the intestines. It controls the churning movements required to digest the food and formation of stool.

4. Vyana: refers to the whole body and mainly chest. Related with cardiac functions.
5. Apana: relates to rectum and genito-urinary tract. Controls evacuation of stools and urine, ejaculation of sperms, and delivery of child.

Locations of Vata: The main locations of Vata in the body are the colon, thighs, bones, joints, ears, skin, brain, and nerve tissues.

Actions:

- All eliminations: fetus, semen, feces, urine, sweat, and a few others.
- Assists with all the metabolisms in the body (Stimulates the Agni)
- Controls all of the various movement of body (both physical & mental), including such things as respiration, heartbeat, motivation and contraction of muscles
- Relays all sensory input from the various sense organs to the brain
- Psychologically, Vata governs communication, creativity, flexibility, and quickness of thought.

Ways Vata Becomes Imbalanced

- Eating Vata-aggravating foods like popcorn, rice, beans, cayenne pepper, coffee and alfalfa sprouts
- Eating while anxious or depressed
- Eating on the run
- Drinking alcohol, coffee, or black tea
- Smoking cigarettes
- Following an irregular daily routine
- Going to bed late at night

How to Balance Vata:

Eat in a peaceful environment.

Engage in wholesome and contemplative activities (like spending time in nature).

Go to bed early.

Meditate daily.

Do gentle physical exercise like yoga, swimming, tai chi, or walking.

One should put efforts to establish regular daily routine to eating schedule; to sleep and to work at regular times. It is very important to regulate vata dosha.

Eat warm, moist, heavy texture food, which is soothing and satisfying. The food with sweet, sour and salty taste is good to balance Vata dosha. Food such as warm milk, butter, cream, warm soups, hot cereal, etc is satisfying. Regular relaxing exercise and avoiding strenuous exercise help. Vata is cold and dry in nature so warm nourishing food stabilizes vata. Cold salads, greens, raw vegetables, iced drinks are not food for persons with vata imbalance. Warm sesame oil whole body massage before bath or head massage before sleep will help balance vata.

Pitta dosha

Pitta derives from the elements of Fire and Water. The Pitta dosha is associated with fire or heat. It is mainly associated with transformation in the body. It is the energy of digestion and metabolism in the body that functions through carrier substances such as organic acids, hormones, enzymes, and bile. Pitta is most closely related to the element of Fire

Qualities of Pitta:

Hot, Sharp, Slightly Oily, Penetrating, Liquid, Light and can be sour and foul smelling when excessively increased

5 Types of Pitta:

1. Pachaka: controls digestion of food by controlling secretion of enzymes.
2. Ranjaka: controls colour of skin and complexion. It converts Rasa (plasma) to Rakta (blood). So white coloured plasma gets converted red coloured blood.
3. Sadhaka: located in brain. Transform the sensory messages to actual perception.
4. Bhrajaka: located under the skin. Regulates body temperature.
5. Alochaka: resides in eyes and is responsible for vision. Rods and cones cells of retina may be related to it.

Locations: The main locations of Pitta in the body are the small intestine, stomach, liver, spleen, pancreas, blood, eyes, and sweat.

Actions: Pitta provides the following functions:

- Metabolism - at various levels from digestion of food to transformation of all other material
- Maintains the proper body temperature
- Vision - converts external images into optic nerve impulses
- Appetite - the feeling of hunger and thirst
- Comprehension - of information into knowledge, also reasoning and judgment
- Courage & Braveness - to face the situation
- It governs all processes related to conversion and transformation throughout the mind and body.
- Psychologically, Pitta governs joy, courage, willpower, anger, jealousy, and mental perception.
- It also provides the radiant light of the intellect.

Ways Pitta Becomes Imbalanced

- Eating Pitta-aggravating food like spicy, hot food.
- Eating while angry
- Drinking coffee, black tea, or alcohol
- Smoking cigarettes
- Over-working
- Being overly competitive
- Staying under sun
- over-indulgence in pungent, sour and salty tastes.

Ways to Balance Pitta

- Eat in a peaceful environment.
- Avoid artificial stimulants.
- Engage in calming activities, like spending time in nature.
- Meditate daily.
- Do calming physical exercise, such as yoga, swimming, tai chi, or walking Eat cool/warm food; try to avoid too hot food and drinks.
- Sweet, bitter and astringent tastes are good to decrease pitta influence.

Complex carbohydrates, milk, sweet fruits, green leafy vegetables are good for pitta.

A glass of warm milk with two teaspoons of ghee will calm down pitta.

Avoid processed foods, oily, spicy heavy and salty foods.

Kapha dosha

- o Kapha derives from the elements of Earth and Water.
- o Kapha is the heaviest of the three doshas.
- o It provides the structures and the lubrication that the body needs.
- o These qualities help to counterbalance Vata's movement and Pitta's metabolism.

Qualities of Kapha: Cool, Heavy, Dense, Sweet, Stable, Oily, Viscous and soft.

5 Types of Kapha:

1. Tarpaka: located in brain. Protects brain from external injury. Related with cerebrospinal fluid.
2. Bodhaka: located in mouth at root of tongue. Responsible for taste sensation of food.
3. Avalambaka: Resides in thorax (chest cavity). Lubricates the chest organs. Related to pericardial and pleural fluids.
4. Shleshaka: located at joints. Prevents them from friction. Linked to synovial fluid.
5. Kledaka: resides in the gut. Protects the mucous membranes of gut from action of fiery pitta.

Locations: Chest, throat, lungs, head, lymph, fatty tissue, connective tissue, ligaments, and tendons.

Actions:

- Strength - to perform physical tasks
- Moistness & Lubrication - to prevent excessive friction from occurring between the various parts of the body
- Stability - to add the necessary grounding aspect to both mind and body
  - o Physiologically, Kapha moistens food, gives bulk to our tissues, and relates to cool bodily fluids such as water, mucous, and lymph.
  - o Psychologically, Kapha governs love, patience, forgiveness, greed, attachment, and mental inertia.

Ways Kapha Becomes Imbalanced

- Eating Kapha-aggravating food like milk products, banana, curd etc.
- Overeating
- Eating to offset emotions (like indulging in sweets when depressed)
- Spending too much time in cool, damp climates
- Not engaging in physical activity
- Spending most of one's time indoors (especially on the couch watching TV!)
- Avoiding intellectual challenges

Ways to Balance Kapha:

o Avoid a luxurious, leisurely lifestyle

o Focus on non-attachment in daily life.

o Make time for introspective activities, like meditation and writing.

o Make a distinction between being nice and being taken advantage of.

o Rise early, with no daytime naps.

o Eat light meals with lightly cooked vegetables, raw fruits and vegetables helps balance kapha.

o Stimulating food, which is bitter, pungent and astringent, are good tastes for kapha dosha.

o Kapha dominated person need to watch the consumption of sweet, salty, and fatty food as they might gain weight easily.

o Butter, dairy, ice cream, cheese, yogurt aggravate kapha.

o Ginger, black pepper, fenugreek, cumin's turmeric these spices should be added to food.

o Use honey as sweetener than any other form of sugar.

o Take honey ginger and lukewarm water to pep up the morning

o Exercise like aerobics, swimming, jogging will help maintain kapha.

Three primary states of existence of doshas:

1. Balanced: All three doshas are present in their natural proportions; also referred to as "equilibrium."

2. Increased: A particular dosha is present in a greater-than-normal proportion; also referred to as an "aggravated" or "excess state."
3. Decreased: A particular dosha is present in a less-than-normal proportion; also referred to as a "reduced" or "depleted state."

Of the three states, the increased or aggravated state leads to the greatest number of imbalances. Such imbalances can arise from dosha-aggravating diet and/or dosha -aggravating life style.

How to balance Doshas:: The key to remember is that like increases like, while opposites create balance. By simply choosing cooling or more alkalizing foods, you can avoid heartburn, while also supporting your underlying make-up. Ayurveda offers specifically tailored recommendations for every individual, ranging from general lifestyle changes to the treatment of dis-ease (literally, an imbalance within our natural state of "ease").

For this reason, Ayurveda can truly be called a system of individualized health care, something remarkably different from the Western model's "one-pill for all" approach. Since the doshas are used to detect imbalances before the manifestation of dis-ease, Ayurveda is also a complete system of preventative medicine.

Tongue Diagnosis

Tongue diagnosis is the vital component of observation diagnosis of TCM to examine the physiological and pathological changes of the human body. If you're like the majority of people, you probably don't give your tongue's appearance much thought at all. After all, western medicine largely ignores the tongue (and the wisdom it offers). But we can make important assessments about our overall health and well-being by observing our tongues' shape, colour, cracks, coating, and more.

Ayurveda Tongue Map

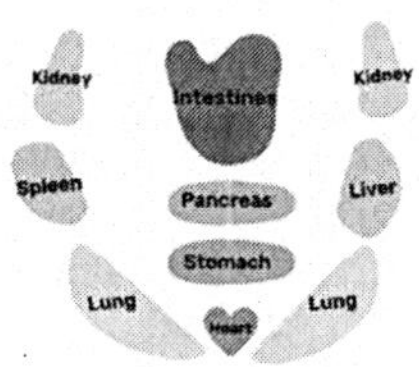

The ancient art of tongue diagnosis also describes quite characteristic patterns that can reveal the functional status of respective internal organs merely by observing the surface of the tongue. The tongue is the mirror of the viscera. A discolouration and /or sensitivity of a particular area of the tongue indicates a disorder in the organ corresponding to that area. A whitish tongue indicates a kapha derangement and mucus accumulation; a red or yellow-green tongue indicates a pitta derangement; and a black to brown colouration indicates a vata derangement. A dehydrated tongue is symptomatic of a decrease in the rasa dhatu (plasma), while a pale tongue indicates a decrease in the rakta dhatu (red blood cells). The front one-third of the tongue relates to the lungs, heart, chest, and neck. Froth in the middle of this area is often a sign of low lung energy with damp and cold lungs and may translate as a cold, bronchitis, asthma, or respiratory allergy. If there is a small depression in the heart area, it often relates to intense grief, sadness, or depression. The central third of the tongue relates to the liver, spleen, stomach, and pancreas. Small ulcers on the tongue in the stomach area may reflect gastritis or peptic ulcer. The rear one-third area of the tongue relates to the lower abdominal organs, such as the small intestine and colon. If this posterior part of the tongue is covered with coating, that is ama or toxins in the colon, indicating low colon energy.

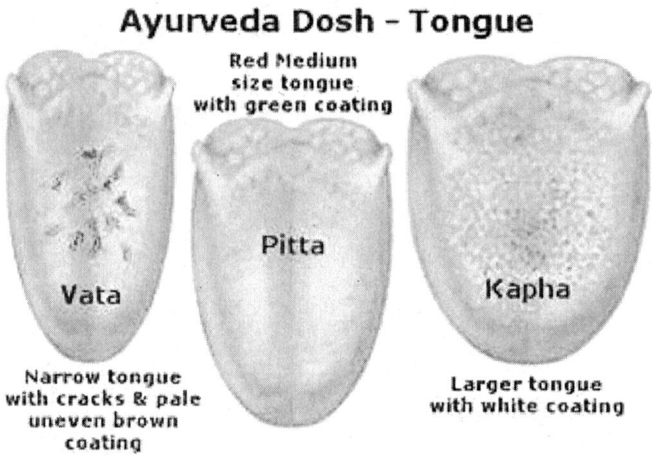

Figure: *Cleansing the Tongue*

One of the best ways to keep the tongue healthy is by scraping it daily. This removes overnight build-up of bacteria and toxins on the tongue. Rather than brushing the tongue, which will only push bacteria and toxins into the tongue, this is done with a tongue scraper or spoon.

To do this, extend the tongue and place the scraper as far back on the tongue as comfortable. Using one long stroke, gently pull the scraper forward so that it removes the unwanted coating on the tongue. Rinse the scraper and begin again if necessary. Ayurveda says that scraping the tongue should only be done in the morning on an empty stomach. Scraping the tongue is a good way to start to observe the tongue and as a result, the health of the internal organs.

Tongue Abnormalities and What They Mean

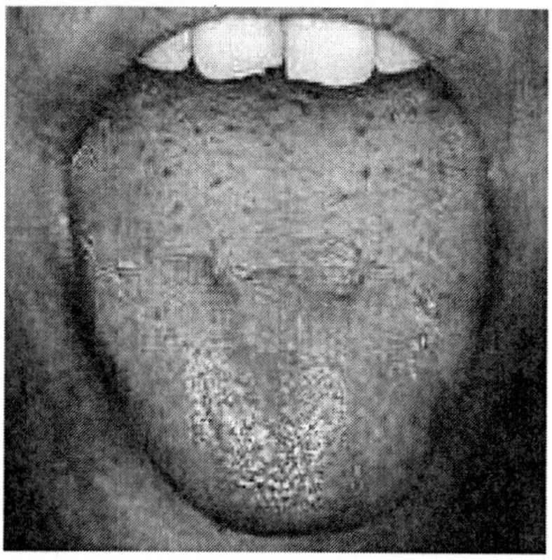

Figure: *Tongue Coating and Location*

If the tongue has any sort of coating on it, this is a very clear indication of toxic build-up in the system and poor overall digestion. The most common area where the coating is typically found is on the back of the tongue, revealing that the toxic build-up is in the colon area. If you see a coating on a different area of the tongue, then that would indicate toxic build-up in the corresponding organ. If the entire tongue is coated, this indicates systemic toxins, meaning the toxins are in the bloodstream and invading the entire body.

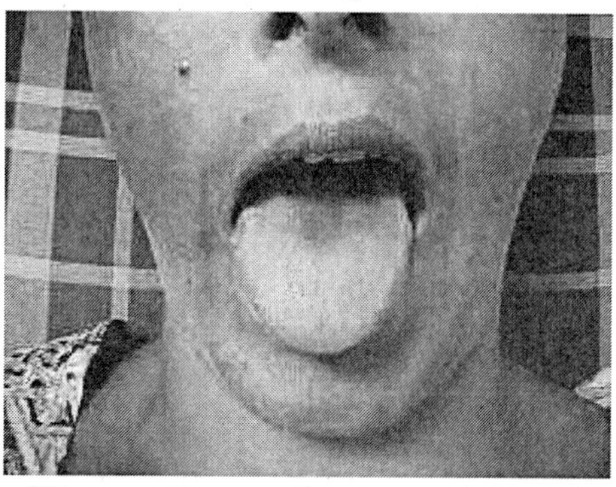

Figure: *Tongue Coating and Colour*

The first line of action is to discover if there are toxins and their location. After that, if you wish to dive deeper into diagnosis, you can look at the colour of the coating which will reveal the doshic imbalance that is involved. If the coating is grey, black, or brown, you can assume Vata toxins; if the coating is orange, reddish, yellow, or green, this indicates Pitta toxins; and finally, if there is a thick, whitish coating, you can think Kapha toxins. This can be quite helpful as each toxin should be treated differently depending on which dosha is involved.

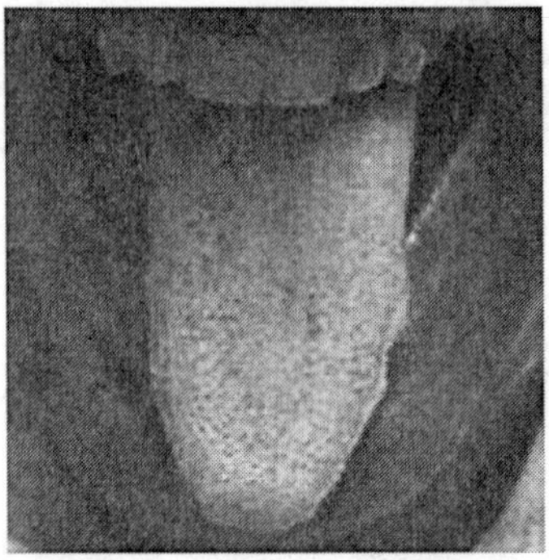

Figure: *Vata Imbalance*

If a tongue is a so-called "Vata tongue", it is typically small, thin, and shaky or trembling in appearance. It may look pale in colour, appear to be dried out, and have a few (or many) cracks. Once again, if there is a coating it will be grey, blackish, or brown in colour and will typically coat the colon area of the tongue. This is a storybook picture of a tongue revealing a Vata imbalance. Vata imbalances typically manifest as anxiety, fear, worry, restless mind, sleep issues, constipation, gas, bloating, and dryness.

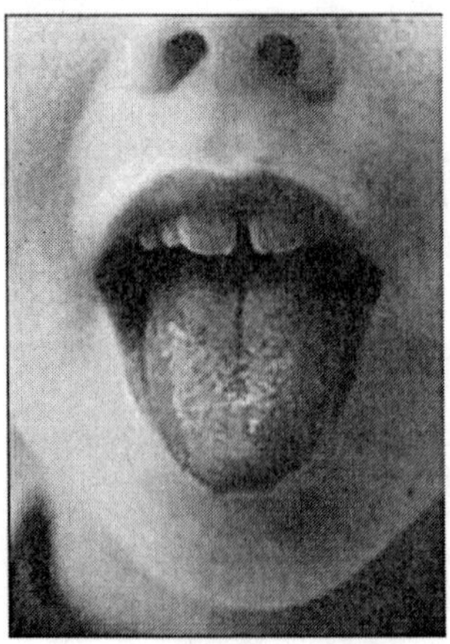

Figure: *Pitta Imbalance*

If a tongue is of a Pitta nature, it may be medium in size, have a sharp or pointy tip, and be excessively red in colour. There may also be red dots on the top of the tongue which reveals excessive heat in the blood. If there is a coating on the tongue, it will be green, yellow, or orange in colour. The coating will typically be located in the small and large intestine area, the liver area, or may also be on the entire tongue revealing toxins in the bloodstream. Pitta imbalances manifest as inflammation, heat, skin disorders (psoriasis, eczema, acne, etc.), anger, irritation, hyperacidity, loose stools, and headaches.

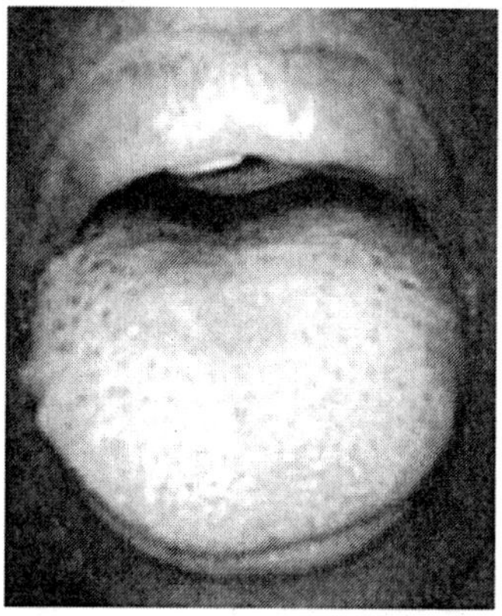

Figure: *Kapha Imbalance*

A tongue revealing a Kapha imbalance tends to be large, thick, and heavy by nature. It may appear swollen, pale in colour, and have thick saliva build-up. If there is a coating on a Kapha imbalanced tongue, the colour of the coating usually will be whitish, thick, and mucusy. The coating may be located in the colon, the kidney area, the lung area, and/or the stomach area revealing increased Kapha in these organs. Symptoms of a Kapha imbalance include heaviness (both objective and subjective), congestion, grief, sadness, depression, lethargy, excessive sleep, day sleeping, slow metabolism, slow digestion, and easy weight gain.

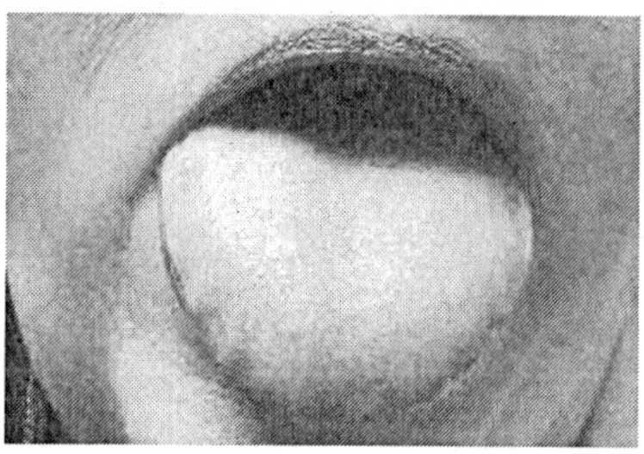

Figure: *Teeth Marks Around the Perimeter of the Tongue*

Unfortunately, it is quite common to see indentation marks along the outside perimeter of the tongue. This is a classic indication that there is malabsorption in the body of essential nutrients. Malabsorption is a lack of ability for your body to absorb specific nutrients and has a wide range of causes. Some of these include poor digestion, inflammation in the GI tract, excessive toxins in the colon, intake of allergenic foods, chronic loose stools, or parasitical infection. Once this issue is removed, the teeth marks should disappear. In certain cases, however, these marks are due to a swollen tongue, revealing inflammation in the system.

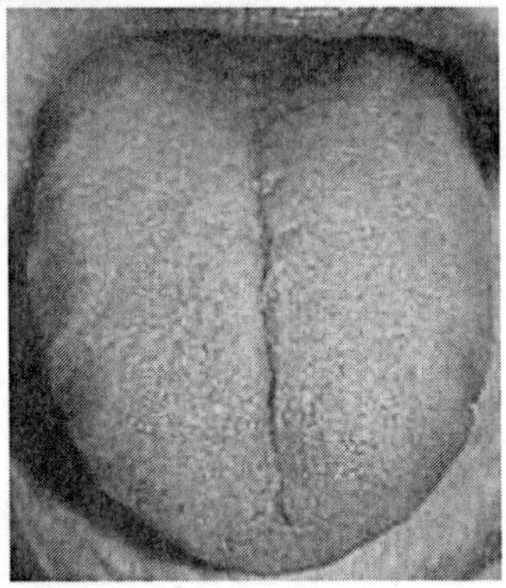

Figure: *Crack, Vertically Down the Center of the Tongue*

This vertical line, which may be located down the center of the tongue, is an indication that there are stresses and emotions being held in the spine. The top of the spine area (cervical spine) correlates to the tip of the tongue and the lower spine (lumbar spine) correlates to the back of the tongue. So, wherever the spine line manifests on the tongue reveals where the tension is being held. If there is any cracking along the spine, this indicates pain, tension, and misalignment at whatever point the crack corresponds to on the tongue/spine. This picture is an example of an individual with complete spinal tension with some misalignment in the neck area.

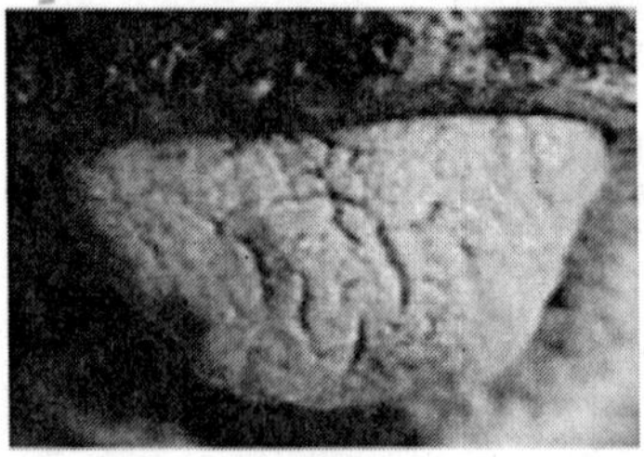

Figure: *Many Cracks all Over the Tongue*

The appearance of multiple small cracks all over the tongue is a clear indicator of a strong, chronic Vata derangement such as high anxiety, fear, insomnia, and possibly a nervous system disorder. If the cracks are only located on one area of the tongue, this may reveal chronic high Vata in that correlating organ (i.e. Vata in the colon). Since the disorder is chronic, Vata pacification should be administered, although this may take some time to heal. Once healed, however, the cracks should begin to clear.

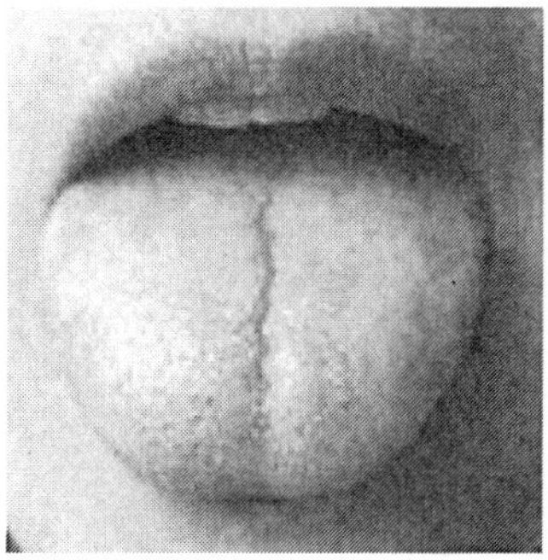

***Figure:** Swollen Tongue*

A swollen tongue may be a sign of inflammation in the body indicating the presence of an allergen such as undesirable food. This can also reveal a Kapha imbalance such as hypothyroidism or fluid retention as well. If one is suffering from a swollen tongue, more investigation should be administered in order to reveal the cause and begin to remove it.

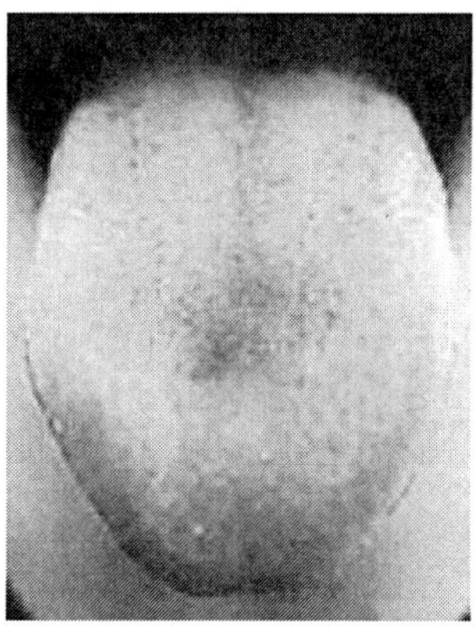

***Figure:** Drooping in the Heart Area of the Tongue*

A hollowness or scooping around the center of the tongue is a common indicator that there is unresolved sadness, grief, or depression in the heart. This picture shows a clear depression in the heart, as well as systemic toxins, due to the coating, and excessive heat in the blood due to the red dots and red edges of the tongue. Each imbalance occurring in our system is often correlated with the other and, therefore, it is often necessary to look at the entire picture.

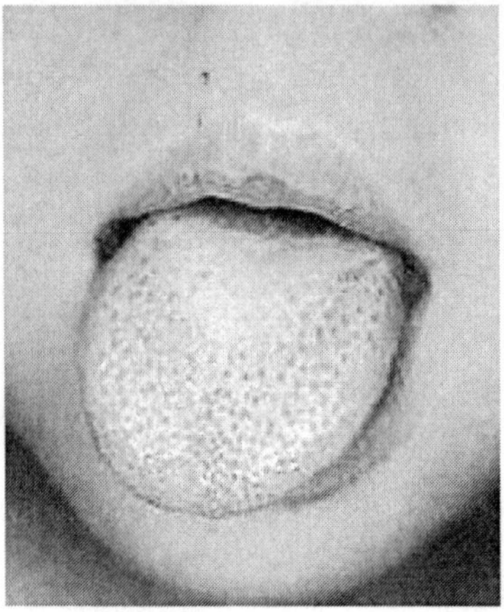

Figure: *Red, Raised Papillae on the Top of the Tongue*

If you see these raised red dots on the surface of your tongue, this typically means there is excessive Pitta or heat in the plasma and blood. Typically, a tongue with these red dots will also be excessively red along the perimeter, confirming this increase in heat. Too much heat can result in loose stools, hyperacidity, ulcer, inflammation, headaches, excessive anger, or irritation. This can be resolved through cooling, Pitta balancing practices, and the appropriate dietary changes.

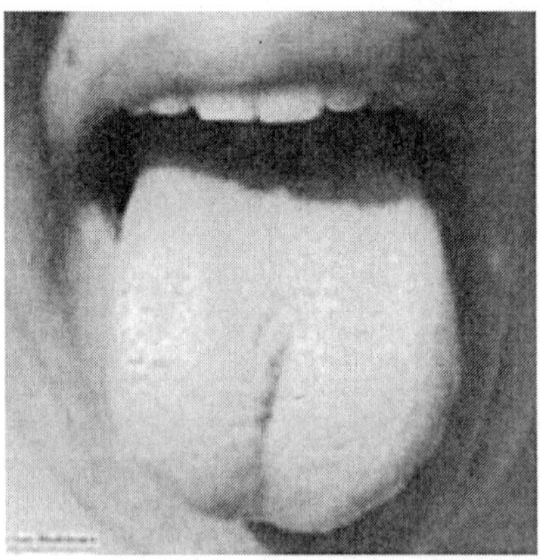

Figure: *Pale Tongue*

A pale tongue is typically a sign of low red blood cells indicating possible anemia. This can be due to excessive blood loss (heavy menstruation or injury); an iron, folate, or B12 deficiency; ulcer;

parasitical infection; certain medications (including NSAIDs); malabsorption; chronic diseases such as cancer, rheumatoid arthritis, or HIV; or many different autoimmune conditions. Anemia can cause fatigue, weakness, poor circulation, frequent bruising, shortness of breath, irregular heartbeat, and cognitive issues. If anemia is suspected, one can look to see if other symptoms are involved, as well as the nails and the pink under the eye (when stretched down) to see if these areas are also pale.

Facial Diagnosis

In Ayurveda, the practice of facial examination is called akruti pariksha. Your face is a storybook that tells the tale of your health and each part of your face correlates to a specific organ. With Ayurvedic facial assessment, it's easy to see where there may be an imbalance or stress on a particular organ.

Although they say you should not judge a book by its cover, it is true that you can read a lot into your health by examining the lines on your face. In Ayurveda, facial diagnosis is a common practice and powerful diagnostic tool, as is reading the tongue, nails, and pulse. Often this is done as a complementary practice to confirm ideas and findings, but also can reveal hidden secrets that may not have been completely clear. By reading the lines on a person's face, one can reveal current disorders, past history of disorders, or even potential disorders to come. Since the lines do not tend to appear overnight, these telltale signs are often revealing chronic (long-term) issues such as malabsorption, low liver energy, weakness in the kidneys, adrenal fatigue, and even emotional disturbances such as unresolved grief.

Common findings with facial diagnosis:

- Malabsorption
- Low liver and/or spleen energy
- Low kidney and/or adrenal energy
- Weak reproductive organs
- Weak prostate; future prostate issues
- High cholesterol
- Low lung energy; chronic respiratory issues
- Chronic worry; high anxiety
- Low libido
- Unresolved, deep-seated grief

- History of high blood pressure (hypertension)
- Endometriosis
- Hemorrhoids
- Future hypothyroid disorder

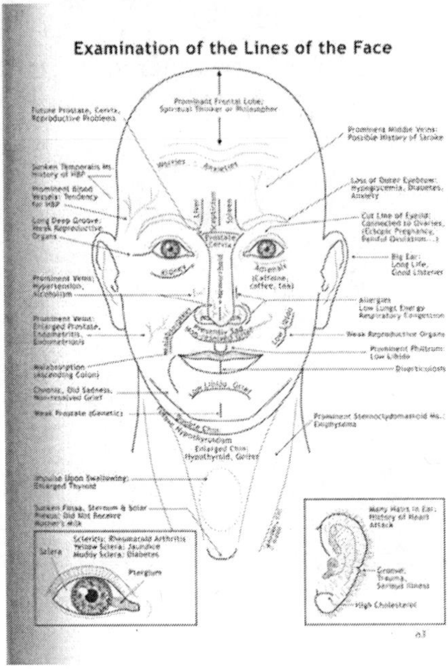

Figure: *Photo Credit: "Textbook of Ayurveda: VOL 2" written & illustrated by Dr. Lad*

As you can see in this lovely illustration above, nearly every line on the face has a meaning to it. The deeper the groove, the more severe and chronic the issue may be. If the line is very slight but detectable, it is most likely pointing to an issue that is a bit more recent and mild. However, these issues should still be addressed since, without proper treatment, a mild disorder may eventually become more severe.

Common Lines on the Face and Their Meaning

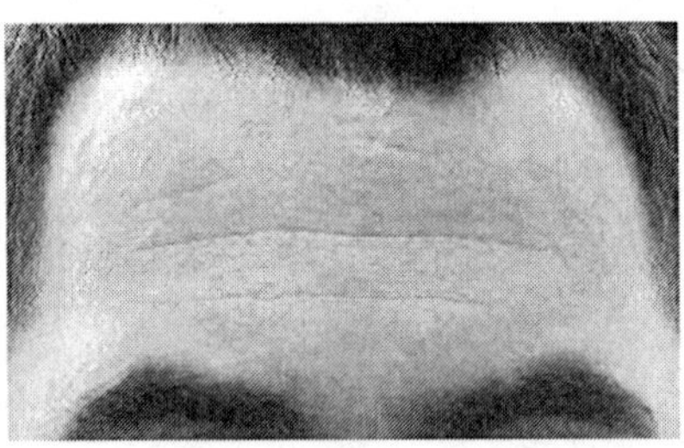

Figure: *Horizontal lines on the forehead:*

If you are experiencing lines that run horizontally across your forehead, it is most likely due to a history of chronic worry and anxiety. These lines are telltale signs of this issue and in today's society are all too common. Excessive anxiety and worry is considered a Vata disorder and can be pacified through Vata-reducing diet, lifestyle, and herbal treatments.

***Figure:** Nasolabial lines:*

Often called "laugh lines," prominent nasolabial lines are actually a clear indication of malabsorption (nothing to laugh about). Malabsorption occurs when our bodies are not absorbing nutrients properly due to weak digestion, improper diet, toxins, inflammation of the GI tract, and other issues. The more prominent the lines, the more serious the issue, and the longer the treatment process. Other physical signs of malabsorption include teeth marks on the perimeter of the tongue and vertical lines going down the nails. Treatment for this issue will vary according to the specific cause of the malabsorption.

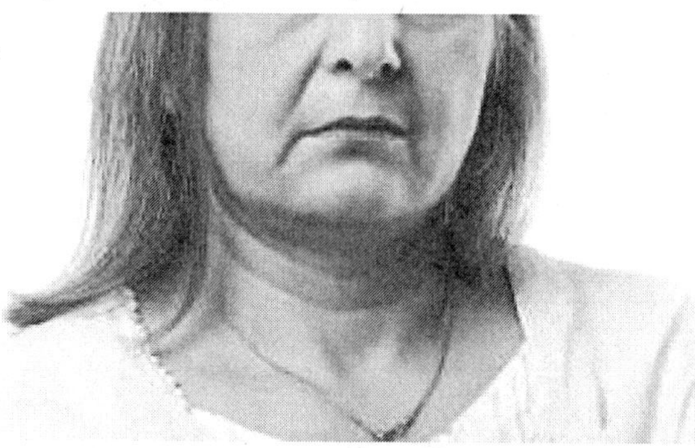

***Figure:** Downward lines on the outer edges of the lips (often called marionette lines):*

If you are noticing downward lines coming from the outer side of the lips (where the upper and lower lip meets), this is an indication of chronic, unresolved sadness and grief. Often called "marionette lines," these lines can be caused by past trauma, unresolved childhood experiences, unresolved issues with loved ones, or a history of depression, among other causes.

Dealing with unresolved grief is not easy, as it can bring up suppressed emotions that have been hidden away for quite some time. Everyone will have their own way to heal from grief, but the first step will be to examine where it is coming from and allow it the freedom to emerge. Some powerful tools for this are meditation, yoga, pranayama, journaling, therapy, and internal reflection.

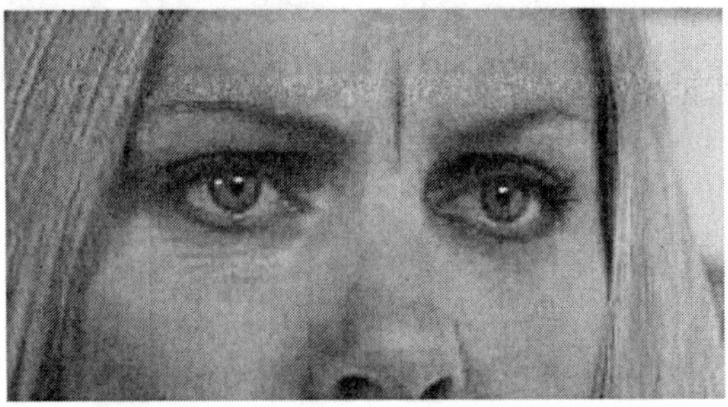

Figure: *Vertical line between the center of the eyebrows:*

A vertical line between the eyebrows that lies fairly center is often an indication of chronic skepticism. It often indicates a long-term Pitta imbalance and can also be related to an individual who is overly headstrong, judgmental, or critical (all Pitta issues). If this is the case, Pitta-pacifying measures should be practiced, especially ones that deal with the mind and emotions.

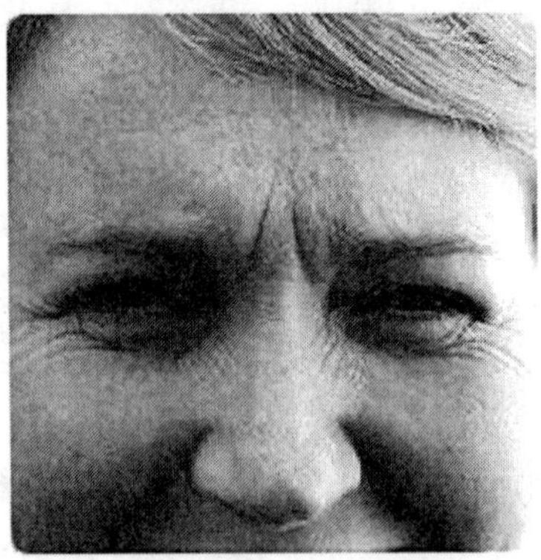

Figure: *Vertical line on the inner eyebrows (right, left, or both):*

A vertical line that forms on the right inner eyebrow (between the brows, but more to the right), is revealing low liver energy, a current liver disorder, or potential future liver issues. Alternately, if the line is forming more towards the inner left eyebrow, this is a sign of low spleen energy and the possibility of a past, future, or current spleen disorder. These organ lines may be separate on some individuals, although commonly they are seen together. As with the skepticism line mentioned above, these lines are often caused by a Pitta imbalance and may stem from deep-seated, unresolved anger (a Pitta emotion).

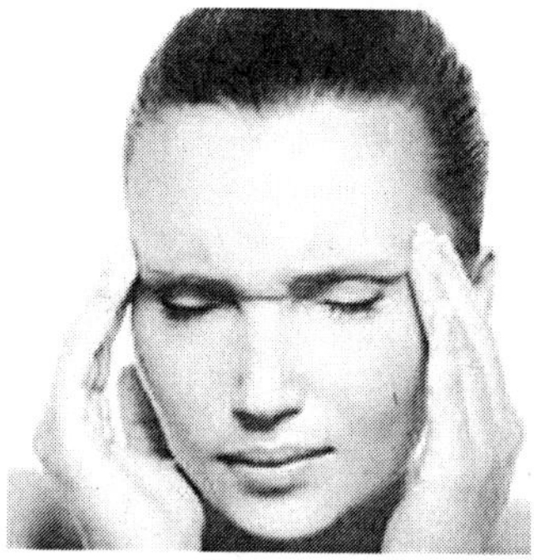

Figure: *Horizontal line between the eyebrows:*

If the line between the eyebrows runs horizontally, this is indicating future prostate, cervix, or reproductive issues due to low energy in each respective area. This line is a bit less common, but may be seen along with a few of the other facial lines indicating weak energy in these areas (read below). Since this line is said to be a future sign of these issues, one can use this knowledge as a guide to prevention, strengthening these organs before potential disease arises.

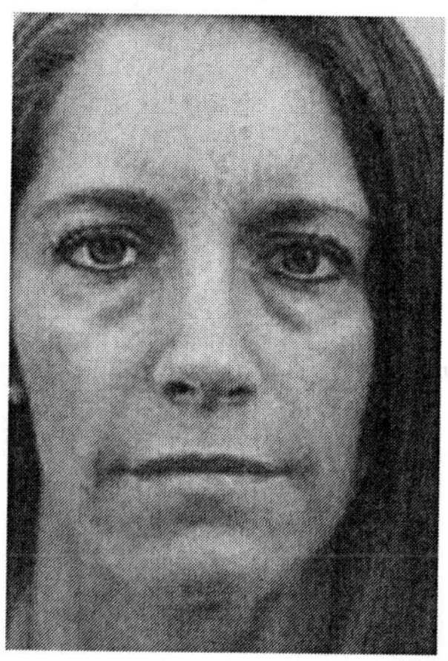

Figure: *Bags and puffiness under the eyes:*

Bags and general puffiness under the eyes seems to be a common issue and annoyance for countless individuals. Many people relate it to being overly tired; however, there is actually a deeper root to this undesirable symptom. Bags under the eyes are a clear indication of low kidney and/or adrenal energy. This can be caused by many things including chronic stress, burnt out adrenals, long-term sleep disorder, excessive caffeine intake, genetics, high blood pressure, or diabetes. Treatment will vary due to the specific cause for that individual. There are several herbs that focus on the health of the kidneys including punarnava and gokshura, and the adrenals such as tulsi, licorice, ashwagandha, and bala. These can be taken while also focusing on a proper diet and lifestyle regimen and, of course, removing the cause.

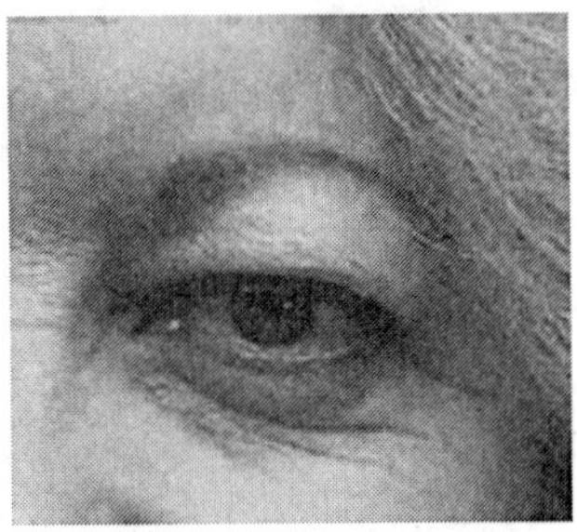

Figure: *Puffiness on the top eyelid:*

If there is puffiness over the top eyelid, this is an indication of low liver energy. This can indicate a current liver issue, but also may be a pre-symptom of a future liver disorder. Therefore, if an individual is experiencing this puffiness, appropriate treatment to heal and strengthen the liver should be administered as soon as possible.

Figure: *Prominent blood vessels on the temples:*

When you see an individual with blood vessels popping out over the temporal region of the forehead, this is showing a tendency of high blood pressure or hypertension. This is often a Pitta issue that is caused by excessive stress and anger (which leads to high blood pressure). Therefore, healing these emotions and treating the overall Pitta in the body and mind will help to reduce high blood pressure and reduce the bulging of the blood vessels.

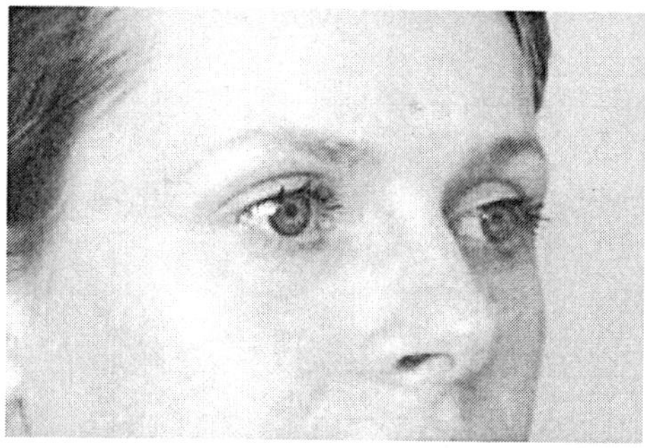

Figure: *Missing outer eyebrow:*

If you have begun to notice thinning of the outer eyebrows, this can be an indication of a few different issues. This hair loss may occur in diabetes, hypothyroidism, low blood sugar issues, or even chronic anxiety. If you are experiencing this issue, look for other indications of these multiple causes to reveal the most likely issue at play. For instance, if you are experiencing sudden, unexplained weight gain, fatigue, depression, and constipation along with the eyebrow hair loss, you are most likely looking at a thyroid issue and, therefore, should have your TSH levels tested. As always, the treatment will vary depending on the specific causes.

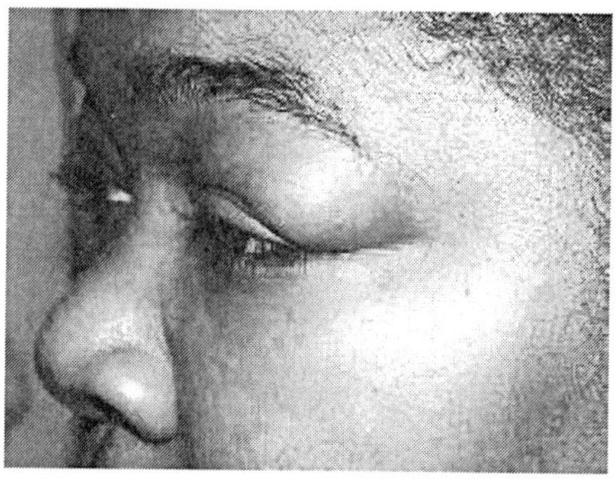

Figure: *Deep groove on the side of the outer eye:*

If you notice a single, deep groove stemming from the outer eye and coming outward (we're not talking about crow's feet), it may indicate low reproductive energy. This can cause issues such as menstrual disorders, infertility, low libido, menopausal issues, impotence, and other related disorders. Often, treatment of these issues involves proper diet, lifestyle, and herbal treatment that will remove the cause and nourish these organs.

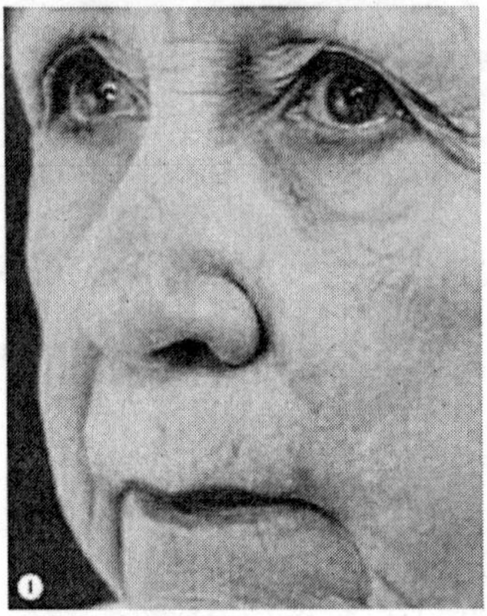

***Figure:** Deep nasal groove:*

If you notice deep grooves on the outside of the nostrils, this is showing low lung energy, chronic allergies, or a history of respiratory illness. This could be a general weakness in the area, although it most likely stems from a history of asthma, bronchitis, pneumonia, or something similar. When this deep groove is seen, one should work to strengthen the lungs with the appropriate herbs, while avoiding potential allergies and other triggers such as overexertion, etc. If there is congestion and mucus in the lungs, there is most likely a Kapha disorder; dryness and tightness will reveal a Vata condition; inflammation and infection presume a Pitta imbalance.

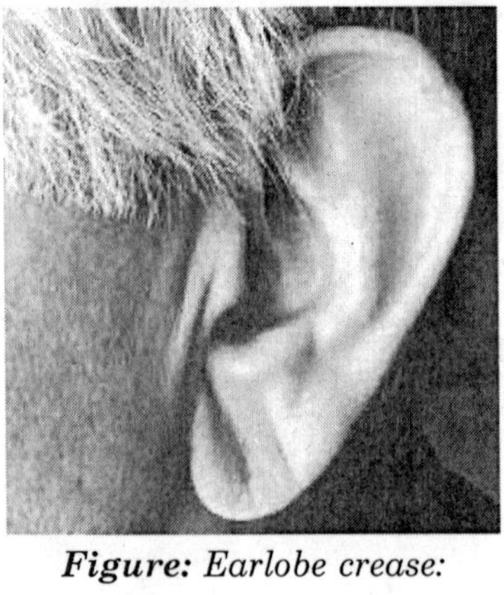

***Figure:** Earlobe crease:*

Amazingly enough, even the lines on your earlobe can indicate your current health condition and future risks. If you see a line that runs downward or sideways on the earlobes, you are most likely seeing a sign of high cholesterol and potential risk for future heart disease. These are both considered a Kapha disorder and, therefore, you will likely benefit from a Kapha-pacifying diet and lifestyle regimen while taking an herbal formula that works to reduce cholesterol levels and strengthen the heart.

Figure: *Prominent philtrum:*

Although a prominent philtrum is often interpreted as an attractive feature, it is actually an indication of a low libido and potentially weak reproductive organs. Therefore, if you are seeing a prominent philtrum above your lip, you may benefit from a rejuvenating regimen that works to strengthen the reproductive organs and increase overall sexual potency.

Figure: *Dimples on cheeks:*

Although there is no denying how cute a nice set of dimples can be, according to Ayurveda they are actually a sign of low reproductive energy. This may be seen as an obvious dimple in the cheek area (pictured here), or can also show up as a vertical line or crease where the dimple typically lies. Either way, this may be an indication of a current low libido, menstrual disorders, hormonal issues, impotence, infertility, or a future indication of issues to come and should be addressed accordingly.

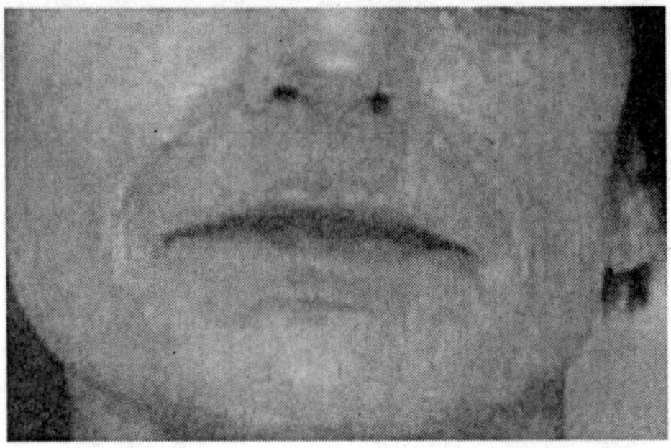

Figure: *Horizontal groove below the lower lip:*

If your chin is sporting a horizontal groove (often curved slightly downwards), this is most likely an indication of deep-seated, unresolved grief held in the body. Alternatively, this may also be a sign of a low libido (or both). If you suspect unresolved grief, this can be remedied by using some subtle tools to release stored emotions, allowing them to be safely processed. This may include yoga, meditation, pranayama, self-care techniques, journaling, therapy, or talking with loved ones. Whatever method resonates with you, make it a part of your routine, moving slowly to avoid releasing too much emotion all at once!

Figure: *Dimple on chin (cleft chin):*

The classic dimpled chin has more meaning than just a unique facial feature. It may be a sign that there is a weak prostate (or cervix in females), and can be a prodromal sign of issues to come in these vital organs. Therefore, an individual with a dimpled chin should take precautions and strengthen the prostate (or cervix) before any obvious disorder occurs.

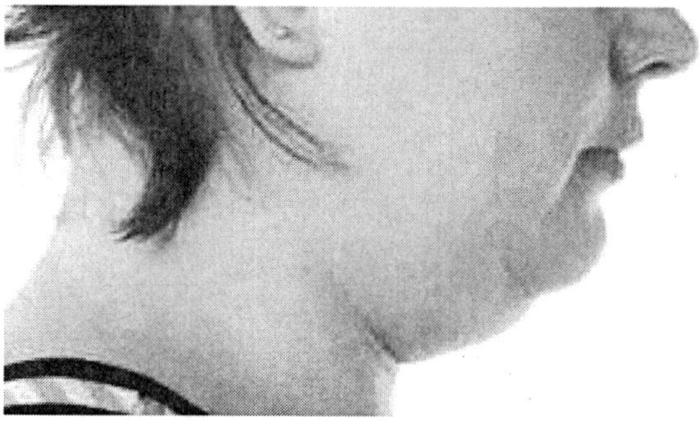

Figure: *Double chin:*

Not surprisingly, a double chin is considered a sign of a Kapha imbalance and can indicate current or future hypothyroidism. If this is the case, the Kapha should be pacified through diet, lifestyle, and herbal treatments while working to increase the metabolism to prevent or treat low thyroid energy.

Conclusion: Now that you have a better idea of what the lines on your face are revealing, the question is: What can you do with your findings? Of course, this will look different for each individual since the causes of these issues may come from genetics, improper diet, improper lifestyle, or general misuse (or all of the above). Once you realize the potential health issues that are prevalent, you can examine further to find out the causes. While you work to remove the causes (this is not always easy), you can simultaneously take herbs, and follow the appropriate diet and lifestyle plan that will help strengthen the affected organs or systems.

For example, if you have several lines pointing to low liver energy, you can examine possible causes. Perhaps you find there are liver issues prevalent in your family and you also have a mild history of consistent alcohol intake and deep-rooted anger (the liver is the organ of anger). You would then work to reduce the alcohol consumption while also taking some liver strengthening herbs such as Guduchi, Kutki and Neem. You can also perform a mild detox to flush out toxins and then go on a Pitta-reducing diet. You will also need to address any anger issues and work to create emotional balance while processing through volatile emotions that have been stored in your body. This can be done through meditation, yoga, pranayama, and other methods of healing the body and mind.

Before trying out any magical wrinkle treatment, first examine a bit deeper and discover what your face is trying to tell you. Although some facial lines are easier to reduce than others, treating the root causes will not only give you a more youthful appearance but will also increase your inner health and wellness.

Ayurvedic Nail Analysis

There are several physical diagnostic tools that are commonly practiced in Ayurveda and one of the main ones includes nail assessment (called Nakha Pariksha). Just as the tongue, hair, skin, and other external attributes are very telling of one's internal health, the nails can be a strong indicator of possible issues occurring in the body as well.

According to Ayurvedic medicine, the nails are a by-product of the bones (asthi dhatu) and, therefore, the health of the bones can be reflected in the health of your nails. In this sense, thin, brittle nails may correlate to thin, brittle bones.

Areas of imbalance that can be seen through nail analysis include:

- Bone health
- Malabsorption
- Lung issues
- Heart issues
- Metabolic conditions
- Inflammation
- Parasites
- Psoriasis and other skin disorders
- Autoimmune conditions such as Lupus (SLE) and alopecia
- Thyroid issues (hypo or hyper)
- Digestive issues
- GI tract issues
- Liver issues
- Vata, Pitta or Kapha disorder
- Vata, Pitta, or Kapha constitution (not by itself, but used as a helpful indicator)

In Ayurveda, everything we do and every trait we carry is a piece of the doshic puzzle of your natural born constitution (known as

Prakriti). Therefore, even our nails can give us some indication which dosha is predominant in our constitution and, also, which dosha is currently out of balance.

Here is a brief chart that gives the typical findings of the nail as it relates to the different doshas.

Dosha	Nail Qualities
Vata	• Thin • Brittle, breaks easily • Dark • Dry • Rough cuticles • Tendency for nail biting (shows Vata imbalance) • May show little to no moons (due to weak digestion)
Pitta	• Soft • Pink • Oily, shiny • Medium in delicacy • Flexible • Smooth • Normal to large moons (luna)
Kapha	• Strong • Thick • Rarely ever break • Shiny, oily, lubricated • Soft cuticles • May show little to no moons (due to sluggish digestion and slow metabolism)

Nail Abnormalities and What They Mean

Longitudinal Lines on the Nails

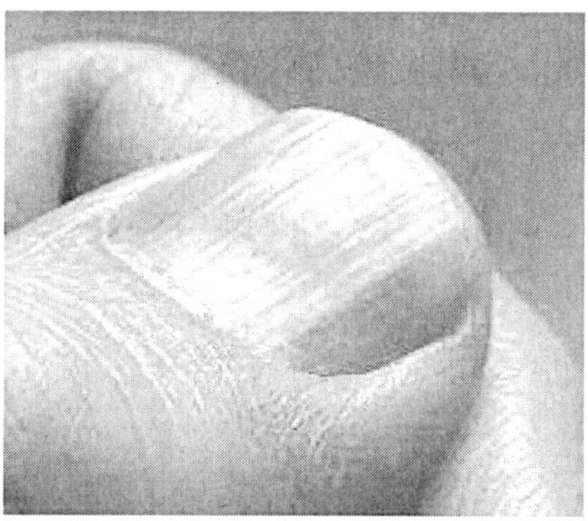

These long lines are all too common for many individuals and typically indicate a clear sign of malabsorption of nutrients in the body. They typically cover the entire nail, from the bottom to the top. Very mild lines that are hard to see without the proper light show a very mild case. The deeper the lines, however, the stronger the deficiency and, therefore, the more important it will be to discover the cause and remove it. Malabsorption can be related to poor digestion, excessive toxins in the system, inflammation in the GI tract, a Vata digestive disorder (Vishama Agni), a Kapha digestive disorder (Manda Agni), a Pitta digestive disorder (Tikshna Agni), or a poor diet in general. Since this is only one piece of the puzzle, other analysis must be further completed in order to establish the actual cause.

Horizontal Lines or Transverse Groove

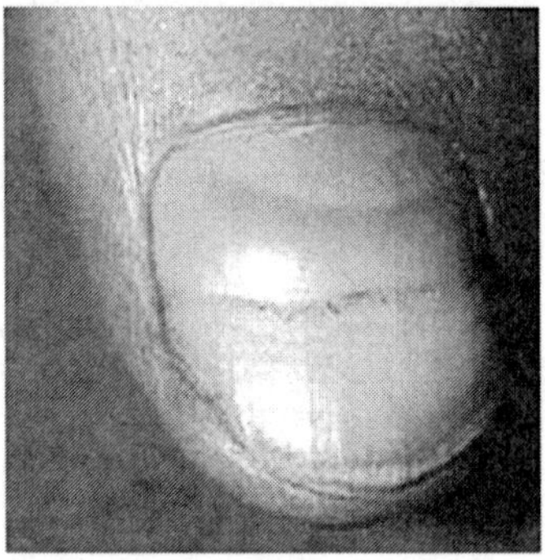

According to Ayurveda, a deep line that runs horizontal to the nail is an indication of a strong illness, infection, or depletion that occurred during the time that specific part of the nail was growing. It also can mean an issue of the metabolism, showing vitiated digestion at the time of growth. If there are multiple horizontal lines on the nail, this indicates a reoccurring issue and most likely is showing a chronic condition (whether metabolic, infection, depletion, etc.) In some cases, these multiple lines can relate to the involvement of an under-active thyroid.

Absence of Moons (Lunula)

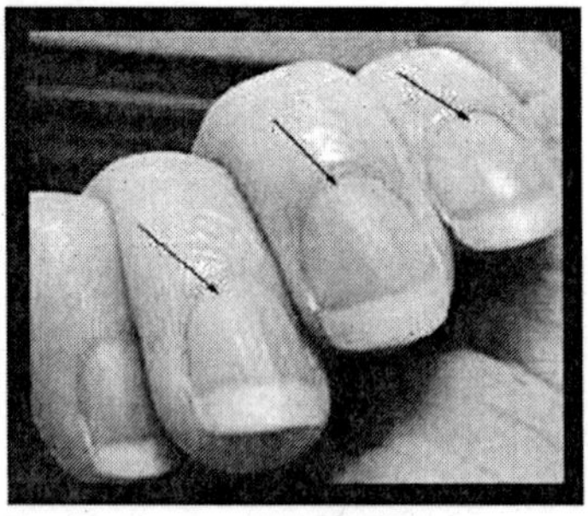

In Ayurveda, the lunula of the nail represents one's Agni or fire in the body. If you look at your nails and notice there are no moons (lunula) or extremely small moons, this is a sign that there is weak digestion or fire in the system. Weak digestion is an indication of poor metabolism and a potential build-up of toxins in the system. It also is a common root cause for most disease and disorder and should be treated immediately.

Large Moons (Lunula)

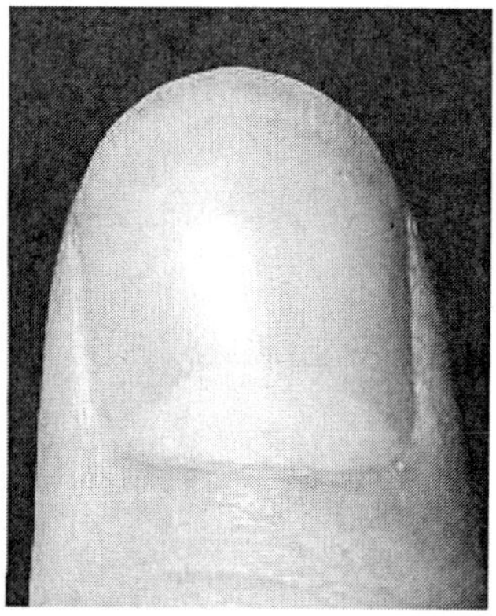

If you have nice, large moons on your thumb to the pinky finger, this represents a strong healthy fire in the system. Ideally, one should have a large moon on the thumb, as they remain strong, but get a bit smaller with each respective finger. However, if they seem larger than "normal" this may show an overactive fire in the body which can lead to Pitta issues such as loose stools, hyperacidity, inflammation, and malabsorption of nutrients. This simply means there is too much fire in the system and cooling practices and diet should be administered. ***Please note that if the whole finger is white, except for a small crescent at the top, this is a different issue typically caused by liver disease.

Red, Puffy Nail Fold (area of skin that borders the nail)

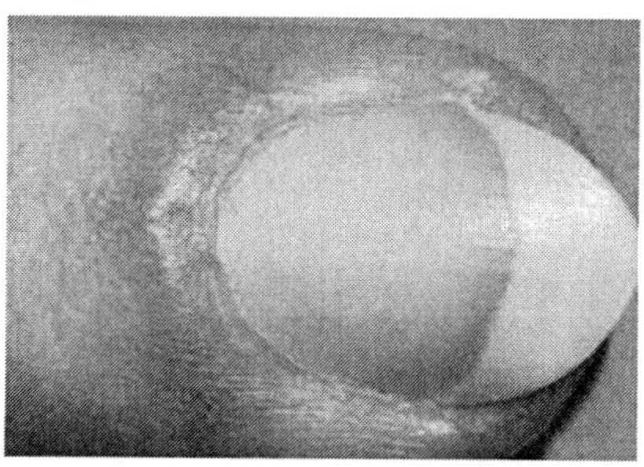

If you notice a red, puffy border along the nail fold, this is typically a sign of parasites or infection in the system. Parasites are prevalent in many individuals and have multiple causes. A few common causes are traveling or living in a developing country, drinking from rivers or lakes, not washing hands properly after elimination, or through a transfer from our furry little friends. Parasites are efficiently treated in Ayurveda through proper diet and herbs. ***A less common cause of the red nail fold can be through Lupus or another connective tissue disorder.

White Spots

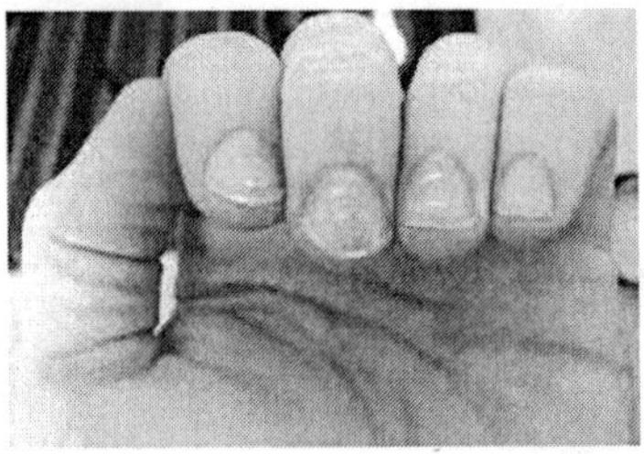

White spots on the nails are very common among a large number of individuals. Of course, if this is just a one-time occurrence, it may just be due to a trauma to that part of the nail. Often, however, this is seen on more than one nail and is a recurring issue. If you are experiencing the latter, this simply means that there is a calcium, zinc, and/or magnesium deficiency in the body. This may be due to a poor diet or could be the result of malabsorption. Malabsorption is a lack of ability for your body to absorb specific nutrients and has a wide range of causes. Some of these include poor digestion, inflammation in the GI tract, excessive toxins in the colon, intake of allergenic foods, chronic loose stools, or parasitical infection. Once this issue is removed, the white spots should stop appearing after the nail has grown out.

Pitting of the Nail

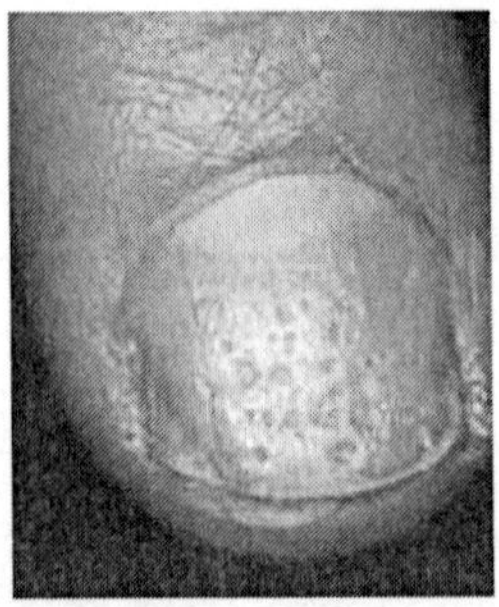

Nail pitting is typically seen in individuals that either have psoriasis, eczema, or another inflammatory skin disorder. It also can occur when an individual has alopecia, Lupus (SLE), or another connective tissue disorder. If you see pitting and do not currently have any of these conditions, this may be a sign that you are at risk for one of these disorders. Therefore, other areas should be investigated to see if there are any other warning symptoms or signs occurring. Skin disorders often have an origin in increased Pitta (aka heat).

Nail Biting

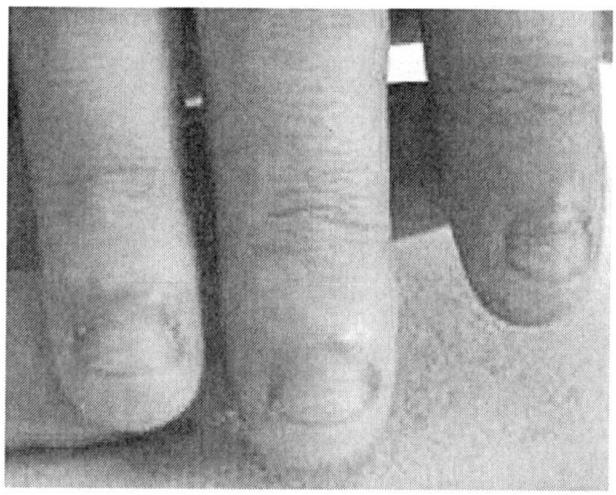

Nail biting is a telling sign of excessive Vata in the system. This is typically a symptom of high anxiety, worry, or fear-all of which are Vata imbalances in the Nervous System. This can be a chronic or acute issue, depending on the individual. Typically, one with a nail-biting habit does it without awareness and rarely has nails that grow beyond the nail bed. Whether an old habit or new, this is a clear sign of high Vata and should be treated accordingly.

Yellow Nails

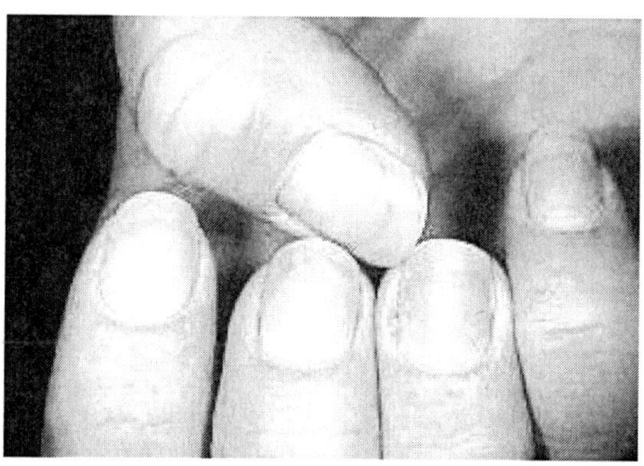

Yellow nails can mean a few different issues and may have a wide array of severeness. One potential issue is a fungal infection. This is more common as you grow older, although any individual can be at risk. A fungal infection can affect one nail selectively or multiple nails at once. Fungal infections can be due to genetics, lowered immunity, liver issues, toxins in the system, or excessive use of nail polish (or a combination of these). Other common causes of yellow nails include jaundice or other liver issues, tuberculosis, lung infections, or certain side effects from medications.

Pale Nails

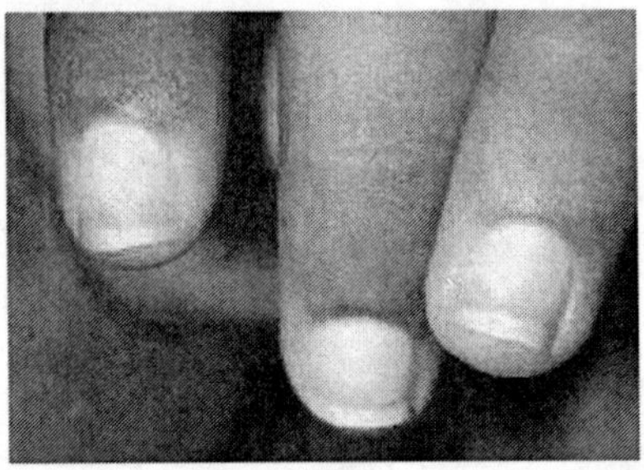

Pale nails typically show anemia (low red blood cells) in the system. This can be due to excessive blood loss (heavy menstruation or injury); an iron, folate or B12 deficiency; ulcer; parasitical infection; certain medications (including NSAIDS); malabsorption; chronic diseases such as cancer, rheumatoid arthritis or HIV; or many different autoimmune conditions. Anemia can cause fatigue, weakness, poor circulation, frequent bruising, shortness of breath, irregular heartbeat, and cognitive issues. If anemia is suspected, one can look to see if other symptoms are involved (or not), as well as examining the tongue and the pink under the eye (when stretched down) to see if these areas are also pale.

Bluish-Purple Nails

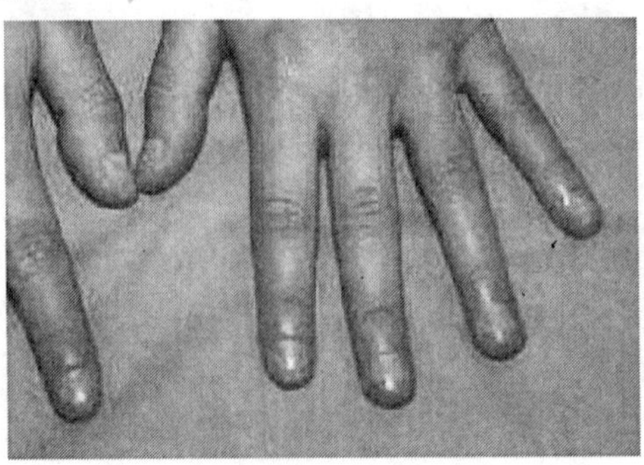

If you see a bluish-purple tint to your nails, this may signify that there is a lack of oxygen in the system causing hypoxia or acute cyanosis (lack of oxygen to the tissues). This can be caused by a chronic issue or a severe acute issue. There may be a pulmonary infection such as chronic bronchitis or a long-term condition such as asthma or emphysema. A great way to increase your lung energy is with regular practice of Alternate Nostril Breathing (aka Nadi Shodhana).

Nail Separation (Onycholysis)

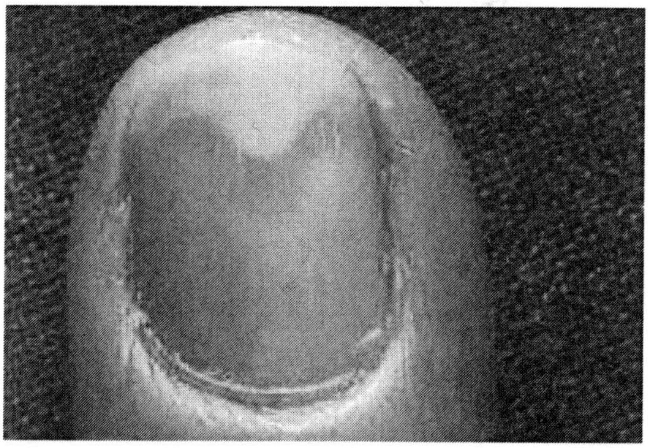

Onycholysis is when the nail begins to separate from the nail bed causing a white discolouration. If the white discolouration becomes yellow, it is most likely that the nail has obtained a secondary infection due to the separation. Onycholysis is commonly caused by skin disorders such as psoriasis, eczema, and dermatitis but also can stem from trauma, excessive manicures, hyperthyroidism, hypothyroidism, primary fungal infection, poor circulation, or inflammatory arthritis.

Clubbed Nails

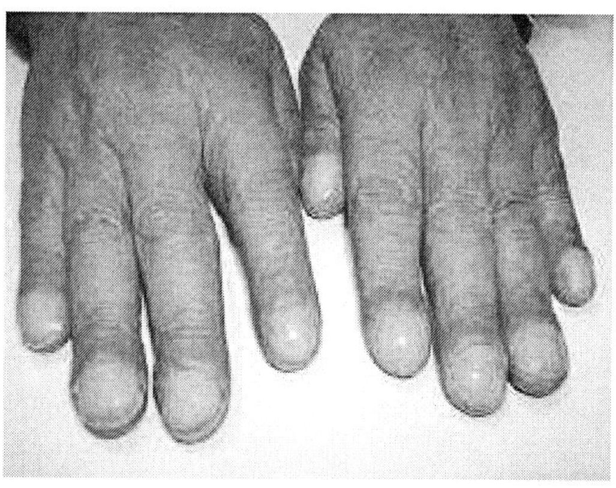

Although not as common as some other nail abnormalities, clubbed nails are often prevalent with heart or pulmonary issues. They may occur in tuberculosis, pneumonia, chronic bronchitis, congestive heart failure, or mitral stenosis. No matter the cause, clubbing of the fingers typically is a sign that the peripheral tissues are not getting a sufficient amount of oxygen and there is low Prana (aka life-force) in the body.

Spooned Nails (Koilonychia)

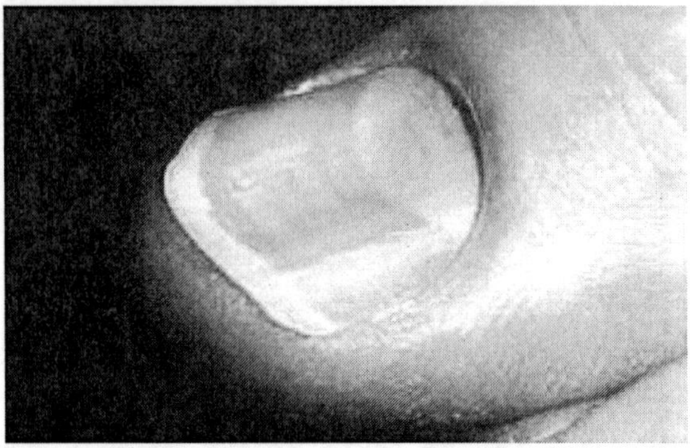

A "spooned" nail is a nail that is flat or concave at the surface, scooping in the center. This can range in severity, with the worst cases causing a splitting of the nail down the middle. The most common cause for the spooned nail is iron deficiency anemia (also see "pale nails" above). Other potential causes are autoimmune issues such as Lupus (SLE), psoriasis, lichen planus or Raynaud's Disease, genetic disorders, vascular disease, or trauma.

Lip Diagnosis

Lip diagnosis in Ayurveda plays an important role in analysing various ailments and applying the proper healing method. Just like other features of the body such as eyes, face, nails and tongue, the lips are also crucial in mirroring the health of the body and disorders of various physical organs. Different features of the lips viz. size, contour, colour, surface and shape must be observed carefully to figure out different disorders. Rough and dry lips indicate a vata derangement or dehydration. Tremors or dryness or lips is also caused due to fear and nervousness. Pale lips of an individual signify a person suffering from anaemia. The lips of a person becomes blackish-brown owing to chronic smoking.

A chronic pitta derangement and the presence of herpes can be figured out by observing the repeated attacks of inflammatory patches along the margins of the lips. Multiple pale brown spots on the lips are indicative of worms in the colon or poor digestion. The lips often become yellow in case a person is afflicted with jaundice. If the lips of an individual become blue it reflects heart disorders and occurs due to lack of oxygen in the lips. Similarly disorders in different organs causes discolouration of various area of lips. A person with vata constitution has thin and dry lips while one having pitta constitution has red lips. Thick and oily lips signify kapha lips.

Ayurveda Perspective On Thin Lips

Thin lips are constitutionally natural for Vata. Since light Vata constitutions tend to have thin skin, they often frequently have thin lips. However, thin lips may also be a sign of deficient ojas (nourishment), especially if your constitution is Pitta or Kapha. Cold, poor circulation, and dehydration may also impact your lips. If your lips are chronically chapped, this may indicate a fungal infection at the corners of your lips. This is called Angular Chelitis. A foot or other fungal infection may cause the lips to become chapped as the infection disrupts the body's normal upward circulation. A fungal infection of the feet creates a heat condition in the leg, causing blood vessels in the leg to dilate, and dryness in the upper body.

Balance Your Body with Diet, Herbs, & Lifestyles Having These Biocharacteristics Everything you eat has an effect on your body, which Ayurveda categorizes in a simple and easy way, using biocharacteristics (gunas). Biocharacteristics are qualities (like cold and hot) that describe the effect a food or herb has on your body. Cooling foods like cucumber, decrease metabolism. Heating foods like chili pepper, stimulate your body and increase metabolism. For 'Thin lips', you should select foods with the following biocharacteristics. Individual results will vary, based on your body type and the root cause of your imbalance.

Eye Diagnosis

Healthy vision is a critical component in everyone's life to see and make sense of the world around us. Practicing preventative eye care includes early diagnosis and timely treatment that results in improved learning and better quality of life. Hence, eye exams every six months lower your risk of health issues related to eye health or vision.

For those who do not know, this is not actually an eye test to determine the physical condition of the eyes. Eye diagnosis gives us the tools to see disease potential in the patient's body (from genetic weakness) and recognise metabolic individuality. This vital information can lead us to explore further diagnostic testing or therapeutic interventions. Above all, eye diagnosis is useful in preventative medicine which is the key to recognising and treating organ weakness or function before it has manifested clinically as a disease. Most of what is known today about eye diagnosis has come to us from Germany, where this form of diagnosis has a very strong and reputable basis.

The term 'eye diagnosis' refers more accurately than 'iris diagnosis' or the more commonly used term 'iridology' which refers specifically to the study of the iris. Eye diagnosis employs the study of other parts of the eye as well including the pupil, sclera, conjunctiva and retina. Therefore eye diagnosis is also, even more correctly, called the study of 'ophthalmological phenomena'.

A good eye diagnostician, like any other health professional must start with the assumption that each patient is an individual. Each person is unique. This means that any system of diagnosis, including eye diagnosis, should not be looked as an exact science but also an art. In practiced hands, eye diagnosis is an extremely valuable tool because the signs in the eye indicate most aspects of a person's state of health.

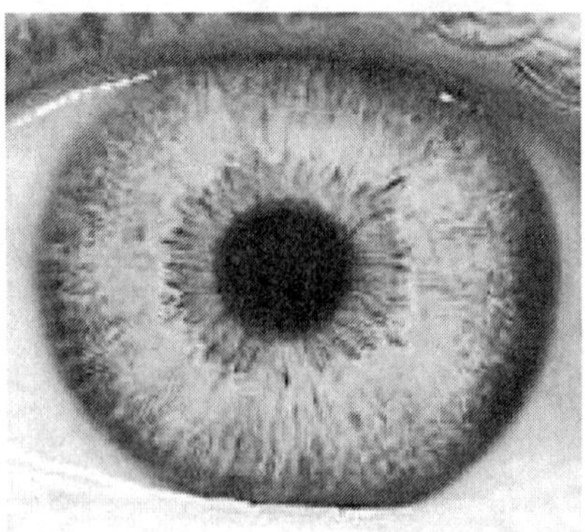

Despite many theories as to how the inherited conditions and predispositions in our bodies, as well as the changes that have taken place during the degradation of our health or for that matter during its improvement, are exactly transposed through to the eyes, is still subject to research. Most theories are essentially based on the fact that the nerves that link our brain to every part of our body as well as the myriads of chemical reactions occurring non-stop in every one of our cells, and a lot of this massive amount of information is reported back to our brain.

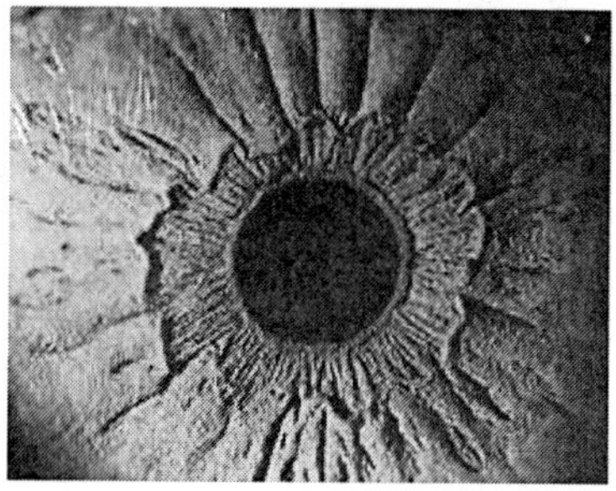

The eyes are simply an extension to the brain and just as the massive amounts of information from our environment get captured by our eyes and get transferred to the brain, information from inside us gets transmitted to the brain which reflects it in our eyes. Indeed the eye's retina and optic nerve are a part of the brain, as during early development a small part of the brain pouches out and becomes the retina and optic nerve.

The eye is therefore the only part of our brain which can be seen directly - it happens when the optician shines a bright light and looks at the retina, the innermost layer of our eye and the optic nerve that carries visual information to the brain, the most complex arrangement of matter in the known universe.

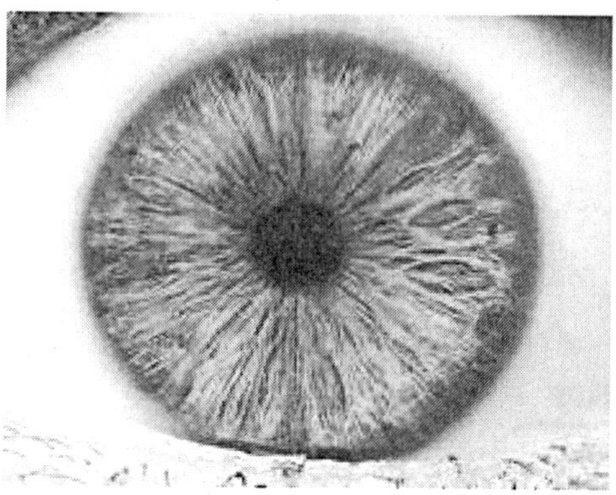

"The eyes are the windows to our body." Although this is an explanation lacking any conventional scientific depth for the moment and does not fully explain what happens in currently known or understood scientific terms, with the advent of quantum mechanics and epigenetics, new frontiers of knowledge are becoming exposed and available for the greater understanding of the role the eyes play, as a diagnostic tool to make us more aware of our body's health.

The ancient science of Ayurveda delivers numerous safe, effective, and preventive methods for maintaining eye health for better well-being. The Ayurvedic Approach to Eye Health provides long-term benefits to replenish and strengthen eye health throughout your life. Ayurveda College in Kerala recommends eye care routines and lifestyle modifications to prevent eye disorders and for a refreshing way of life. The holistic approach of Ayurveda aims at deep cleansing of the eyes by assisting lubrication and revitalization of optic nerves to improve vision.

The Ayurvedic Approach to Eye Health: In the modern scenario, we put our eyes through inbound stress with the overuse of digital exposure resulting in doshas imbalances. From an ayurvedic point of view, eye issues are an expression of an imbalance of the three doshas - Vata, Kapha, and pitta. Hence, the imbalance of doshas results in several ailments that cause eye strain, irritation, inflammation, and dryness. However, regardless of the generation gap, people switch to the Ayurveda tradition for detoxification of the body for better eye health. Ayurveda treatment remedies replenish eye health with cooling, calming, moisturizing and soothing qualities to empower eye vision. Ayurveda adheres to diet regulations and lifestyle recommendations to counterbalance the excess heat and intensity that the eyes are experiencing with eye-related ailments. Hence, the Ayurveda eye detoxification program nourishes optic nerves that help to relieve eye strain and the deteriorating effects of prolonged exposure to digital screens. The time-tested scientific approach of Ayurveda corrects the normal flow of fluids, essential nutrients, and waste material in and out of the optic cells by eliminating toxins accumulated in the optic nerves.

Eye Problems From an Ayurvedic Point of View: The Ayurveda perspective of treating eye disorders restores the lost balance between these life-sustaining forces in a natural way. The accumulation of cellular toxicity gained from a sedentary lifestyle, poor diet, and unhealthy nutrition leads to several eye disorders such as Dry eye syndrome, Burning in the eye, Vata diseases in the eyes, Curved eye, Conjunctivitis, Night blindness, Squinting, Myopia and Computer Vision Syndrome. Ayurveda courses in India help to gain awareness regarding various eye disorders and prevention techniques for better eye health.

The holistic approach of Ayurveda cleanses internal optic nerves by removing dust from the cornea and thereby moisturizes the dry eye. Also, the Ayurveda treatment approach aids in the improvement of eye disturbances and thus, improves the clarity of the vision. Hence,

Eye problems from an ayurvedic point of view are cured for thousands of patients with proven benefits in correcting the abnormal deviation of optimal eye health.

Importance of Eye Care: Better eye vision is one of the wonderful senses that can be easily connected with the emotions of surroundings. Hence, it is an obvious task to protect your eyes from developing various eye disorders and thereby reduce the odds of blindness or low vision. The sooner you diagnose eye-related ailments, the more likely you are to get a cure with Ayurveda naturally. However, annual eye appointments with high-end Nutrition and Hydration can take care of our eyes and help us to stay away from common eye disorders. Hence, it is essential to take steps ahead to take necessary precautions to protect your eyes and lead a quality life.

Causes of Poor Eyesight: Poor eyesight may be rooted in certain lifestyle habits and other health concerns. Hence, preventative measures should be taken into account to protect your eyesight by addressing the root cause of poor vision. Let us consider common causes of poor eyesight that disturbs one's daily routine.

- Aging
- Over-exposure to UV rays
- Excess consumption of alcohol and certain drugs
- Improper usage of contact lens
- Smoking and tobacco use
- Diabetes
- Skipping visits to an eye consultant
- Failure in wearing protective goggles
- Family medical history
- Too much screening time

Ayurvedic Treatments for the Eyes: Netra Tharpanam is an eye rejuvenating treatment in which warm medicated oil is poured into a covering over the eyes. The procedure may nourish the surrounding tissues of the eyes which helps to improve vision. Nasya has prescribed the Ayurveda technique to eliminate eye dryness that occurs from respiratory and allergic conditions. Netradhara is an ayurvedic medicated oil wash for rejuvenating eyes to get relief from computer vision syndrome and dry eyes. Shirodhara is a complete relaxation technique in which a continuous stream of oil, milk or medicated buttermilk is poured over the Third Eye for complete rejuvenation and helps in eliminating eye-related ailments.

Ayurvedic Remedies to Strengthen the Eyes: Ayurvedic Remedies to Strengthen the Eyes aims at correcting the imbalances of Vata dosha in the body and the eyes, thereby relieving the symptoms of eye disorders, and the digestive fire. Consider the below Ayurveda solutions to prevent eye-related weakness and stress.

- Practice eye exercise to eliminate pressure on optic nerves
- Wash eyes with cold water for lubrication
- Stay hydrated to prevent eye dryness
- Eat a balanced diet for the nourishments of optic nerves
- Get sound sleep
- Wear protective eyewear in dust-borne surroundings
- Don't skip meals
- Try to eat at regular intervals
- Get regular eye exams twice a year

If your eyes are feeling irritated, dry, red, watery, painful, fatigued, or swollen, approach the School of Ayurveda and Panchakarma, the leading Ayurveda treatments in India for exclusive eye care. Start your journey towards comprehensive wellness with our unique range of Ayurvedic eye care solutions. There exist several Diploma courses in Netra Rogas for a better understanding of the importance of eye health and how it affects our daily routine. Our expert team of Ayurveda practitioners indulges in various secret eye care routine practices to achieve the goal of nourishing vision. Our recommended natural blend of lifestyle routine along with nutrient-rich diet help to lead a quality lifestyle with better vision.

Chapter 3

Causes of Diseases in Ayurveda

Introduction

Diseases, according to Ayurveda are caused by the imbalance in the three doshas. The predominance of a dosha in an individual's constitution indicates his or her vulnerability to a particular disease. Diseases in Ayurveda are classified according to the origin of their causes.

It is important to first understand the approach of Ayurveda towards diseases and their prevention if one wishes to delve into the nuances of this form of natural treatment. The great sages who compiled the texts that define modern Ayurveda have carefully laid down instructions on how diseases must be identified and treated. Diseases can be broadly divided into the Sarira (physical) and the Manasa (mental), and their sub-divisions go deep into the root causes of ailments. External and internal factors combine to cause sickness, and the vaidyan must carefully mix perception, experience, and knowledge to chart a course for the patient's recovery.

Ayurvedic medicines are distilled from natural herbs that are used as the primary source. The concept of dravya is extremely important, as this substance, a combination of the Five Great Elements, is used to prepare Ayurvedic medicines. These medicines, administrated according to the condition of the patients and the severity of the ailment, have helped vaidyans serve patients for eons.

Lifestyle and Routine

In recent decades, life style as an important factor of health is more interested by researchers. According to WHO, 60% of related factors to individual health and quality of life are correlated to lifestyle (1). Millions of people follow an unhealthy lifestyle. Hence, they encounter illness, disability and even death.

Ayurveda's Role in Longevity: Unlocking the Secrets to a Healthy and Fulfilling Life

Longevity, the pursuit of a long and fulfilling life, has been a cherished goal for many individuals throughout history. Ayurveda, the ancient Indian system of medicine, offers a holistic approach to achieving longevity by promoting balance and harmony in all aspects of life. In this article, we will delve deeper into the various facets of Ayurveda, including its principles, practices, herbs, healing therapies, and lifestyle habits that contribute to longevity. We will also explore the correlation between Ayurveda and modern science, share success stories of individuals who have benefited from Ayurvedic longevity practices, discuss the criticisms and challenges faced by Ayurveda, and explore the future implications of Ayurvedic longevity on individual well-being.

Ayurvedic Principles for Longevity: To understand the role of Ayurveda in promoting longevity, it is important to familiarize ourselves with the underlying principles of this ancient science. Ayurveda revolves around the concept of three doshas-Vata, Pitta, and Kapha-and their balance. Achieving longevity involves keeping these doshas in check by regulating digestion, detoxifying the body, and living in harmony with the environment.

1. Balance of Doshas: Maintaining a balance of the doshas is crucial for overall well-being and longevity. This can be achieved by understanding your unique dosha constitution and making lifestyle choices, such as consuming a diet that aligns with your dosha type, adhering to a routine tailored to your constitution, and adapting to seasonal changes.

2. Importance of Digestion: In Ayurveda, digestion, or Agni, is considered the cornerstone of health. A robust Agni ensures efficient nutrient absorption and elimination of waste products. To promote longevity, Ayurveda emphasizes consuming a well-balanced diet consisting of whole foods, fresh fruits, vegetables, and legumes, while avoiding processed and unhealthy foods that can disrupt digestion.
3. Detoxification: Regular detoxification, known as Panchakarma, is an integral part of Ayurveda. Panchakarma involves five cleansing methods, including Vamana (Emesis), Virechana (Purgation), and Nasya (Nasal cleansing), among others. These therapies help eliminate toxins from the body, rejuvenate the organs, and promote longevity.
4. Living in Harmony with Nature: Ayurveda recognizes the profound influence of the environment on an individual's health and lifespan. Living in a balanced and natural environment, surrounded by clean air, water, and a harmonious atmosphere, contributes to overall well-being and longevity. For eg. Ritucharya, a Dincharya that informs how to make small efforts to make yourself healthy and happy per day or adapt as per seasonal changes.

Ayurvedic Practices for Longevity: Ayurveda offers a wide range of practices that promote longevity by enhancing overall health and well-being. Incorporating these practices into your daily routine can have a profound impact on your longevity journey.

1. Yoga and Meditation: Yoga and meditation are fundamental practices in Ayurveda. Yoga postures, combined with

conscious breathing, help maintain physical flexibility, balance, and strength. Meditation promotes mental clarity, emotional balance, and spiritual growth, contributing to overall well-being and longevity.

2. Daily Routines (Dinacharya): Ayurveda emphasizes the importance of a disciplined daily routine, known as Dinacharya, to maintain optimal health. This routine includes practices such as yoga, meditation, oil pulling, tongue scraping, and specific times for waking up, eating, and sleeping. Following a consistent daily routine promotes a healthy body, mind, and spirit.
3. Seasonal Routines (Ritucharya): Ayurveda acknowledges the impact of seasonal changes on the body and mind. Ritucharya involves adapting your lifestyle, diet, and daily routine according to the changing seasons. This practice helps maintain balance, prevent seasonal imbalances, and supports longevity.
4. Ayurvedic Diet and Nutrition: Ayurveda places great emphasis on a balanced and personalized diet for longevity. It recommends consuming fresh, organic, and locally sourced foods that suit your dosha constitution. Ayurvedic nutrition also incorporates the use of herbs, spices, and medicinal preparations that help balance the doshas and promote overall health.
5. Breathing Exercises (Pranayama): Pranayama, a set of yogic breathing exercises, helps balance the doshas, calm the mind, and increase vital energy. Regular practice of pranayama enhances overall health and well-being, contributing to longevity.

Ayurvedic Herbs and Supplements for Longevity: Ayurveda harnesses the healing power of herbs and natural supplements to support longevity. These herbs, when used appropriately, can promote overall well-being and enhance longevity.

1. Ashwagandha: Ashwagandha, an adaptogenic herb, helps the body adapt to stress and promotes overall well-being. It supports healthy cortisol levels, boosts energy, and enhances vitality, contributing to longevity.
2. Brahmi: Brahmi is a renowned herb known for its cognitive-enhancing properties. It improves memory, concentration, and overall brain function, thus supporting longevity.

3. Triphala: Triphala is a combination of three fruits-Amalaki (Indian Gooseberry), Bibhitaki, and Haritaki. It aids digestion, supports detoxification, and enhances overall health, making it beneficial for longevity.
4. Turmeric: Turmeric, with its potent anti-inflammatory properties, plays a vital role in Ayurveda. It supports the body's natural healing mechanisms, promotes overall health, and contributes to longevity.
5. Guggul: Guggul, derived from the resin of the Commiphora mukul tree, has been used for centuries in Ayurvedic medicine. It promotes healthy blood circulation, supports joint health, and enhances overall well-being, thus contributing to longevity.

Ayurvedic Healing Therapies: Ayurveda offers unique and effective healing therapies that help promote longevity by rejuvenating the body, mind, and spirit.

1. Panchakarma: Panchakarma is a comprehensive detoxification process that aims to eliminate toxins and restore balance in the body. This therapy involves five therapeutic procedures: Vamana (Emesis), Virechana (Purgation), Basti (Enema), and Nasya (Nasal cleansing). Panchakarma helps remove deep-seated toxins, revitalize the organs, and rejuvenate the body, promoting longevity.
2. Abhyanga: Abhyanga is a therapeutic full-body massage using warm herbal oils. It helps improve blood circulation, lymphatic drainage, and overall well-being. Regular abhyanga promotes longevity by reducing stress, nourishing the tissues, and enhancing vitality.
3. Shirodhara: Shirodhara involves a continuous stream of warm oil poured onto the forehead. This therapy calms the

mind, reduces stress, and enhances cognitive function. By inducing a deep state of relaxation, Shirodhara contributes to longevity by promoting mental well-being.

4. Nasya: Nasya is the administration of herbal oils or medicated substances into the nasal passages. This therapy helps relieve congestion, clear the sinuses, and support respiratory health. Nasya also has a rejuvenating effect on the mind and promotes overall longevity.
5. Marma Therapy: Marma therapy involves stimulating vital energy points in the body through gentle pressure or massage. By activating these energy points, marma therapy helps balance the doshas, improve circulation, and promote overall well-being. This therapy contributes to longevity by restoring harmony and vitality in the body.

Ayurvedic Lifestyle Habits for Longevity: Ayurveda emphasizes the importance of adopting healthy lifestyle habits that promote longevity and overall well-being.

1. Quality Sleep: Adequate and restful sleep is crucial for rejuvenation and overall health. Following a consistent sleep routine and creating a conducive sleep environment promotes longevity.
2. Positive Mindset: Cultivating a positive mindset and emotional well-being is essential for longevity. Practices such as gratitude, mindfulness, and self-reflection contribute to a positive outlook on life and support overall well-being.
3. Social Connections: Maintaining healthy social connections and nurturing relationships play a significant role in longevity. Strong social support networks contribute to emotional well-being, reduce stress, and promote a fulfilling and long life.

4. Regular Physical Activity: Engaging in regular physical activity is vital for maintaining optimal health and longevity. Practices such as yoga, walking, or any form of exercise that suits your body type and age support overall well-being.
5. Stress Management: Stress management is crucial for longevity and well-being. Ayurveda offers various techniques such as meditation, breathing exercises, and relaxation practices to manage stress effectively. By reducing stress levels, these practices promote longevity and support a healthy mind and body.

Ayurvedic Factors Affecting Longevity: Several factors influence longevity according to Ayurveda. Understanding these factors helps individuals make informed choices to support their well-being.

1. Genetics: Genetic factors play a role in an individual's life span. While we cannot alter our genetic makeup, adopting Ayurvedic principles and practices can help optimize our health and potential for longevity.
2. Environment: The environment in which we live, including factors such as air quality, water quality, climate, and surroundings, can impact our overall health and longevity. Creating a supportive and harmonious environment enhances well-being and promotes longevity.
3. Age: The age at which an individual begins to practice Ayurvedic principles can influence their overall longevity. However, it is never too late to adopt Ayurvedic practices and make positive changes to support health and well-being.

4. Physical Health: The overall physical health of an individual is a significant factor in determining longevity. By addressing any existing health concerns and maintaining optimal physical well-being, Ayurveda supports a long and healthy life.
5. Mental Health: Mental health plays a crucial role in longevity. Ayurveda recognizes the mind-body connection and emphasizes practices that promote emotional well-being, cognitive health, and overall mental balance.

Ayurveda and Modern Science: Ayurveda has garnered attention from modern science, leading to numerous studies exploring its principles and practices. While Ayurveda is a traditional system of medicine, its holistic approach aligns with the principles of integrative medicine, emphasizing disease prevention and overall well-being. Modern scientific research is shedding light on the mechanisms and efficacy of Ayurvedic practices, bridging the gap between ancient wisdom and contemporary knowledge.

Ayurvedic Longevity Success Stories: There are numerous success stories of individuals who have embraced Ayurvedic practices and witnessed significant improvements in their overall well-being and longevity. These personal experiences serve as inspiring examples of the effectiveness of Ayurveda in promoting a healthy and fulfilling life.

Ayurvedic Challenges and Criticisms: Ayurveda, like any other system of medicine, faces certain challenges and criticisms. Some of the common criticisms include a lack of regulation, cultural appropriation, questions regarding scientific validity, concerns about affordability and accessibility, and ethical considerations regarding the sourcing of herbs and products. It is important to acknowledge and address these concerns to ensure the responsible and effective practice of Ayurveda.

The Future of Ayurvedic Longevity: Ayurveda is gaining global recognition as an effective means of promoting longevity and overall well-being. The future of Ayurvedic longevity is shaped by several factors, including emerging wellness trends, ongoing research, innovation in Ayurvedic formulations and therapies, globalization, and increased cultural awareness. As Ayurveda continues to evolve, its impact on individual health and well-being will continue to grow, offering new possibilities for achieving longevity.

Ayurvedic Longevity and You: Incorporating Ayurvedic longevity practices into your life can be a transformative journey towards better health and well-being. It is essential to approach Ayurveda with guidance from qualified practitioners and adopt personalized approaches based on your unique needs and goals. Ayurveda recognizes that each individual is unique, and by embracing personalized practices, you can unlock the potential for longevity and lead a fulfilling life.

Benefits and Drawbacks: Adopting Ayurvedic practices for longevity offers numerous benefits, including improved overall health, enhanced well-being, and increased vitality. However, it is important to note that Ayurveda is a complementary medicine and should not replace conventional medical treatment for severe medical conditions. It is always advisable to consult with your primary healthcare provider before making significant changes to your lifestyle or incorporating Ayurvedic practices.

Conclusion: Ayurveda offers a holistic approach to promoting longevity and overall well-being. By embracing its principles, incorporating its practices, and utilizing Ayurvedic herbs and therapies, individuals can unlock the potential for a healthier and more fulfilling life. Ayurveda's emphasis on balance, personalized approaches, and integration with modern science provides a comprehensive framework for promoting longevity. However, it is important to approach Ayurveda responsibly, seek guidance from qualified practitioners, and consult with healthcare providers before making significant lifestyle changes. By integrating Ayurvedic principles into our lives, we can tap into the wisdom of this ancient system and embark on a transformative journey towards improved health, vitality, and longevity.

Suggestions For A Creative Healthy Life

In a world filled with fast-paced living and quick fixes, Ayurveda stands as a time-tested system that has nurtured vitality and longevity for centuries. Our article is your gateway to discovering the immediate benefits and lifelong advantages this holistic approach offers.

If you're seeking a path to vibrant health, increased vitality, and a life filled with energy and purpose, then this guide is for you.

Ayurveda is a holistic science that deals with ancient medicines that originated in India. Its principles are based on the essential connection of mind and body and that mental imbalances can lead to physical illness.

Ayurveda is not considered just as a system of medicine - it is a way of living. It teaches us how to live harmoniously with our environment and bodies and emphasizes the importance of preventative care and lifestyle choices in maintaining good health.

If you are searching for measures to improve your life and health, then ancient Ayurvedic techniques may be just what you need. In this piece, we will help you understand some of the most popular and effective Ayurvedic methods you can use to improve your life.

1. What is Ayurveda

Ayurveda has been practiced in India for centuries for better health and happier living. As per history, in previous centuries, men and women in India followed Ayurvedic behaviour regularly and could lead healthy lives. They could even do challenging tasks with ease. They were very active and flexible and led a healthy life despite the lack of technology and development to cut off today's fast-paced life in which pollution and unhealthy food have exhausted us physically and mentally.

Fortunately, this holistic art as an aid to reach the masses worldwide. We should be thankful for the efforts made by individuals and groups who have made significant efforts to bring to light the lost art of yoga. Before we go into in-depth knowledge about Ayurveda, let us first try to know the three doshas in Ayurveda.

2. The Three Doshas

The three Doshas are the basic principles of Ayurveda, and understanding them is critical to taking advantage of the benefits Ayurveda offers. The three Doshas are Kapha, Vata, and Pitta. They represent the five elements (space, air, fire, water, and earth) and are thought to control our body and mind. Each Dosha has unique characteristics and functions, and understanding each can help us balance our lives. Vata is associated with movement, creativity, and flexibility, and it controls physical and mental activities, breathing, and cell division.

Pitta is associated with heat and the metabolic processes necessary for digestion, absorption, and assimilation. It is responsible for digestion, metabolism, and absorption of nutrients. Kapha is associated with earth and water, responsible for moisture and structure and maintaining body balance. Each of these Doshas is equally important, and when they are in balance, the person will have suitable physical, mental, and spiritual health. Balancing the Doshas can help improve our overall well-being, enhance our relationships, and create lasting peace and joy.

3. The Five Elements

The five elements of Ayurveda are the basis of Ayurvedic principles. Ayurved help us gain a deep-rooted awareness of these aspects should be your first step in understanding this ancient healing system.

The first element of Ayurveda is the earth, which is associated with abundance and stability. It is also seen as a physical foundation that supports life, and the earth is often connected with feelings of security.

The second element is water, an essential component of Ayurvedic principles seen as a source of emotion, expression, and connection. Water energy provides a cooling and soothing quality associated with balance, fluidity, and relaxation. The third element is fire, which is symbolized by passion and drive. Fire represents energy, expansion, and courage and is seen as a source of transformation and empowerment. The fourth element is air, associated with thought, communication, and action. Air energy encourages growth and change and offers clarity and insight.

The fifth element is space, which is the ground of all existence. Space is associated with clarity and awareness, allowing us to find peace and contentment. This element is essential for understanding more profound meanings and our place in the universe. Understanding how these elements interact and affect our lives is integral to Ayurveda. Good health and well-being can result when these elements are in harmony within ourselves and our environment.

4. The Benefits of an Ayurvedic Lifestyle

When Ayurvedic principles are incorporated into lifestyle, many changes which help regulate health can be noticed. These are some of the vital benefits of living with an Ayurvedic mindset:

- Improved digestion and last longer feeling of fullness after meals
- Better sleeping patterns
- Increased mental clarity, creativity, and concentration
- Improved immunity
- Balanced mindset and emotions

- Decreased inflammation levels
- Enhanced spiritual growth

Incorporating Ayurveda into your daily helps cultivate balance and harmony in your life, leading to improved health and wellness. Additionally, practicing yoga, meditation, and mindfulness helps to bring additional relief to your body, mind, and soul.

By following Ayurveda, you can experience proper balance and harmony in your mind, body, and spirit. Ayurveda is about recognizing your true Self and taking steps to support better health.

5. Tips for Getting Started with Ayurveda

Ayurveda promotes using simple steps to achieve balance and harmony in your overall health. Here are five tips for getting started with an Ayurvedic lifestyle:

- Figure Out Your Dosha Type - Knowing your body type opens the door to better understanding your lifestyle needs and which habits may benefit or harm your health. The three types of dosha in Ayurveda are Vata, Pitta, and Kapha. So, let's take a quiz to figure out our body type.
- Follow an Ayurvedic Diet - Eating for your dosha type helps to provide balance and health. For example, those with a Vata dosha may benefit from more warming and grounding foods.
- De-Stress Through Mindful Practices - Yoga and meditation are favourites of the Ayurvedic lifestyle. Taking time to explore mindfulness practices helps to bring harmony to mind and body.
- Take Time to Connect - Ayurveda promotes a healthy connection with the outdoors. Prioritize spending time outside, such as going for a walk-in nature, to reap the benefits of Ayurveda.
- Get a Professional Evaluation - An Ayurvedic physician, or vaidya, can provide guidance and support. Individuals may be able to develop a customized approach after evaluating their individual needs.

Longevity-Enhancing Ayurvedic Herbs

Ayurveda uses a variety of herbs known for their capacity to extend life and improve general health to tap into the power of nature. To energise the body and boost vitality, these plants are incorporated into everyday rituals and activities.

Source: Canva

Rasayana: Rejuvenation for Longevitys The notion of Rasayana, which translates to "rejuvenation," lies at the heart of Ayurveda's strategy for extending life. Rasayana therapies make use of particular herbs and techniques to boost energy, slow down ageing, and encourage good health. Rasayanas are meant to improve mental clarity, balance the doshas, and nourish all bodily tissues.

Key Longevity-Enhancing Herbs

- Ashwagandha: Known as an adaptogenic herb, Ashwagandha helps the body adapt to stressors and balances energy. It supports the nervous system, improves sleep quality, and boosts immunity, all of which contribute to a longer, healthier life.
- Amalaki (Indian Gooseberry): A potent source of Vitamin C and antioxidants, Amalaki supports immune function, detoxification, and healthy digestion. It rejuvenates body tissues, enhances skin health, and promotes longevity.
- Turmeric: With its active compound curcumin, Turmeric exhibits anti-inflammatory and antioxidant properties. It supports joint health, aids digestion, and contributes to overall well-being.

These herbs, among others, are often used individually or in formulations to support longevity and vitality. Integrating these herbs into one's diet, lifestyle, and Ayurvedic practices can yield transformative effects on overall health and contribute to a life of longevity and wellness.

Ayurvedic Detoxification: Panchakarma for Longevity

Detoxification is crucial for achieving longevity and good health, according to Ayurveda. A key component of Ayurvedic methods for purging toxins and reviving the body is panchakarma, a thorough detoxification procedure.

Source: Canva

Toxin Elimination and Longevity: Panchakarma detoxification aids in the removal of accumulated poisons (ama), which can disturb dosha equilibrium and obstruct biological processes. These poisons are thought to hasten aging and lead to a number of health problems. The body's natural healing processes are triggered by ama cleansing, which enhances energy, digestion, and mental clarity.

Panchakarma Therapies and Benefits

- Vamana (Emesis): This therapy involves controlled vomiting to expel excess Kapha-related toxins. It clears the upper respiratory and digestive tract, promoting lung and heart health.
- Virechana (Purgation): Utilising herbs, Virechana eliminates excess Pitta-related toxins through the bowels. It supports liver function, enhances digestion, and improves skin health.
- Basti (Enema): Basti targets Vata-related imbalances by administering herbal enemas. It nourishes tissues, lubricates the intestines, and promotes vitality.
- Nasya (Nasal Therapy): Nasya involves administering herbal oils through the nostrils to cleanse the head and neck region. It improves respiratory function, mental clarity, and sensory perception.
- Raktamokshana (Bloodletting): A less common therapy, Raktamokshana purifies the blood by removing impurities. It can be beneficial for skin disorders and chronic conditions.

Panchakarma therapies are effective instruments for rejuvenation since they are tailored to a person's constitution. These treatments lengthen and improve the quality of life by improving the body's resilience, vitality, and general wellbeing by purging the body of toxins and reestablishing balance.

Physical Hygiene

Practicing good personal hygiene is important for helping keep the body healthy and clean. Good personal hygiene involves keeping all parts of the external body clean and healthy. It is important for maintaining both physical and mental health.

In people with poor personal hygiene, the body provides an ideal environment for germs to grow, leaving it vulnerable to infection.

On a social level, people may avoid a person with poor personal hygiene, which may result in isolation and loneliness.

Types of personal hygiene

There are many types of personal hygiene: The following list is a good starting point for someone looking to build a personal hygiene routine:

Dental: Dental hygiene involves more than just having white teeth. A good dental hygiene routine can help prevent issues such as gum disease and cavities. It can also prevent bad breath.

Body: Several million sweat glands cover the human body. When bacteria break down sweat, the process creates a smell or body odor.

Washing the body will help prevent skin irritation, as well as removing the bacteria that cause body odor. Washing the hair removes oil and keeps a person looking clean and fresh.

Hand washing: Regular hand washing is one of the best ways to avoid spreading communicable diseases.

The Centers for Disease Control and Prevention (CDC) recommend washing the hands at certain times:

- before, during, and after preparing food
- before eating food
- before and after looking after anyone who is vomiting or has diarrhea
- before and after treating a cut or wound
- after going to the bathroom
- after changing diapers or cleaning up a child who has used the toilet

- after blowing the nose, coughing, or sneezing
- after touching garbage or dirty surfaces or objects
- after handling pets or pet-related items, such as food

Nails: Fingernails may harbor dirt and germs, contributing to the spread of bacteria. It is easier for dirt and germs to collect under longer nails, so keeping them short can help reduce the risk of spreading infections.

How to maintain good personal hygiene: Knowing how to maintain good personal hygiene can make it easier to build a routine. A person should have some basic knowledge of the following types of hygiene:

Dental hygiene: For a healthy mouth and smile, the American Dental Association (ADA) recommend brushing the teeth for 2 minutes at least twice a day - once before breakfast and once before bed. People should use an ADA-accepted fluoride toothpaste and replace the toothbrush every 3-4 months. The ADA also advise people to floss daily. Learn more about good dental hygiene here.

Hand Washing

The CDC outline five simple steps for effective hand washing:

1. Wet the hands with clean, running water, then turn off the tap and apply soap.
2. Lather the hands by rubbing them together with the soap, remembering to reach the backs of the hands, between the fingers, and under the nails.
3. Scrub the hands for at least 20 seconds, which a person can time by humming the "Happy Birthday" song twice.
4. Rinse the hands well under clean, running water.
5. Dry the hands using a clean towel or air dry them.

Learn more about proper hand washing here.

Body: It is advisable to shower or bathe daily, using soap and water to rinse away dead skin cells, oil, and bacteria. People can pay special attention to areas that accumulate more sweat, such as the armpits, in between the toes, and the groin area.

They should also wash their hair with shampoo at least once a week, or more if necessary. Applying deodorant when fully dry can help prevent body odors. Learn more about how often to shower here.

Nails: Using sanitized tools to trim the nails and keep them short is one of the best ways to ensure that no dirt can collect underneath them. Scrubbing the underside of the nails with a nail brush can form part of a person's hand washing routine.

Menstrual and genital hygiene: It is important to change sanitary products regularly and to wash the hands before and after changing tampons, pads, or any other sanitary products.

As vaginas are self-cleaning, using soap to clean the vagina can cause an imbalance of its natural bacteria and lead to infections. The vulva (the external part of the vagina) should only need cleaning once a day using a mild soap and water.

People with an uncircumcised penis can clean it by gently pulling back the foreskin and washing underneath it with warm water or soap.

Learn more about vaginal hygiene here.

Learn more about identifying and removing smegma here.

Teaching children hygiene

Parents and caregivers should teach children how to keep themselves clean from a young age.

For example, they can start using toothpaste to brush a child's teeth when they reach the age of 12 months. When the gaps between a child's teeth close, it is important to start flossing. Encouraging children to help clean themselves as soon as they are old enough is a good way to instigate a proper personal hygiene routine.

Factors that can negatively impact hygiene Poverty and lack of access to clean water can both have a detrimental effect on a person's personal hygiene. A person's mental health can also affect how they take care of themselves. People who are living with certain conditions, such as a psychotic disorder, severe depression, or drug or alcohol use disorder, may find it very difficult to keep up a personal hygiene routine. Conditions that poor personal hygiene can signal

While personal hygiene can cause certain health issu s, it can also be a side effect of some of them. People living with Alzheimer's disease and other types of dementia often have poor oral hygiene.

In some cases, the inability to maintain a hygiene routine could result from depression. Depressive symptoms, such as reduced energy levels and impaired cognitive function, can make a self-care regimen more difficult to keep up.

Negative effects of poor personal hygiene: Poor hygiene is a sensitive topic, and talking to a person about it can be difficult. As a result, a person with poor personal hygiene could become isolated from other people. Poor personal hygiene may also have an effect on the workplace. Companies may be more likely to offer jobs and promotions to individuals who appear to take care of their health and presentation. Poor personal hygiene can be particularly problematic in the food industry.

There are also many health implications of having poor personal hygiene, with the CDC listing the following as hygiene-related diseases:

- athlete's foot
- body lice
- chronic diarrhea
- tooth decay
- head lice
- hot tub rash
- pinworms
- pubic lice
- scabies
- swimmer's ear
- ringworm

Hygiene Routine Tips

Helpful tips for creating a hygiene routine include the following:

- Make it a habit: With daily practice, a new habit can become a regular part of life. Choose one area to focus on and practice until it becomes second nature.
- Set reminders: Using the notes app on a cell phone can be a great way to avoid forgetting any tasks.
- Use rewards: A sticker chart can be a brilliant incentive for children to maintain their personal hygiene.
- Invest in nice toiletries: Using products that smell good may encourage some people to stick to their personal hygiene routine.

Ayurvedic Hygiene Practices

Ayurveda is a well know system of medicinal practice which originated in India, and that is based on a treatment that aims on creating a balance between the basic elements of human life i.e. the wind, water, air and fire .This medicinal practice mainly involves use of natural herbs and plants to from medicine along with a good deal of focus on a person's dietary habits, lifestyle choices and internal well being. One major area under Ayurvedic way of life is the hygiene practices.

Hygienic living, according to Ayurveda, comprises of several lifestyle practice like regular bathing, teeth cleansing, proper care of eyes, skin care and occasional massage or application of some herbal oils in the body which help in rejuvenation and cleansing. Discussed below are some of the hygiene methods as per Ayurveda.

Ayurveda for Eyes: The eyes are considered to be the greatest gift of God and the most important of the five human senses. Eyes need to be well taken care of since they are the reflection of good health and well being. Bright sparkling eyes enhance personality and attractiveness of a person. Ayurveda has many suggestions for hygiene and health of eyes, listing a few below.

- Wash your eyes with light warm water 10-15 times in the morning. This helps in cleansing but do avoid extreme temperature exposure to eyes.
- Use cotton wads dampened with rose water and place it over your eyes. The cooling effect of organic rose helps your eyes to relax.
- Use of "Ashwagandha" helps cleansing and strengthening vision.
- Aniseed is also vital for eye health and to fight cataract diseases.
- Indian Gooseberry and Marigold is also useful is preventing ocular issues. Especially helpful in situations of conjunctivitis.

Ayurveda For Oral Hygiene

Oral Hygiene is most important for your teeth and to keep you away from irritating bad breath.

Ayurveda recommends brushing your teeth three times a day. Use Ayurvedic herbal tooth pastes for the same for best results. In addition to the dental care at home, do visit your dentist regularly to check for tooth diseases like cavities and get the mouth cleansed.

For fresh breathe and oral hygiene chew mint leaves, seeds of fennel or cloves during the day. People who are prone to respiratory infections and allergies are susceptible to oral hygienic problems. In such cases visit a Ayurvedic professional who can prescribe medicine to check production of mucus. Avoid dryness in mouth by having plenty of liquids.

Ayurveda For Skin

Ayurvedic treatments can lead to maintaining of good skin hygiene, and is believed to be capable of treating any kind of skin problems like acne, pigmentation etc.

- For a healthy skin, Ayurveda recommends a proper diet. Digestion simulating foods with high fibre content like fruits, grains and vegetables are believed to help maintain good skin hygiene by preventing excess oil production which is facilitated by spicy and oily or sweet food. Food intake should be followed with a lot of water intake.
- Steaming and cleansing with mild soap .Sandalwood and buttermilk can be very effective in cleaning and hygiene.
- Using orange peel to scrub the skin and applying lemon juice twice a day adds positively to skin health and hygiene,

Ayurvedic Anointing of The Body: Ayurveda believes messaging Ayurvedic oils in your body not only causes a health skin and betters hygiene, but also invokes feeling of being loved. For best results, you need a massage of 15 minutes per day of good Ayurvedic oil. Benefits are as follows-

- Removes unwanted dirt and filth from the body, adding to hygiene.
- Nourishment to body tissues
- Good sleep pattern
- Improves blood circulation

Mental Hygiene

The term "mental hygiene" refers to daily activities that support and maintain mental health. Public health guidelines tell us that we need to do small tasks daily to maintain our physical and dental hygiene, like showering and brushing our teeth. We are now extending the same concept to mental health.

Good mental health refers to a perfect linking of emotional, psychological, and social aspects in one's life. Adverse childhood experiences and their prolonged exposure may extend to adulthood, resulting in mental trauma, or some kind of medical illness. A person is said to be emotionally/physically fit, they should enjoy a good balance of mind, body, and soul. Let us go through the entire article to know how Ayurveda helps in improving Mental Health.

The traditional science of Ayurveda proves the long-term solution to unresolved conditions of mental trauma by rejuvenating physical and psychological factors in one's life. Ayurveda brings out its natural approach to regulating emotional behaviour through herbal medications and lifestyle modifications. Panchakarma Course in Kerala energizes the mind's doshas and mental disturbances through a comprehensive detoxification program and thereby improves mental clarity and mood swings. The ayurvedic approach to mental health helps to reduce depressive and anxious episodes in one's life and is effective in reducing a series of mental health disorders.

The Mind: According to Ayurveda The mind is considered the launchpad between the senses and the soul. It is an extraordinary organ that controls both sense-related and functional activities of the body. It has unique characteristics to correlate with every emotion of life - happiness, fear, anger, shame, contempt, disgust, guilt, distress, interest, surprise, and joy.

A person's mind depends on three qualities like sattva, rajas, and tamas in which one's character is modulated. An uncertain proportion of these qualities and a dynamic imbalance of doshas may upset the mental balance. Marma Training in Kerala finds a natural solution to fight negative elements and thereby relieves sleep deprivation, stomach-related issues, and mood swings, hence improving quality of life.

The Origins of Mental Illness: Mental illness occurs due to any sort of brain damage, Stressful life situations, and chronic medical conditions that may lead to various forms of mental health disorders such as OCD, depression, mania, PTSD, and psychosis. Hence, mental illness comes under a vast category in which its unauthenticated behaviour affects emotion, thinking ability, and attitude.Ayurveda College in Kerala sets a customized treatment approach to stabilize the imbalance of doshas that cause mental illness through herbal massage, nasal breathing, meditation, and yoga practices.

Why is Ayurvedic Prevention for Mental Disorders Important: Ayurveda's approach to treating any ailments does not include the treatment of any single disease alone. Ayurveda follows a therapeutic regime to remove toxins that inhibit the natural energy flow in the body. Ayurveda prevention of mental disorders aims at the relaxation of Ojas to pacify the conscious mind for better mental and physical health. Ayurveda practitioners conduct a detailed analysis of a patient with respect to their medical history, lifestyle pattern, and diet regime and recommend an effective therapeutic solution to improve their cognitive abilities.

Certain herbal medications along with their purificatory treatments address the underlying root cause of the mental disorder and are able to find an effective solution for the cause of mental illnesses such as Stress, Migraines, Dementia, Mood swings, Emotional disturbance, and insomnia. Ayurveda seeks realistic behaviour of physical and mental health through holistic light to recognize their actual self for mental nourishment. This systematic technique of mindfulness nourishes the brain cells to achieve positive signals that trigger good thoughts, observations, concerns, feelings, and opinions.

Ayurvedic Tips for Enhancing Mental Health: Ayurvedic management of mental health brings both Agni and doshas in balance and enhances a sense of good contentment and well-being.

Following a healthy lifestyle with a nutritious diet can relieve signs of mental disorders to a great extent. Also, Ayurveda treatment can calm or relax your body tone in the natural way of the detoxification process.

Diet and Lifestyle Modifications for Mental Health: Paying attention to what you eat and when you eat are inevitable factors one could consider for good mental strength. Ensure we follow a strong brain-healthy diet and healthy lifestyle routine to support better mental emotions. Here is a list of healthy eating tips for the betterment of mental strength.

- Stay hydrated to flush out toxins in your body
- Avoid high levels of processed food such as fried chips, sugar-filled snacks, and soft drinks.
- Practice leisure time apart from a busy work schedule
- Eat seasonal fruits and veggies
- Enhances the intake of healthy fats for appropriate brain functioning
- Chew well for better digestion
- Exercise regularly
- Have a sound sleep
- Make a good social connection with friends and family
- Always consume freshly prepared warm foodstuff

- Consume food that contains omega-3 fats which are present in oily fish like tuna, salmon, mackerel, perch, herring, and sardines.

Ayurveda Therapies for Enhancing Mental health: The application of medicated herbs with personalized therapies can calm and relax the mind, body, and soul. Ashwagandha is one such magical herb to improve cortisol levels and thereby increases the proper functioning of brain cells. Brahmi can accelerate positive impact on memory, concentration, and intelligence and helps to reduce the signs of negative emotions in mental health. Turmeric can improve blood circulation and helps to prevent the brain cells from developing mental disorders.

Virechana is a type of panchakarma therapy in which bitter purgative herbs are introduced to induce vomiting and thereby cleansing of the body takes place to relieve the stress associated with mental disorders. Shirodhara is the Ayurveda technique of pouring medicated oil onto the center of the forehead and is effective in people who suffer from insomnia, sleep disorders, anxiety, depression, and other forms of mental disorders. Satvavajaya chikilsa induces positive thoughts regarding self-awareness, family, and social responsibilities. This therapy is effective in treating mental disorders that are caused due to emotional disturbances.

As a whole, you are well aware that Ayurveda can relieve the signs of mental disorders naturally without having any side effects. If you or your loved ones are experiencing any mental health issues such as stress or depression, get in touch with the School of Ayurveda and Panchakarma for the best possible outcomes. We have 25 years of experience in delivering the true spirit of Ayurveda for overall well-being.

Chapter 4

Ayurvedic Treatment

Introduction

Ayurveda treatment starts with an internal purification process, followed by a special diet, herbal remedies, massage therapy, yoga, and meditation. The concepts of universal interconnectedness, the body's constitution (prakriti), and life forces (doshas) are the primary basis of ayurvedic medicine.

Some popular Ayurvedic treatments used to treat various diseases are panchakarma treatment, Shirodhara, Abhyangam, Kati Vasti, Nasya treatment, Elakizhi, Njavara Kizhi, etc. These therapies are administered by a certified practitioner and may take a little longer to show positive effects.

Considered by many scholars to be the oldest healing science, Ayurveda is a holistic approach to health designed to help people live long, healthy, balanced lives. The term Ayurveda is taken from the Sanskrit words ayus, meaning life or lifespan, and veda, meaning knowledge. It has been practiced in India for at least 5,000 years, and has recently become popular in Western cultures. The basic principle of Ayurveda is to prevent and treat illness by maintaining balance in the body, mind, and consciousness through proper drinking, diet, and lifestyle, as well as herbal remedies.

There are two main types of Ayurveda: traditional and Maharishi. Maharishi is a version of traditional Ayurveda based on translations from the classical texts by Maharishi Mahesh Yogi. Both types of Ayurvedic practitioners:

- Prescribe herbs

- Believe that disease results from an imbalance in the doshas (basic energy types)
- Use many of the same remedies for treating illness

Maharishi Ayurveda emphasizes the role of supreme consciousness in maintaining good health and promotes transcendental meditation (TM) as a way to experience the pure consciousness of the universe. It also highlights the expression of positive emotions and the need to attune your life to the natural rhythms of your body.

How does it work: According to Ayurvedic beliefs, just as everyone has a unique fingerprint, each person has a distinct pattern of energy, a specific combination of physical, mental, and emotional characteristics. Ayurvedic practitioners also believe there are three basic energy types called doshas, present in every person:

- Vata. Energy that controls bodily functions associated with motion, including blood circulation, breathing, blinking, and heartbeat. When vata energy is balanced, there is creativity and vitality. Out of balance, vata produces fear and anxiety.
- Pitta. Energy that controls the body's metabolic systems, including digestion, absorption, nutrition, and temperature. In balance, pitta leads to contentment and intelligence. Out of balance, pitta can cause ulcers and arouse anger.
- Kapha. Energy that controls growth in the body. It supplies water to all body parts, moisturizes the skin, and maintains the immune system. In balance, kapha is expressed as love and forgiveness. Out of balance, kapha leads to insecurity and envy.

Everyone has vata, pitta, and kapha. But usually 1 or 2 are dominant in a particular person. Many things can disturb the energy balance, such as stress, an unhealthy diet, the weather, and strained family relationships. The disturbance shows up as disease. Ayurvedic practitioners prescribe treatments to bring the doshas back into balance.

From a Western medical perspective, stress relief seems to be one of the ways Ayurveda works to help fight illness. For example, studies have found that transcendental meditation (TM), a component of Maharishi Ayurveda, lowers anxiety. Other studies have found that Ayurveda lowers blood pressure and cholesterol, slows the aging process, and speeds recovery from illness. Many herbs used in Ayurvedic medicine have antioxidant effects, meaning they may help protect against long-term illnesses, such as heart disease and arthritis. Many

Ayurvedic practitioners also recommend a vegetarian diet which is believed to be better for your heart than diets containing red meat.

What should I expect from an Ayurvedic treatment: Ayurvedic treatment focuses on rebalancing the doshas. On your first visit, the practitioner will take a detailed medical history, check your pulse, feel your abdomen, examine your tongue, eyes, nails, and skin, and listen to the tone of your voice. The practitioner will also ask you questions about your general health, paying special attention to your lifestyle, diet, habits, and surroundings. The practitioner will then recommend ways to restore your natural dosha balance, which almost always includes changes in lifestyle, especially diet. Practitioners draw from more than 20 types of treatment. The most commonly prescribed include:

- Pranayama. Breathing exercises. Practicing pranayama helps you feel calm.
- Abhyanga. Rubbing the skin with herbal oil to increase blood circulation and draw toxins out of the body through the skin.
- Rasayana. Using mantras (repeated words or phrases) during meditation combined with certain herbs for rejuvenation.
- Yoga. Combining pranayama, movement, and meditation. Yoga has been shown to improve circulation and digestion, and to reduce blood pressure, cholesterol levels, anxiety, and chronic pain.
- Pancha karma. Cleansing the body to purify it and reduce cholesterol. Practitioners use methods that cause sweat, bowel movements, and even vomit to cleanse the body of toxins.
- Herbal medicines. Prescribing herbs to restore dosha balance.

What is Ayurveda good for: The goal of Ayurvedic medicine is to prevent diseases. Studies have suggested that Ayurveda may be effective at reducing the risk of heart disease. For example, one study found that Ayurveda helped reduce plaque and reverse the thickening of artery walls known as atherosclerosis in both healthy adults, as well as adults at high risk for heart disease. Atherosclerosis is a slow, complex disease in which cholesterol, fats, and other substances build up in the inner lining of an artery. This buildup, known as plaque, can lead to heart attack and stroke.

Combining yoga with certain Ayurvedic herbal remedies may reduce pain and disability in people with chronic pain conditions, such as arthritis and fibromyalgia.A number of Ayurvedic herbal remedies have been examined, though high-quality studies are lacking. For example, guggul (Commiphora mukul), a traditional Ayurvedic medication used to treat high cholesterol, is widely used in India. It appears to block production of cholesterol in the liver, lowering cholesterol levels. Fenugreek (Trigonella foenum graecum) seeds can lower LDL (bad) cholesterol and triglycerides (fats in the blood), and raise HDL (good) cholesterol levels. Its effects seem to come from its ability to lower the absorption of cholesterol in the intestine, and may be related to the high fibre content of the seed. The high fibre content of fenugreek seeds may also help control blood sugar if you have diabetes.

Other Ayurvedic herbs are being studied as treatments for many health conditions, including:

- Alzheimer disease
- Anxiety
- Asthma
- Cancer
- Dementia
- Dysmenorrhea (painful menstruation)
- Herpes
- High blood pressure
- Parkinson disease
- Perimenopausal problems
- Premenstrual syndrome (PMS)

Ayurvedic herbs combined with conventional medications may also be helpful for:

- Acne
- Chronic constipation
- Chronic fatigue syndrome (CFS)
- Irritable bowel syndrome (IBS)
- Obesity
- Uterine fibroids

Are there any risks: Most Ayurvedic therapies, such as pranayama and rasayana, are unlikely to have negative side effects in people who are psychologically healthy. People with serious mental health issues may benefit from these therapies. But they should only pursue them under the guidance of a knowledgeable psychiatrist or psychologist.

Ayurvedic herbs may interact with medications. Like all herbs, they are not right for every person. So speak with your physician. In addition, heavy metals such as lead and mercury have contaminated some Ayurvedic herb supplements. Ask your health care provider about choosing quality supplements for you and your family. Be sure to talk to your doctor before trying Ayurveda, especially if you take medicines or have to eat a special diet (to control diabetes, for example).

Determining The Individual Constitution

While modern medicine is largely limited to treatment of ailments and dealing with manifest symptoms, Ayurveda as a way of life runs much deeper, looking at individuals not just as made of carbohydrates, amino acids, and minerals, but also as mental and spiritual beings with prana or life energy that sustains life. An individual owes its existence to the five great elements.

The ancient science of Ayurveda is vast and based on insightful principles that don't just help you stay healthy and live longer but also make this journey more beautiful and full of vitality and dynamism. Food and medicine, social behaviour, seasonal changes, and the impact of everything we do on our nervous system and brain-the Ayurvedic approach takes all of this into account in crafting the appropriate treatments.

In addition to sustainable and healthy living, Ayurvedic principles also give beautiful glimpses of the basis of creation. In fact, the core of Ayurveda is Sankhya philosophy, which says that in the entire universe there are only two ultimate entities that exist-namely the Prakriti, that is the primordial matter and the Purusa, which is the universal spirit.

The Five Elements

One of the ways in which primordial matter reveals itself in the perceivable universe is through the five primary elements. Our body also is made up of these five elements and upon death dissolves back into these five elements in nature. Our five senses of sight, touch, sound, smell, and taste are based on these five primary elements-fire, air, space, earth and water respectively-and therefore our respective sense organs-eyes, skin, ears, nose, and tongue-function based on them.

The Fire Element

Fire has the power to transform the state of any substance. In the human body, it is the fire element that leads the conversion of food into energy. Digestion, absorption, and assimilation of food are taken care of by this element in addition to regulation of body temperature. An imbalance in the fire element manifests in the form of metabolic disorders, mental ailments, skin diseases, and fever.

The Air Element: Air is mobile in nature. In our body, it is the air element in the form of oxygen that keeps cells alive and functioning. Our movement, respiratory system, and nerve impulses are governed by the air element. Dry and light in nature, the air element is formless and transparent. Its imbalance leads to nervous system related disorders, respiratory issues, abnormal blood pressure, and pains in muscles.

The Space Element: Space is the medium for sound to travel. In addition to governing our auditory senses it is responsible for our intuition and wisdom. An imbalance of space elements in the body can manifest as thyroid issues, or problems related to speech or hearing, etc.

The Earth Element: Earth forms all the solid mass in our body-bones, tissues, teeth, nails, skin, and hair. The nature of earth elements is hard, stable, slow, dry, heavy, and thick. Imbalance of the earth element leads to weight gain or loss, weakness, increased cholesterol, or bone density changes.

The Water Element: Water is present in our body in the form of all bodily fluids, including saliva, blood, sweat, and semen. It is water that governs our emotions and also makes cohesion possible in everything including tissues.

The Tridoshas and Their Roles: The five elements combine with one another to form intelligent life principles called tridhatus that govern all the processes in the body and are responsible for certain physical and behavioural traits. These tridhatus are vata, pitta, and kapha; in vitiated form they are referred to as doshas. Each of these doshas is dominant in different time periods of the day and night, in different seasons of the year and in different areas of the body. The ritucharya, meaning seasonal regimen, and the dincharya, the daily regimen suggested by Ayurveda, are based on living in accordance with nature and performing daily activities in accordance with the dominant dosha at the specific time of the day or year. Such a lifestyle helps keep doshas in balance. The regimens take care of cleansing and detoxification of the body in addition to modifying one's diet and lifestyle in accordance with seasons.

Vata: Ether and air elements combine to form the vata dosha. Vata is mobile and hence governs all bodily movements, nervous system, respiratory system and takes care of the elimination of waste material and toxins from the body. The primary site for vata dosha is the lower part of the body including lower back, thighs, large intestine and pelvic regions. Vata also dominates the nervous system, skin and ears.

There are five different types of vata that govern different types of movements in the body:·

1. Prana Vayu is the kind of vata that governs respiratory system and mental activity.
2. Udana Vayu governs speech and movement in the upper body.
3. Vyana Vayu takes care of nourishment and circulation in the whole body and movement of body parts.
4. Samana Vayu helps in secretion and movement of digestive juices and in absorption of nutrients.
5. Apana Vayu takes care of downward movement which is needed for elimination of urine, feces, menstrual blood, semen and for giving birth.

Pitta: Fire and water elements combine to form the pitta dosha. Responsible for the metabolism, pitta mainly impacts the blood, eyes, skin and middle part of the body including liver, stomach, spleen, small intestine and gallbladder.

Pitta also has five sub-types:

1. Sadhaka pitta governs intellect and memory, and drives the transformation of words to knowledge.
2. Alochaka pitta takes care of perception from visual senses to the mind, drives creativity and intuition.
3. Pachaka pitta mainly deals with digestion and assimilation of food and regulation of body temperature.
4. Ranjaka pitta is responsible for formation of blood.
5. Bhrajaka pitta imparts luster to the skin and regulates the temperature and colour of the various body parts.

Kapha: Water and earth elements combine to form the kapha dosha. Kapha provides protection and lubrication to the body organs such as mucous lining of stomach, cerebrospinal fluid for brain and synovial fluid in the joints. The upper part of the body is where kapha mostly resides. The sites for kapha include the respiratory tract, upper stomach, mucous membranes, joints and head.

Kapha has five subtypes:

1. Trapaka kapha nourishes and lubricates the brain cells and nervous system and is responsible for carrying stimuli to the brain.
2. Bodhaka kapha takes care of perceptions like taste
3. Avalambaka kapha takes care of the chest region.
4. Kledaka kapha works in the gastro-intestinal tract.
5. Shleshaka kapha lubricates the joints.

The Constitution of Your Body: The five elements can combine in innumerable different proportions to form different body types, or constitutions. This constitution is determined by which of the three doshas are predominant in an individual and is the outcome of conditions that prevail at the time of conception and during the gestation period. The constitution of an individual generally remains the same throughout one's lifetime and plays an important role in determining his physical appearance, nature and behaviour patterns.

A vata body type is more prone to problems caused by gas in the gastrointestinal tract and hence needs to limit the intake of foods that are difficult to digest like millets and corn and might find wheat more suitable whereas for a kapha type person millets and corn might be more suitable than wheat. Ayurveda has different sets of guidelines for the different constitutions. Knowing your constitution can help you maintain better health by understanding what lifestyle and food will be best for you and what are the situations and food that might cause trouble for you.

Nadi Pariksha (Pulse Diagnosis): This ancient non-invasive method of determining one's constitution by analyzing the person's pulse behaviour yields surprisingly accurate results. Apart from determining the constitution, pulse diagnosis method is also used to find out what doshas are out of balance and hence diseases resulting from imbalance of those doshas can be prevented even before they manifest.

Pitta Constitution

According to Ayurveda, your constitution is established at conception, cemented at birth, and remains constant over the course of your lifetime. It influences your physiology, your physique, your likes and dislikes, your tendencies and habits, your mental and emotional character, as well as your vulnerabilities toward imbalance and disease. It is defined by the particular combination of vata, pitta, and kapha that you were born with, and it represents your body's natural state of equilibrium. Because your constitution serves as your blueprint for optimal health, understanding it-with the help of curiosity and self-awareness-can be truly enlightening. Our intention here is to introduce you to your constitution and to give you some of the tools necessary to begin to develop a deeper understanding.

It's important to know that we all have all three doshas in our constitutions: vata, pitta, and kapha. But the ratio between them-the specific quantitative and qualitative relationship between the three-is entirely unique to you. That said, as a pitta type, your constitution is distinctly pitta-predominant, and you probably have a lot in common with other pitta types who share that core distinction.

What Ayurveda Knows About You: While there is undoubtedly no one quite like you out there, it is remarkable how accurate Ayurveda can be in predicting who we are-based simply on the broad strokes of our constitutions. As you read through this introduction, and start to piece together the ways in which pitta has shaped your constitution, you will probably begin to see your particular strengths and vulnerabilities more clearly. And as your understanding of your constitution expands, your capacity to use these insights to your advantage will also improve. Below are a number of traits that you can likely attribute to your constitution.

Physical Characteristics: Please keep in mind that distinguishing physical characteristics should always be considered within the context of your ethnicity. For example, traits like eye colour, skin colour, or hair type are assessed in comparison to others with a similar heritage.

You probably have a well-proportioned skeletal frame that is medium in size, much like your overall bone structure and build. Your musculature is naturally lean but athletic, and your weight probably tends to remain fairly steady. Your face is generally heart-shaped, and you may have sharp facial features like a pointed nose and a tapered chin. Your eyes are probably medium in size, light in colour, and can be sensitive to bright light, while your gaze is piercing. Your skin and scalp are relatively fair, slightly oily, reddish in colour, and may be especially sensitive or reactive. Your hair is soft and fine, might be prone to early graying or balding, and may either include reddish hues or be conspicuously red. Your body temperature tends to be consistently warm or hot, your extremities are usually warm to the touch, and you sweat easily, so you do not likely tolerate especially hot weather, intense sun, or difficult physical labour. In fact, you probably prefer to remain cool, and may like cooler, drier climates best. Your natural internal heat may also make you somewhat predisposed to inflammatory types of disorders.

Personality: Mental and Emotional Tendencies: You are generally intelligent and discerning-with good concentration and memory, articulate speech, and a mind that is as keen, insightful, and studious as it is focused and driven. In fact, you almost certainly love a good intellectual challenge. You are probably known for being ambitious, hard-working, disciplined, dependable, and wise, but you may sometimes feel like your iron will or your competitive nature win out over other aspects of who you are.

In fact, pitta types often ignore the needs of their bodies in favour of satisfying their raw sense of ambition and their desire to be productive. There is little doubt that you tend to love learning and that you have a natural capacity for problem solving, systems, and organizational tasks. You also likely have a refined sense of taste-in food and elsewhere in your life-and while you probably make money easily, you may often spend it on luxuries. You tend to be highly principled, charismatic, and you are equipped with natural leadership qualities. On the other hand, you may have a bit of a temper, and when your perfectionist tendencies take over, you can become highly critical of both yourself and others.

Digestion: You very likely have a strong and consistent appetite, and you are almost certainly blessed with naturally strong digestion, which can sometimes propel a lack of awareness around tendencies to overeat or overindulge. Nevertheless, when you are healthy, you probably enjoy a wide range of foods without issue. However, chances are you do not view eating as a particularly productive activity, so you may often multi-task while eating, rush through your meals, and chew less thoroughly than is ideal. Slowing down and offering your full attention to each meal would probably be highly beneficial for you. Your bowels likely move rather frequently (sometimes two or three times per day), and your stools are naturally soft and oily, which means that when you are healthy, you never have to worry about being constipated.

Energy Levels, Stamina, and Sleep: You have a lot of energy to offer the things that you are passionate about, and while your stamina is moderate by nature, your will is quite strong, which gives you the capacity to push yourself when you so desire. In fact, you are highly capable of convincing both yourself and others that you have far more reserves of strength and stamina than you do in reality. This is one of pitta's primary challenges.

You require a moderate amount of sleep-six to eight hours, on average-and if possible, you prefer to sleep in absolute darkness. You generally sleep well, even if your sleep is sometimes interrupted, and in all likelihood, you prefer a relatively firm bed with fewer covers. You can definitely be a night owl, and sometimes, you are most productive late at night. However, when you stay up late, you may find it much more difficult to turn your mind off and surrender to sleep. Most pitta types do well to retire by about 10 p.m.

The Qualitative Nature of Pitta

Does this sound like you? It's astonishing how helpful the doshas can be in making sense of both our strengths and our weaknesses. In this next section, we hope to ground your understanding even further by exploring the primary qualities of pitta, how they can impact both the physiology and the mind, and how they can either support or challenge your health-depending on whether they are balanced or aggravated.

As you read through this section, you may begin to notice some of the ways in which each quality manifests in your system, giving you a glimpse into some of the more subtle aspects of your particular constitution. In time, it is precisely this type of deepening self-awareness that can inform your understanding of how best to promote optimal health and balance in your life.

Pitta Is Light: Lightness often manifests as a trim, fit physique, easeful digestion, light-heartedness, a bright and alert mind, a magnetic or charismatic personality, lightly-coloured eyes, and fair skin. In excess, it can cause a flighty ungroundedness, light-headedness, excess upward moving energy (think headaches or baldness), low blood sugar, or sensitivity to sunlight.

Pitta Is Sharp: A sharp mind is characteristically inquisitive, penetrating, quick, and highly capable of mastery. Sharpness is also behind decisiveness, discernment, a strong appetite, penetrating digestive capacity (that easily breaks down ingested food), and sharp vision-whether literal, figurative, or both. In excess, it can lead to a short temper, sharp words, the capacity to judge one's self and others harshly, and sharp hunger.

Pitta Is Hot: The hot quality creates a healthy blush in the cheeks, a naturally strong digestive fire, the capacity to stay warm in cold conditions, and gives the personality passion. In excess, it can manifest as skin rashes and breakouts, burning sensations, inflammatory disorders, excess acidity, and hot emotions like anger and rage.

Pitta Is Oily: Oiliness makes for naturally soft and lubricated skin, smooth movement in the joints, and it bolsters our capacities to relax, accept nourishment, and give or receive love. In excess, it can lead to oily skin and hair, acne, excess mucus, or an especially manipulative (think slippery) personality.

Pitta Is Liquid: The liquid quality supports proper salivation, healthy digestive juices, an appropriate capacity to sweat, and fluidity of movement throughout the digestive tract, blood, joints, and body. In excess, liquidity can dilute the digestive fire, cause bleeding gums, bleeding disorders in general, a tendency to bruise easily, and excessive sweat.

Pitta Spreads: The spreading quality can manifest as charisma and charm, the capacity for spreading influence, and may lead to exceptional achievement, broad recognition, and even fame. In excess, it is often behind a spreading rash and the capacity to create a toxic emotional environment.

Kapha Constitution

Kapha is essentially composed out of earth and water components. It is heavy, slow, cool, sleek, smooth, delicate, thick, stable, gross, and cloudy. Kapha provides structure and robustness to all things; it gives the cohesiveness needed to maintain a particular form. Kapha additionally hydrates all cells and frameworks, lubricates the joints, saturates the skin, maintains immunity and safeguards the tissues. Kapha is often associated with water energy, and with love and compassion.

The kapha body is physically solid, compact and wide with extensive thighs, hips, bums, and chest and has a tendency to be perpetually overweight. Kapha types ordinarily have large, appealing eyes that are blue or dark in colour. Their skin is fair, cool and always glowing. Kapha hair is thick, extravagant, and abundant, typically blond or dark, and wavy. Kapha individuals tend to over-produce mucus and other milky secretions, and their voices are delicate, regularly obstructed by excess mucus. Kapha types are extremely elegant, have a natural, erotic sensuality about them, and are generally very fertile.

Kapha individuals love heat and they suffer in cold, damp climates. Kapha types emanate strength and balance, to such an extent that vata and pitta types are frequently replenished by simply being in their essence. Kapha types are dedicated however they generally prefer to lay low, even to the point of lethargy. Due to their inclination towards laziness, kapha types do best to focus on a non-sedantory life, following a strict schedule that keeps them moving. Among all the doshas, kapha types can persist and advantage from the most intense forms of exercise. Ideally, a kapha type would rise before 6 a.m., take a bath and perform a solid workout before breakfast.

Kapha Dosha Characteristics

- Large, broad body frame
- Moderate appetite
- Deep and sound sleep
- Pleasant & deep voice
- Moderate sweating
- Good Stamina
- Low Thirst
- Calm & Polite Nature
- Tendency to gain weight
- Smooth & glossy skin

Tips For Balancing Kapha

Diet To Be Consumed

- Consume low fat milk. Always boil milk before drinking it which makes it easy to digest, try adding turmeric or ginger to the milk before boiling it in order to diminish any Kapha-increasing qualities in the milk.

- Eat lighter fruits like apples and pears. Avoid heavy and sour fruits like oranges, banana, dates, figs, pineapples, coconuts, melons and avocados. These fruits can increase Kapha in the body.

- Reduce consuming sugar products since they aggravate kapha in the body. However, honey can be consumed, it is excellent in balancing kapha.
- Beans can be taken except tofu
- Avoid eating nuts
- Grains can be taken especially barley and millet. Avoid consuming too much wheat and rice because it increases kapha
- All spices can be taken except for salt
- Avoid tomatoes, zucchini, cucumbers, sweet potatoes as they increase kapha

How To Consume The Diet

With regard to pacifying Kapha, how we eat can profoundly affect our level of progress. Kapha does well to stick to three meals each day, and sometimes only two meals are adequate. It's likewise best to eat your meals at consistent times from one day to the next. You can additionally kindle a sluggish digestive fire around 30 minutes before lunch and dinner by chewing a piece of fresh ginger with a pinch of sea salt, a couple of drops of lime juice, and about ¼ teaspoon nectar. This readies the digestive framework to get the food and to process it viably. Amid meals, it is essential to eat in a quiet and peaceful domain and to give your complete attention to the process of being nourished so that your body shows satisfaction. This will help lessen overeating and emotional eating, which frequently torments kapha. Fast foods, desserts and exorbitant amount of bread and other comfort foods can be particularly kapha provoking. However, it might be difficult to stay away from all kapha-exasperating nourishments. Though, the impeding capability of these nourishments can be limited by ensuring that they are served warm, with the help of heating medicinal plants, and taken in small quantities as recommend by Ayurveda. Lastly, because kapha digestion is generally slow and has a tendency to manage vitality with or without food, occasional fasts or cleanses can be exceptionally useful. A fruit or juice (think apple or pomegranate), or a more extended mono eating routine of kitchari can be exceptionally supportive.

Kapha Sleep And Energy Cycles

Kapha individuals can sleep for long durations, for the most part on their stomachs or in the fetal position. They commonly sleep for eight to twelve hours for every night and can indulge on more sleep than they truly require. Ideally, kapha types require to sleep for around seven hours each night.

If a kapha individual sleeps past 6 a.m. when kapha becomes dominating in the environment they may find it quiet hard to get up from the bed, and may encounter an enduring feeling of heaviness and laziness throughout the day. Thus, kapha individuals do really great when they wake up before 6 a.m.

Vata

According to Ayurveda healing, there are three life energies: the "vata," "pitta," and "kapha" doshas. Vata dosha reportedly consists of air and space and has links to change, mobility, and movement. Ayurveda is one of the world's oldest healing systems. It originated in India and encourages a holistic healing approach using a combination of diet, exercise, and lifestyle changes. According to Ayurveda, the world comprises five elements: space, water, earth, fire, and air. These elements combine to form three life energies - vata, pitta, and kapha - which define each person's constitution. Each person is a unique combination of the three doshas, but they usually have one or two dominant doshas.

Balance among all three doshas creates equilibrium and good health. Ayurvedic medicine recommends certain dietary and lifestyle habits for vata-dominant people that aim to balance their three doshas. Read more to learn about the characteristics, diet, and lifestyle habits of the vata dosha.

What is the Vata Dosha

Vata combines air and space, also called ether. It has links to change, mobility, and movement.

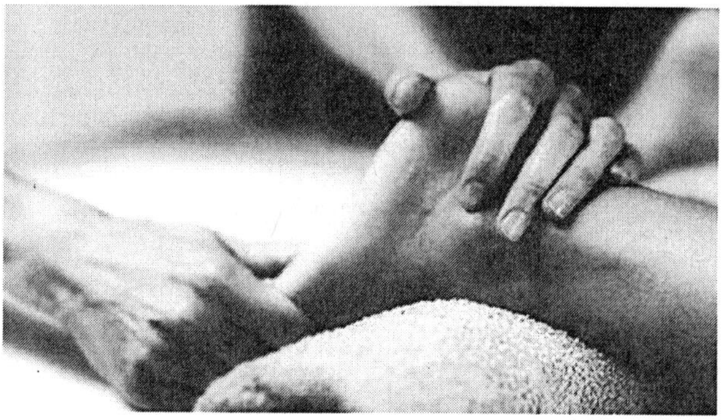

According to Ayurveda medicine, it relates to the nervous system and controls breathing, blinking, and circulation. Proponents of the medicine system also say vata is also irregular, rough, flowing, spacious, cold, light, and dry.

People who believe in this healing say those who are vata-dominant are energetic, creative, and flexible. They may also have insufficient or moderate weight, dry skin, and fine hair. The pitta dosha is a bodily energy that reportedly comprises mostly fire with some water. People believe it helps regulate digestion and may have links to immunity, metabolism, and body temperature.

Pitta may also have associations with activity, transformation, and change. It is said to be hot, oily, light, intense, and sharp. The kapha dosha is a bodily energy that reportedly contains water and earth. It provides stability to the body, moisturizes skin, and heals wounds. It also has links to cohesion, structure, and lubrication. Kapha is reportedly wet, heavy, solid, slow, sticky, cool, dense, and oily.According to Ayurveda, it is important for a person to balance the doshas. This will maximize the positive benefits of each dosha and mitigate negative effects.

Vata Dosha Characteristics

Vata people often have a small or thin frame and dry skin and hair. They are sensitive to cold weather and may have cold extremities, circulation issues, and joint pain. Their personalities can be entertaining, dynamic, and enthusiastic.

They are also said to be creative, perceptive, and sensitive people. Physically and mentally active, they often multi-task and talk quickly. Vata people may be easily overwhelmed and be prone to changeable moods. When vata people become aggravated, their emotions may manifest as fear, anxiety, and nervousness.

Vata Dosha Diet

In Ayurvedic medicine, healthy digestion is the foundation of good health. It recommends eating foods that balance the dominant dosha.

Vata individuals should eat foods that increase kapha qualities, such as heaviness, stillness, and smoothness. This is said to balance the coldness and lightness of vata. Some vata individuals have shifting, sensitive digestive patterns and variable appetites. They tend to skip meals or forget to eat, which can lead to unintentional weight loss. They may also experience gas, bloating, and constipation.

According to Ayurveda, they should choose warm, moist, and heavy foods that are easily digestible. They should avoid cold and raw foods as well as stimulants such as nicotine and caffeine.

Sweet, salty, and sour foods balance vata people, while pungent, bitter, and astringent foods may be aggravating to them.

A vata dosha diet may include:

- Beverages: Buttermilk, warm teas, nut milk, and warm or room temperature water
- Meat and eggs: Beef, chicken, turkey, and eggs
- Grains: Rice, oats, quinoa, and wheat
- Fruits: Berries, peaches, mangoes, melons, bananas, avocados, coconuts, and cooked apples
- Vegetables: Carrots, beets, squash, lentils, mung beans, sweet potatoes, and green, leafy vegetables
- Spices: Ginger, basil, bay, cinnamon, nutmeg, cloves, parsley, and turmeric
- Nuts and seeds: Almonds, chestnuts, cashews, pistachios, and sunflower and pumpkin seeds
- Oils: Ghee, avocado oil, coconut oil, sesame oil, and extra virgin olive oil

Lifestyle habits: According to Ayurveda, several lifestyle habits can balance a vata person.

Since vata relates to movement and stimulation, many of these practices are calming, soothing, and relaxing. For example, they can also take a relaxing bath or diffuse essential oils.Activities to relieve stress and bring attention inward include meditation, yoga nidra, and restorative yoga poses. People can also try calming breathing exercises that include Nadi Shodhana, Ujjayi, and Bhramari.

The science of Ayurveda: While Ayurveda is a long-standing tradition, there is a lack of large, in-depth studies supporting its benefits. However, some smaller studies back certain Ayurvedic concepts and practices.

According to a 2015 study, a person's dosha can affect sleep quantity and quality. People with a vata constitution took more time to fall asleep and felt less rested in the morning. They also had more disrupted sleep, which can reduce sleep quality due to fewer periods of deep or slow-wave sleep.

A 2019 review suggests Ayurveda may be beneficial in treating type 2 diabetes. It found that herbs, such as bitter melon, fenugreek, and holy basil, may boost immunity and lower blood sugar levels.

People can take herbs in supplements form or use them for hot oil and powder massages.

Chapter 5

The Panchakarma

Introduction

Ayurveda is an elegant system of healing, first described around 5,000 years ago in ancient Vedic texts as comprehensive teachings on preserving and maintaining health. The fact that this ancient medicine is still in use today is a testament to the wisdom it holds when it comes to understanding the human potential to achieve a happy and wholesome life.

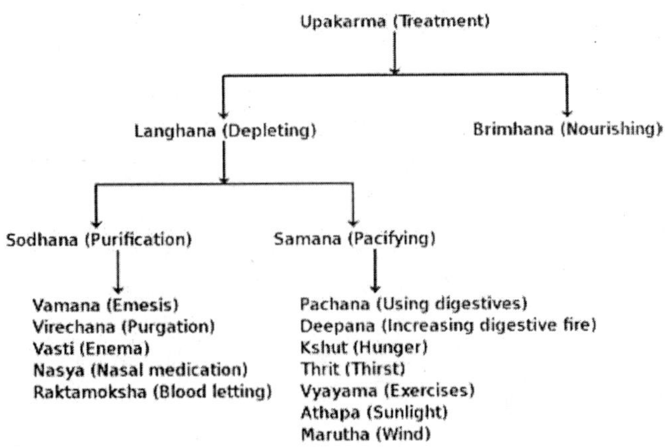

Primordial in essence, Ayurveda serves to awaken your body's ability to restore balance using principles that are seemingly basic and yet profound. These same principles are mirrored in many indigenous cultures today, especially when it comes to the importance of restoring harmony or balance to cultivate good health. In addition, woven into Ayurvedic teachings is a sense of love and compassion for each person's healing journey and a reminder to regard yourself in the same way. One of the first things you will learn about or experience when starting to delve into the world of Ayurveda is the cleansing and rejuvenation process called panchakarma, where you quite literally clean the slate and start anew.

What Is Panchakarma: Panchakarma eliminates accumulated impurities from the mind-body physiology; it is essentially a detoxification program. Pancha in Sanskrit means "five," and karma means "action" and refers to five different purifying and rejuvenating procedures in Ayurveda.

When it was initially designed thousands of years ago, there weren't as many causes for unhealthy accumulations in the body, but it was still necessary to create this sophisticated panchakarma detox program. Today, as improper diet, stress, and environmental hazards abound, panchakarma can be of great help.

A panchakarma program takes place over the course of several days, allowing plenty of time and space to rest and process the experience. Each step in the program is purposeful and is meant to ultimately restore your body's innate healing ability. Your body knows how to cleanse itself quite efficiently and is well-equipped to remove waste through various channels such as:

- Sweat glands
- Blood vessels
- Urinary tract
- Intestines

Since your body has its own detoxification system, what's the purpose of panchakarma? Think of a car that is well-maintained and how long it can be kept running. Give it good oil and the attention it needs, and it will reward you with many good years. Ignore your car and its parts start to wear out and overall functioning is less than optimal. While you are more complex than a car, the same concept applies. Sometimes your body and mind need a little help. You need all your parts to be running smoothly to feel healthy and energized. In order to do so, a little conscious effort is needed.

Panchakarma helps to gently clear the channels of removal in the body so that everything runs smoothly and efficiently, like a well-oiled machine. In the process, your mental and emotional bodies go through their own cleansing process as well. The mind and body are intricately connected according to Ayurveda. What you do to one affects the other.

For example, when you feel stress you will always feel it somewhere in your body. Or, when you have a good workout, your mind feels light and clear.

Classic and Modern Panchakarma

As with anything that has been around for a very long time, panchakarma has evolved throughout the years and the modes of practice have differed throughout India. For a little history, here are the five classical elements that make up panchakarma therapy as they were originally written:

1. Basti: Herbalized oil enemas
2. Nasya: Nasal irrigation
3. Vamana: Therapeutic vomiting
4. Virechana: Purgation
5. Raktamokshana: Bloodletting

Some of these treatments have been modified for obvious reasons. A panchakarma program today will usually include the following:

- Herbal oil massages
- Steam baths
- Cleansing enemas
- Nasal administration
- Gentle laxatives (senna)
- Specialized diet

These therapeutic processes are still based on the five actions and the effects are powerful and long-lasting. Using your body's channels of detoxification the entire program is designed to not only heal your body but facilitate a deep-rooted release of stress that has sometimes been stored for years. For many, panchakarma ends up being an unexpected and powerful journey into the healing process.

It's important to understand a few fundamental concepts of Ayurveda to help fully appreciate what makes panchakarma effective even at the most subtle levels.

Ayurvedic Definition of Good Health

What is the definition of good health? Ask on an individual basis and you'll find many definitions based on such things as life experiences, culture, and health history. With any good journey, it's helpful to know where you are going-what the goal is. Then, steps can be taken to seek out ayurvedic healing accordingly.

Here is the Ayurvedic definition of good health in Sanskrit, followed by the general translation:

Sama dosha, sama agnischa

Sama dhatu mala kriyah

Prasanna atma indriya manahwww

Swastha iti abhidhiyate

One whose doshas are balanced, whose digestive fire is balanced,

whose bodily tissues and elimination processes are functioning normally,

and whose senses, mind, and self are filled with bliss;

such a one is called a healthy person.

Ayurveda teaches that your natural state is one of health, happiness, and an inner sense of well-being. As the above definition confirms, this can be achieved when your body is clear of toxins, your mind is at peace, your emotions are calm and happy, your wastes are efficiently eliminated, and your organs are functioning normally. This sounds great, but how do you not only get to this point but also maintain it? This is where Ayurveda shines.

The Importance of Detoxification

According to Ayurveda, good health depends on your body and mind's ability to metabolize all of life's experiences, both good and bad. This is why digestion, or agni, is important as it relates to the metabolization of life on all levels. Agni means gastric fire, enzymes, and metabolism and determines how efficiently you are able to convert information in the form of food, emotions, and experiences into nourishment. When agni, and the gastrointestinal tract (or GI tract for short), is strong, everything is broken down and absorbed into your mind-body physiology as appropriate. Anything that is not useful is eliminated from your body and mind. Start to notice how you personally metabolize the world around you and how it affects you.

When agni is weak, it leads to improper digestion of food, experiences, and emotions and results in an accumulation of undesired impurities usually referred to as toxins. Ayurveda refers to these incompletely metabolized materials as ama and is viewed as toxic residue. The presence of ama clogs the channels in the body that are in charge of waste removal and circulation. Thus, proper assimilation and nourishment are denied to the mind-body physiology.

Ama is described as:

- Heavy
- Thick
- Cold
- Foul

Agni is described as:

- Light
- Clear
- Hot
- Pure

Which one describes how you feel? When ama has accumulated over a period of time, mental and physical functioning is diminished and it feels like it takes a lot of energy to get anything done. The body is working overtime to perform what it usually does with ease. It is difficult to restore balance and harmony until the impurities have been eliminated. Once ama is reduced and agni is strong, you can tackle life a lot easier.

In the world is busy, stressful, and toxic that places a huge strain on your physical and mental systems, especially over time. While you may not see it with your eyes, you most assuredly feel it. Stress is a huge problem and is the cause of many ailments. How can you focus on creating a happy life that Ayurveda promotes when you feel like crap The first step is clearing out the gunk, or ama, through panchakarma and then learning tools to maintain good health.

Signs You Might Benefit from Panchakarma: The signs of ama accumulation can be obvious. If you notice you have any of the following symptoms, you might benefit from a panchakarma program:

- Thick layer of coating on the tongue
- Tired throughout the day, especially after meals
- Body aches and pains
- Uncontrollable cravings
- Foggy mind
- Bad smelling breath, odor, and flatulence
- Constipation or diarrhea

The Panchakarma Treatment: Are you convinced you need panchakarma? Here is what to expect. Depending on the facility, your panchakarma program may slightly vary. It's always under the supervision of a medical doctor and/or an Ayurvedic physician. The program is specialized and is tailored to your mind-body constitution or dosha(s). It is often recommended to stay in-house for treatment in order to get the most out of the experience.

There are three main components of the panchakarma process:

- Preparation phase (poorva karma)
- Principal procedures (pradhana karma)
- Post-therapy procedures (paschat karma)

The preparation phaseis designed to prepare your body for elimination of imbalances. It includes steps that are meant to soften and help encourage the release of stored toxicity. The therapy called Snehana (oleation) refers to both internal and external oleation of the body.

You are instructed to take increasing quantities of herbalized oils by mouth, which are designed to lubricate your digestive system. The Chopra Center's recipe for Bliss Balls include ingredients that are meant to stoke agni as well as provide lubrication. In addition, the preparation phase may also include ginger tea as well as herbal supplements such as triphala and guggulu.

During the principal procedures phase, now that your body has been prepped, your focus is on the elimination of toxins. This is where the five classical therapies would take place. Instead, alternative treatments are given that provide similar benefits and include the following:

- Bastis, or herbalized enemas, are administered. They are made up of herbalized oils that flush out your intestinal tract, accessing the deeper tissues and eliminating fat-soluble toxins. While it may not sound appealing, the whole process is meant to be gentle. Senna can be used as part of this phase as an additional gentle laxative.
- Nasya, or nasal applications, are medicinal oils that are applied throughout the nasal passages, clearing the sinuses and draining excess mucus. If you suffer from chronic sinus problems or allergies, you may find relief. This step can feel soothing and calms your mind.
- Swedana, or sweat treatments, are next. Dry and wet saunas open up your pores and begin to rid the body of impurities

through your sweat glands. It helps to dilate circulation and speeds up the elimination of impurities that have been loosened by oleation. It also encourages a general state of relaxation.

- Abhyanga, or oil massage, is the external oleation of the body. The type of oil along with the herbs used to prepare the oil are based on the recommendations of the overseeing doctor. In panchakarma, massage serves as a way to provide oil to the tissues, loosen impurities, and encourage those impurities to start making their way out through your channels of elimination. Each day is a different massage treatment and is scheduled in a specific order that is optimal for cleansing.

The post-therapy procedures, also considered the rejuvenation phase, is the time to implement the tools that have been taught to help sustain the new and improved you. Ayurveda emphasizes the need to rekindle one's agni to prevent unhealthy accumulation. This is accomplished through regular practice of the following:

- Yoga
- Meditation
- Dosha-specific diet
- Daily abhyanga
- Pranayama

The feeling of lightness and clarity accompanies this time. Impurities have been removed from your body, thus you feel more energized and it's easier to make healthier choices. Rasayana means "that which is nourishing" and defines the mindset that you must consider during this time. Incorporate more natural foods, spend time in nature, exercise, and choose experiences that make you happy in addition to putting into practice agni-enhancing techniques.

Example of a typical day:

- Wake up with sunrise and practice gentle yoga and meditation.
- Drink a cup of spiced tea with cumin, ginger, cardamom, fennel seeds, and other spices and herbs for your dosha.
- Enjoy a light breakfast.
- Begin your first treatment of the day, such as an oil massage.
- Spend time in the dry or wet steam room to release toxins.
- Eat a detoxifying lunch of kitchari, lentils, and rice in healing spices.

- Walk around in nature or sit and meditate. Try to detach from technology!
- Take naps as needed.
- Undergo another treatment, such as the herbalized basti.
- Consume a light dinner of more kitchari or cooked vegetables and rice.
- Read, meditate, or journal and then head to bed.

Why Should You Try Panchakarma Treatments?

You don't have to be sick to benefit from panchakarma. If you are healthy, then you will become stronger and have more energy. If you are sick, it will gently encourage you back to health in a natural way. Prevention is important! Anything you can do to maintain a state of balance will help in the long run and ensure a long wholesome life. Here are a few of the benefits of doing panchakarma:

- Eliminates impurities from your body and mind
- Restores your mind-body constitutional balance (or doshas), improving health and wellness
- Strengthens your immune system and you become more resistant to illness
- Reverses the negative effects of stress on your body and mind thereby slowing the aging process
- Enhances your self-reliance, strength, energy, vitality, and mental clarity
- Brings about deep relaxation and a sense of health and well-being

How Often and When: Traditionally, Ayurveda suggests doing panchakarma with the change of the seasons, so about three times per year. Any time you experience transitions, things can get out of balance and accumulations occur. Anytime you feel out of sorts or ill, consider panchakarma. The whole process helps to remind you about the importance of taking care of yourself and honoring where you are at and what you need in the moment.

Your body and mind thrive when given moments of respite and some peace. Panchakarma not only rejuvenates your body and mind but also teaches you about yourself. The value of knowing what good health feels like, even if it's just a glimpse, provides a sense of hope that it's possible to live in this world and feel good. Give panchakarma a try!

Vaman

Vaman is one of the five therapies of panchakarma in Ayurveda. Vaman means therapeutic vomiting which is a medicated emesis.

It is targeted to expel increased kapha dosha out of the body it causes certain types diseases such as cold, cough etc.

Kapha is situated in the chest region expelling in from the oral route is very easy hence vaman treatment is designed to expel it out first forcefully brought from the extremities and different organs into the stomach and then vomiting is induced.

Importance

1. Kapha disorders and associated Pitta disorders or diseases originating or settled in the place of Kapha will be relieved either permanently or for a longer period of time.
2. It helps to prevent the forth coming diseases due to Kapha and Pitta.
3. Most of Ayurvedic drugs are administered by oral root. First it goes to the Amashaya (stomach), which is the main seat of Kapha. Digestion of food also starts from Amashaya. If there is accumulation or aggravation of Kapha in Amashaya, the digestion of food or drug cannot takes place properly. With the help of Vamana Karma, Amashaya Shuddhi (cleansing) occurs, so the digestion of drug and food takes place properly.

Vasantika Vamana (emesis in spring season): In Ayurvedic texts, Vamana procedure is indicated for the expulsion of Kapha Dosha. Kapha Dosha is aggravated in Vasant Rutu; hence, Vamana is indicated in spring season approximately in the month of March and April.

Go to: Vasantika Vamana-Contra-Indications/Indications Almost everybody can undergo Vasantika Vamana except those suffering from the diseases contraindicated for Vamana like bleeding from the upper channels like mouth, upper GIT, bronchial tree, emaciated, very old, pregnant woman, persons with hypertension and heart diseases, exclusively Vata constitution and Vata disorders.

Especially it is highly beneficial for volnteers of Kapha and Kapha-Pitta constitution and patients suffering with Kapha disorders and associated Pitta disorders or diseases originating or settled in the place of Kapha like bronchial asthma, allergic bronchitis, rhinitis, sinusitis, COPD, productive cough, migraine, hyperacidity, indigestion, anorexia, obesity, overweight, dyslipidemia, diabetes mellitus, skin diseases like acne vulgaris, psoriasis, eczema, dermatitis, Lichen Plannus, vitiligo, urticaria, falling and graying of hairs, inflammatory and swollen joint disorders of early stage, depression, drowsiness, excessive sleep, epilepsy, certain auto immune diseases etc.

Diagnostic procedures: The persons were examined on the basis of Dosha, Dushya, (tissues and excreta), Desha (habitat), Prakriti (constitution), Bala (strength), Kala (season), Agni (digestion and metabolism), Vaya (age), Satva (psychological make up), Satmya (adaptability), Ahara (diet) etc and fit persons for Vamana were only selected after having a written consent.

Vamana protocol: It can be divided into three steps

- Purva Karma (preoperative preparation)
- Pradhana Karma (operative procedure/induction of Vamana)
- Pashchat Karma (post operative care)

Purva Karma (Pre-operative)

preparation) Pachana and Deepana (digestives and appetizers)

Trikatu Churna 2 g, Chitrakadi Vati/Amapachana Vati 2 tab TID with warm water for three days. Abhyantara Snehana (internal oleation) Shuddha Ghrita/Siddha Ghrita or Tail (plain/medicated ghee/oil) was given in increasing dose for three to seven days as per the requirement till achieving the signs and symptoms of proper Snehana.

Abhyanga (massage) and Swedana (fomentation) After proper Snehana on next day, Abhyanga was done with Bala Taila followed by Sarvanga Swedana two times a day for one day and next day morning before administering Vamana again. Abhyanga with Bala Taila followed by Sarvang Swedana was done.

Dietetic guidelines during Purva Karma

Diet during the days of Snehapana

(i) Patients were advised to take moderate quantity of liquid and warm food, easy to digest mixed with little fat, which is neither sticky nor complex and to drink lukewarm water.

Diet on previous day of Vamana: Patients were advised to have plenty of milk, curd, sweets like sesame and Jaggary Laddu, Jalebi, Khicadi made from black gram, sesame, jaggary and rice or Dahi Wada.

Counselling before Vamana

- (i) Patients were informed about different steps involved in this procedure.
- (ii) A well-informed written consent was obtained.
- (iii) Patients were advised to relax and remove the negative thoughts.

Pradhana Karma (nduction of iVamana): It includes

- (I) Administration of Vamana Yoga

Table 1 Average quantity of drugs used for Vamana Karma

Drugs	Average
Dose of *Madanaphala* (g)	5.81
Quantity of *Ksheera* (ml)	1130.29
Quantity of *Yastimadhu Phanta* (ml)	3202.9
Quantity of *Lavanodaka* (ml)	2489.13

- (II) Observations during Vamana Karma
- (III) Observations regarding four criteria

(I) Administration of Vamana yoga: This was done in the following way.

a. Position of patients:

Patients were asked to sit on a comfortable Vamana chair of the height of knee joint.

b. Examination of vital data:

Pulse and blood pressure were recorded before, during and after completion of Vamana Karma.

c. Administration of food articles and drugs:

Vamana was induced in the early morning between 6 am and 9 am.

1. Patients were asked to drink milk stomach full (Aakantha pana) approx. 2 l, Peya (thin rice gruel) mixed with ghee was also given for some patients.
2. Then patients are given Vamana Yoga - medicinal formulation (Madanaphala Pippali (powder of seeds of Randia dumetorum) 4 parts, Vacha (Acorus calamus) 2 parts, Saindhava Lavana (rock salt) 1 part and Honey Q.S.) to induce emesis

For collecting vomitus, a wide mouth vessel was kept ready. Now the patient is instructed to vomit without much straining. The urge may be excited by opening wide the lips, the palate, the throat and by slightly bowing the upper part of the body. The dormant urge may be excited by tickling the throat with two well manicured fingers.[3] During the act of emesis when actual bout is being thrown out, forehead and chest of the patient was held, umbilical region of the patient was pressed and back of the patient was gently massaged in upward direction.

3. During the procedure, Vamanopaga Kashaya (supportive decoction to continue vomiting) like decoction/hot infusion of Yashtimadhu (glycyrriza glabra) after each Vega was administered repeatedly to support the act of vomiting till the appearance of Pitta (bile) in vomitus.

- (II) Observations during Vamana Karma: Record of input, output and other observations were maintained.
- (III) Assessment of Vamana: It was assessed as Pravara (highest), Madhyama (moderate) and Hina (lowest) Shuddhi (cleansing) on the basis of four criteria as per the classical texts.

1. Vegiki criteria: It is on the basis of number of bouts like 4, 6 and 8 Vega (projectile vomiting bouts) for Hina, Madhyama and Pravara Shuddhi respectively. In addition to projectile bouts, smaller bouts in every aspect than Vega (Upavega) were also recorded.
2. Maniki criteria: It is on the basis of the quantity of elimination of Dosha, like 1, 1½ and 2 Prastha for Hina, Madhyama, Pravara Shuddhi, respectively (Prastha = 540 ml).

   This is calculated from the total quantity of output minus the total quantity of input.
3. Antiki criteria: It is on the basis of endpoint, it is advised to continue Vamana till the appearance of Pitta in the vomitus which marks the end of Vamana.
4. Laingiki criteria: It is on the basis of positive signs and symptoms produced after Vamana.

Pashchata Karma (Post operative care): When Vamana Karma was completed, patients were kept on close observation and on special dietetic and behavioural restrictions which are considered as "Pashchata Karma" for some days till achieving Agnideepti and Bala. This may be classified as follows.

Dhumapana and Gandusha (medicated smoke and gargling): After Samyaka Vamana, patients are advised to inhale the medicated smoke, gargle and wash mouth, hands and feet, then to rest for about an hour.

Behavioural and dietetic restrictions: Patients were advised to avoid loud speeches, sitting or standing in one position for long duration, excessive walk, excessive rage or excessive depression, exposure to excessive cold, heat, dew, to flowing winds, long journey, night waking, day sleep, to retain or provoke urges. Frequently, untimely, excessive, less, contradictory and heavy diet were also avoided.

Samsarjana Krama: (special dietetic schedule): It has to be planned on the basis of type of purification achieved by Vamana i.e. for Hina, Madhyama and Pravara Shuddhi, three, five and seven days respectively. Generally, in all the patients after Vamana Karma, the Peyadi Samsarjana Krama is advised as dietary regimen as follows with little modification. On the day of Vamana, thin rice gruel without spices and fat once a day; on second day thick rice gruel without spices and fat twice a day; on third day rice and liquid soup of green gram and rice without spices and fat twice a day in moderate quantity; on forth day liquid soup of green gram and rice with spices and fat twice a day in moderate quantity and on fifth day onwards normal diet was given.

Enema Basti

A major component of Ayurveda's Panchakarma cleanses, Basti is imperative for the purpose of clearing disease due to Vata Dosha and promoting longevity. Basti, which is an Ayurvedic enema, is a suppository that can be made of either tonifying or purifying substances. While receiving a medicated solution in the rectum you may experience elicit apprehension, the practice was developed to render the experience as harmonious as possible. This therapy boasts extensive benefits, treating both the physical body and the mind. With a wide spectrum of applicability, Basti possesses the capability to treat very specialized conditions. It can treat circumstances of either excess or deficiency, solely depending upon which constituents are to be used.

Typical Beneficiaries of Basti:

- People afflicted with ailments of Vata Dosha.
- Those whose limbs have become stiff or contracted.
- Individuals who are afflicted with fractures and dislocations.

- Abdominal disorders/ailments of the pelvic region.
- Nervous disorders.
- Issues of improper circulation.

Home Site of Vata

As is true with all the Doshas, the body will always contain a location where specific Doshic energy can be habitually found. This location is also typically the first area a disturbance/ailment will be discovered. Vata Dosha is found predominantly within the large intestine. The large intestine is an area of the body that is allotted a hollow cavity/space to allow for the passage of stool. This "space" is exactly why Vata Dosha, being comprised of Ether (Space) and Air, prefers to target this area with imbalance. In the preliminary phase of the disease, the earliest signs of Vata derangement are commonly observed as gas and constipation.

If Vata is not able to be balanced in an appropriate extent of time, it then travels into the blood and lymph. This subsequently allows Vata to relocate into the deeper tissues by using these channels as a highway for transportation within the body. While the circulatory and lymphatic systems were designed to transport nutrients to the rest of the body by design, with imbalance they function to transport disease as well. The colon is a major point of nutrient absorption in the body and can be thought of in a similar mannerism to the root of a tree. When a tree is well irrigated (Cleansed) and nurtured through the soil (Digestion), it allows the tree to grow large and tall, building branches, and producing flowers, and even fruits. The catalyzation of the growth process, all begins with a healthy root system! The same principle is observed within the human body. With the application of a successful Basti treatment, the body will become well nurtured, which in turn leads to overall health improvements and well-being.

Panchakarma Application

Ayurveda's most powerful detoxifying cleanse is known as Panchakarma. Pancha means five while karma means action, making Panchakarma a summarization of these five main therapies or actions. According to the Charaka Samhita, an ancient text wherein most of this system of medicine was recorded, Panchakarma is articulated as Vamana (Therapeutic emesis), Vierechana (Therapeutic purgation of the bowels), Nasya (Oleation of the nostrils), Anuvasana Basti (Oil enema), and Niruha Basti (Water enema). A later classical text, titled the Shushruta Samhita, thereafter classifies Rakta Mokshana (Bloodletting) as the fifth Panchakarma therapy.

The two Basti therapies were then combined into a single category of "Basti". The original Panchakarma classification attributing 2/5 of the cleanse's success to Basti, demonstrates how pivotal the practice can be when clearing disease from the body. This is in large part due to the basic principles of Panchakarma theory at its core. Toxins (Ama) are loosened from their location within the body through the process of internal and external oleation. As they are loosened, they are then forced to retreat into the GI tract through the use of sudation (Heat) and fomentation (Sweating).

Once the Ama has been relocated into the GI tract, it can then be purged out of the body through the Panchakarma, as mentioned above, therapies. Typically, Bastis are alternated in-between tonifying and purifying types. This is to prevent the body from becoming overly depleted and dried out through the utilization of the purifying Niruha Basti (Water-based enemas). It is common practice to perform an Anuvasana Basti (Oil-based enema) both before and after a Niruha Basti is received for this precise purpose. This practice of "bookending" a Niruha Basti also ensures that Vata is kept grounded and at its root, which is one of the fundamental objectives of the therapy overall.

Before and After Basti Care

Just as the absorption of herbs and/or oil can affect our digestion during oral ingestion, digestion is also affected when these substances are assimilated into the rectum. After a Basti is administered, the absence of hunger will generally be observed for three to four hours.

However, longer durations without the sensation of hunger are not uncommon to experience either. Due to the sensitivities imposed upon the digestive and eliminatory systems, proper care should be taken both prior to and after the therapy, to ensure that no imbalances occur within the person. During a Panchakarma, the pre-care protocol is known as Purva Karma (Preparatory actions). This procedure will typically involve a light diet, internal and external oleation, and fomentation (The application of heat). It customarily will continue for between three to twenty-one days.

The purpose of Purva Karma, is to loosen up Ama and bring any excess Dosha back into its home site contained within the digestive/ eliminatory systems (Known as the Mahavaha Srotas - "The Great Channel"). Once the Ama and Dosha have been brought back into the Mahavaha Srotas, they can then be purged from the body through the cleansing practices of a Panchakarma. Following a Panchakarma, certain post-cleanse (Praschat Karma) practices should be emphasized to ensure the proper recovery of the patient transpires. First and foremost, there should be appropriate management of Agni (Digestion). This rehabilitation of the Agni is known as Samsarjana Krama. The dietary regimen issued prior to the cleanse during Purva Karma is very similar to the Agni re-optimization process during the Praschat Karma (Post-cleanse). A light diet, consisting primarily of Kitchari, or other rice/dal combinations is emphasized. Kitchari is an extremely easy-to-digest meal. In fact, a majority of the stress and energy placed upon the digestive system when conventional meals are ingested is negated when kitchari is substituted. With less stress on the digestive system, the other bodily systems which were purged, are better able to recover.

Kitchari is so effortlessly digested mainly because of its ingredients and the way in which it is prepared. Mung beans and rice are the two main stars of this dish. Mung beans, which are one of the easiest beans in the legume family for the body to process, are soaked; This kickstarts the assimilation process. Dal cooked together with soaked rice and a plethora of digestive spices allows for a heightened integration of digestive aptitude. This dish is a complete protein; Therefore, it will provide the necessary nutrition for the day, all the while reducing strain on digestion. Once the Agni has been properly restored in the patient, life will more or less return back to normal. The Praschat Karma usually lasts for a period of one to three weeks. It is common for the body to become much more sensitive to triggers in the diet than it was prior to the cleanse during this time. These sensitivities can propel the person into a heightened awareness around their own digestion. Food sensitivities show which aspects of the diet we have predispositions towards not digesting properly. Every Dosha has foods that they digest better or worse than the other Doshas. Learning which manner the body reacts to certain foods can lead to an optimized state of digestion as a result of eating foods that are more in alignment with the person themselves. Dietary predispositions are easily enunciated through the knowledge of a trained Ayurvedic practitioner. However, seeing and understanding how the body reacts firsthand, is an important tool in the continued understanding of its well-being. These food triggers should be minimized or even eradicated from the diet altogether.

If a standalone Basti therapy is taking place without the other components of the Panchakarma cleanse, a similar pre-cleanse (Purva Karma) and post-cleanse (Praschat Karma) should be observed when possible. These will both have a more moderate and abridged means of execution. The modified steps are outlined below:

Modified Pre and Post Care Guidelines for Basti

Modified Purva Karma (Pre-cleanse)	Modified Praschat Karma (Post-cleanse)
A light diet of kitchari or broth should be ingested for 1-3 days following the Basti.	If the urge to defecate becomes pronounced, let the body evacuate the Basti.
Oil massage (Abhyanga) should be received for 1-3 consecutive days prior to the Basti. An Abhyanga should also take place just prior to the Basti therapy.	No food should be taken for 3-4 hours following a Basti.
Light sudation and fomentation should follow the Abhyanga massage.	A light diet of kitchari or broth should be ingested for 1-3 days following the Basti.
Ingestion of 1 Tbsp of ghee (Or oil) per day for 1-3 days prior to the Basti (The oil can be taken in food, or on its own).	

Receiving a Basti

In order to receive a Basti properly, the Large Intestine should be evacuated prior to the start of the therapy if possible. This removes possible obstruction of the channel due to fecal matter, thus allowing the medicated liquid to travel deeper into the colon. An Anuvasana Basti should never be received when the sensation of hunger is perceived. If hunger is present, the Basti will be drawn upwards towards the small intestine and stomach which disrupts the effectiveness and absorption of the medicine into the body. To prevent this from happening, a light meal consisting of kitchari or broth should be ingested one to two hours prior to the therapy's commencement. In the case of Niruha Basti, the stomach should be empty before receiving the water decoction. The reasoning behind this is that following the complete digestion of more food, the Doshas retreat more easily into the gastrointestinal tract, allowing them to be easier purified by the Basti. Also, as the Niruha Basti is not retained for a significant period of time, there is not the same risk of it retreating upward into the body as was the case with the Anuvasana Basti.

Guidelines for Receiving Anuvasana Basti and Niruha Basti

Anuvasana Basti	Niruha Basti
The stomach should not be empty during an Anuvasana Basti- Eat a small light meal 1-2 hours prior to the Basti.	If possible, a bowel movement should take place before the Basti begins.
If possible, a bowel movement should take place before the Basti begins.	Niruha should be passed immediately after the conclusion of the therapy.
If it is possible to retain the oil, maintain it inside the colon for nine hours to provide maximum absorption.	

Nasal Administration Nasya

Nasya Treatment involves the instillation of medicated oils or powders into the nostrils. This therapeutic process aims to nourish the nasal cavity, sinuses, and upper respiratory tract, promoting optimal functioning of these areas. Nasya Treatment mainly treats head, throat, and eye problems.

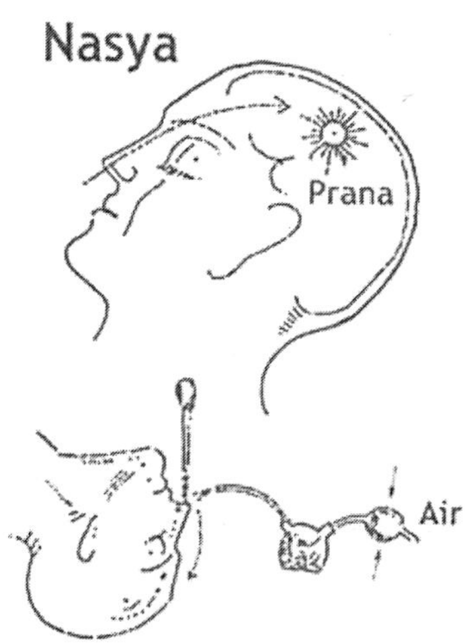

The nose is the door to consciousness and the pathway to our inner pharmacy. Medications that are administered via the nasal passages affect the mind, prana vata, tarpaka kapha, sadhaka pitta, and majja dhatu. Administer nasya on an empty stomach an hour before or after a shower or exercise. Lie down with the head tilted back and put 5 drops of nasya in each nostril. Sniff deeply, then remain lying for a minute or so, to allow the nasya to penetrate.

General Indications

General Contraindications

Stiffness or pain of head, neck, or jaw
Children (under 7)
Headache and Migraine
Old age (over 80)
Sinus pain and congestion
Pregnancy
Toothache, loose teeth, receding gums
Menstruation
Hoarseness of voice
Just before or after shower/bath
Twitching or drooping eyelids
Indigestion or full stomach
Tingling sensations on face
Diarhhea
Obstruction in throat
Hunger or Hypoglycaemia
Uvulitis, Tonsillitis, Laryngitis, Pharyngitis
Thirst or Dehydration
Speech disorders and loss of speech
Exertion
Bell's Palsy (facial paralysis)
Intoxication
Goiter
Physical exercise
Glaucoma

Acute fever

Pituitary or space-occupying tumor

Grief

Unconsciousness/fainting

Just having done purgation or basti

Depleted sexual energy

Same time as neti pot nasal cleansing

Any disorders above clavicle area

Types of Nasya

1) Virechana (cleansing) nasya: dry powers or herbs are blown into the nose. Commonly used substances include vacha (calamus), brahmi (gotu kola), and jatamamsi.

Specific Indications

Kapha disorders

Headache or heaviness in the head

Cold

Sticky eyes

Runny nose, sinusitis, chronic rhinitis

Hoarseness of the voice due to kapha

Cervical lymph congestion

Attachment, greed, or lust

Adenitis

Bacterial infections

Epilepsy

Skin diseases

Drowsiness

Parkinsonism

Additional Contraindications

2) Bruhana (nutritive) nasya: especially good for vata dosha. Strengthening and tonifying substances are administered through the nose. Commonly used substances are ghee, salt, shatavari ghee, ashwagandha ghee, medicated milk, and various oils.

Specific Indications

Vata disorders

Vata-type headache or migraine

Dryness of voice

Dry nose or sinuses

Nervousness, anxiety, fear, negativity

Dizziness or emptiness

Ptosis

Bursitis

Stiffness of the neck

Cervical spondylosis

Insomnia

Additional Contraindicatisons

3) Shamana (sedative) nasya: medicated decoctions, teas, the fresh juice of herbs, or medicated oils specific to the dosha are used. Substances used include brahmi ghee (for pitta), vacha oil (for kapha or vata), and tikta ghee (for vata or pitta).

Specific Indications

Pitta disorders

Blue patches on skin: infradermal hemorrhage

Alopatheia

Blephritis

Psoriasis

Additional Contraindications

4) Navana nasya: decoctions, fresh juices, and oils are mixed together and administered according to the aggravated dosha. Used for pitta-vata or pitta-kapha disorders. Among the substances used include brahmi juice (for pitta) and vacha juice (for kapha or vata).

Specific Indications

Aggravated doshas

Additional Contraindications

5) Marshya: A little ghee or oil is inserted into the nostrils with the little finger. This, along with gentle massage, helps to

relieve stress and opens the deep tissues. It can be done on a regular basis or occasionally as desired.

Prati marshya: Marsha done on a daily basis.

Specific Indications

Stress

Dryness

Bloodletting Rakta Moksha

Rakta Moksha, also called bloodletting, is a traditional Ayurvedic treatment method for the removal or displacement of impure blood from the affected body part. Rakta Moksha therapy is also regarded as one of the five ama elimination procedures in Panchakarma.

Rakta dhatu is one of the seven dhatus or bodily tissues. When the Rakta dhatu is healthy, it enhances the individual's complexion and enables the proper nourishment of the muscles and other tissues. In its vitiated state, it leads to several diseases like mukhapaka (oral ulcers), raktapitta (epistaxis), vaivarnya (discolouration of skin), kushta (skin diseases), gulma (tumor), etc. Some of the factors that produce toxins in blood, according to Ayurveda, are:

- Excessive consumption of salt, sour, unctuous, and heavy foods
- Alcohol intake
- Overeating
- Sleeping immediately after meals
- Excessive exposure to sun or heat
- Stress

By letting out the blood through Rakta Moksha Ayurveda therapy, all the problems caused due to vitiated blood can be eliminated. It can be performed along with other therapies like Virechana, Vamana, Nasya, and Basti to balance the doshas as well as the energies that control the biological functions in the body.

Rakta Moksha Procedure

There are two categories in the way the Rakta Moksha treatment is performed

Shastra Visravana: Shastra Visravana therapy is performed using metal instruments. In this therapy, the blood is let out through two procedures:

- Siravyadha (puncturing the vein)
- Pracchana (creating several incisions over the skin)

Anushastra Visravana

The therapies in Anushastra Visravana are performed without using metal instruments. They are of four types:

- Jalouka Vacharana: Application of jalauka or leeches are preferred in cases of vitiated Pitta doshas in blood.
- Alabu: Due to the bitter, dry, and pungent nature of calabash gourd, it is useful for bloodletting in Kapha dosha vitiation. This procedure involves making multiple incisions on the skin and then extinguishing an ignited wick over the affected area to create a vacuum that drains the blood out.
- Shrunga Vacharana: Here, the Shrunga or horn of a cow is used to bring out blood in Vata dosha vitiation.
- Ghati Yantra: The method of extracting blood is similar to Alabu therapy, but it uses a pot instead of the gourd.

Indications

- Leukoderma
- Psoriasis
- Leprosy
- Eczema
- Urticaria
- Hives
- Varicose veins
- Enlarged liver or spleen
- Acute appendicitis
- Trigeminal Neuralgia

Contraindications

- Rakta Moksha is contraindicated for the following
- Young children
- Old age
- Pregnancy
- Menstruation
- Anemia

- Jaundice
- Tuberculosis
- Diabetes

Rakta Moksha Benefits

- Expels out disease-causing vitiated blood from the body
- Prevent tumors and edema
- Helps to balance Pitta dosha aggravation
- Beneficial in bleeding disorders
- Prevents allergies and repeated hives
- Helps to manage high blood pressure and arthritis
- Treats chronic diseases, such as psoriasis

Palliation

Snehana

Warm, medicinal oils are applied in large amounts all over the body. Medicated oils like Mahanarayan oil or Sahacharadi oil are used in different people according to the requirement. Essential oils may also be employed according to the doshas. Along with the application of oil, intake of oil or ghee (snehapana) is also recommended. Oils help loosen and liquefy toxins and concerns in the skin and blood (called the outer disease pathway), dislodging and removing the heavy, sticky toxins from the smallest channels.

Thus, toxins begin to drain from the central disease pathway (deeper tissues) and start to flow into the GI tract. Secretions are also activated, enabling easier dosha transport of toxins (ama) and wastes (malas) as they return to the GI tract for elimination. Oil lubricates and protects tissues from damage, as ama returns to the GI tract. Finally, since Váyu is responsible for movement, oil lubrication restores proper Váyu functioning, allowing for a proper flow of wastes and toxins to their removal sites.

Swedana: According to Ashtanga Hridayam, after oleation steam, sweating therapies are employed for effective dislodging and liquefying of toxins and improving digestion. Svedhana causes the body's channels to widen, enabling ama to easily flow from the tissues back to the GI tract and improve circulation. Heat allows the skin and blood (outer disease pathway) to be cleansed. This relieves, cleanses, and reduces fat tissue and muscle tension. Heat also restores balance to Váyu and

Kapha (i.e. removing coldness and stiffness) and reduces the heavy, sticky nature of ama. Once toxins are back in the G.I. tract, they are ready to be completely expelled from the body through Panchakarma therapy. Internal (e.g., spicy herbs) and external (e.g. jacuzzi, sauna) heat are used to dislodge wastes and toxins.

Abhyanga: Ayurvedic Self-Massage

The necessity of self-care emerged in an all new way during the pandemic. Why? Because suddenly, almost overnight, many people had more time for it. Some meditated, baked, exercised, took bubble baths, spent time with loved ones in socially distanced circles, and slowed the pace of life. Hopefully, any reframing that healthier habits brought in 2020-2022 hasn't disintegrated. But if it has and you've once again stepped into the overwhelm of a packed schedule, the ayurvedic practice of abhyanga may help you reconnect with yourself - and improve your overall wellness in the process. Here's a look at what abhyanga is, the potential benefits, how to practice it, and more.

Definition of Abhyanga: Abhyanga is a type of massage performed with oil, often warmed between the palms before application, that you practice on yourself or receive as a therapy. It's derived from the Sanskrit words anga (movement) and abhi (different, against, or contrary). Abhyanga is a practice in ayurvedic medicine from India, one of the oldest medical systems in the world, according to the National Center for Complementary and Integrative Health (NCCIH). This traditional medical system approaches health in a holistic way, such as through a seasonal ayurvedic diet, yoga and meditation practices, herbal remedies, oil pulling, and dry brushing.

Traditionally, abhyanga is one of the dinacharya, or daily practices, for maintaining health, or as part of the pretreatment procedure of panchakarma (a more intensive "detox" treatment regimen), per the aforementioned published review.

How Abhyanga Works: In ayurveda, abhyanga may work in several ways. "Skin is one of the biggest organs in the body. It plays a role in elimination and immunity," says Sukumaran. Both the oil and massage may improve health in different ways. Massage itself can be de-stressing, and the oil may act as a moisturizer for the skin to keep it supple and hydrated. Properly hydrated skin allows the skin's barrier to stay intact, which is important because the skin is your immune system's first line of defense, notes a review on skin, immunity, and aging.

According to Banyan Botanicals, ayurveda practitioners believe that oil self-massage may also lead to:

- Better circulation (of blood and lymph fluid)
- Improvement in sleep
- Healthy vision
- Increased longevity

The practice encourages you to put yourself first by carving out time and ritualizing self-care; in theory, this has a positive ripple effect on your wellness. "Abhyanga is one of the most important self-care rituals. When we care for our most precious thing - our bodies - it leads to higher self-esteem and self-respect," says Sukumaran, from her personal experience.

Possible Health Benefits of Abhyanga: Note that more research is still needed to better understand the possible perks of abhyanga. To date, most Western, aka conventional, research examines the general health benefits of ayurveda and its applications for specific populations, and research on abhyanga, specifically, is lacking. If you're looking to incorporate a low-risk, self-care practice (or traditional form of massage therapy) into your new routine, here are some potential benefits of abhyanga.

May Help Relieve Stress: Anyone who's visited a spa for a massage or asked a partner or friend for a simple shoulder rub knows just how stress-relieving a massage might be.

"Abhyanga helps soothe and calm the nervous system," says Katie Silcox, an ayurvedic teacher and author of Glow Worthy, based in Charlottesville, Virginia. She refers back to the state of being a baby, where most people receive lots of skin-to-skin contact - something that happens rarely outside of intimacy today. As you practice self-massage, "you're taking yourself back to that time, reminding yourself through your physiology that you are loved, safe, and valued for who you are. This is a deep spiritual ritual you can do for yourself," she explains, from her personal experience.Some research corroborates this potential benefit, showing that healthy people who received abhyanga massage from a therapist for an hour reported lower perceived stress levels. It's important to note, however, that studies on the self-massage form of abhyanga are lacking.

May Improve Circulation: The touch in massage stimulates your circulation, and conventional massage therapy has been shown to lower blood pressure levels, according to an earlier study. That research looked at 10-15 minutes of Swedish massage (a different massage technique) and found that these blood pressure benefits persisted for at least three days after the massage.Though there is no research yet on abhyanga specifically for improved circulation, this may be a possible benefit scientists will explore someday.

May Promote Better Sleep: Massage therapy, in general, has been shown to improve sleep, including for people with insomnia or those who have pain conditions, according to the American Massage Therapy Association (AMTA).

For many people, a popular time to practice abhyanga is before bedtime. Having soothing pre-bed rituals free of technology and other stressors and distractions may help your body wind down in preparation for sleep. "[Some] people report that abhyanga before bed helps their sleep," says Silcox, of her teaching experience. As you'll learn below, abhyanga can be done in just 15 minutes, but busy people may benefit from performing a light massage in the shower for just a minute or two, she adds.

May Aid Skin and Hair Health: During abhyanga, you'll likely massage both your skin and scalp, which means you may apply the oil to your hair as well. One review noted that the oil may nourish your skin to make it soft, elastic, and strong. Likewise, regular applications of oil to your scalp may boost the health of the skin here, as well as the hair follicles, improving scalp dryness, itching, and even dandruff.

The act of massaging this oil onto skin is believed to dilate small blood vessels to increase circulation, which may deliver nutrients to skin and hair follicles, per past research. Finally, rubbing your hands on your skin exfoliates it by removing dead skin cells, which is another reason why your body may feel softer when you're done.

Abhyanga Safety and Side Effects: The good news? A self-massage practice is usually safe. "Abhyanga is something that does really help almost everyone," says Silcox, in her experience. Research suggests there are certain health conditions that may make abhyanga inappropriate for certain groups. Those can include people with osteoporosis, skin disease, fractures, varicose veins, atherosclerosis, cancer, and an open wound, among others. Talk to your doctor first to determine if abhyanga oil massage on yourself or as a therapy is right for you.

Who Might Want to Try (and Avoid) Abhyanga: Most people can safely practice oil self-massage; it's used in India by both adults and children, says Sukumaran. Of course, if self-massage hurts in any way, you should avoid areas of pain. By performing a light, stroking self-massage, you're able to control the pressure and areas of focus.

Massage is the rubbing or kneading of the body's soft tissues. Massage techniques are commonly applied with hands, fingers, elbows, knees, forearms, feet or a device. The purpose of massage is generally for the treatment of body stress or pain.

In European countries, a person professionally trained to give massages is traditionally known as a masseur (male) or masseuse (female). In the United States, these individuals are often referred to as "massage therapists;" In some provinces of Canada, they are called "registered massage therapists."

In professional settings, clients are treated while lying on a massage table, sitting in a massage chair, or lying on a mat on the floor. There are many different modalities in the massage industry, including (but not limited to): deep tissue, manual lymphatic drainage, medical, sports, structural integration, Swedish, Thai and trigger point.

Chapter 6

Disease Process

Introduction

In Ayurveda, there are six stages of disease: Sanchaya (accumulation), Prakopa (aggravation), Prasara (dissemination), Sthana Samshraya (localization), Vyakti (disruption), and Bheda (manifestation). There are no symptoms or vague complaints during the first four stages.There are numerous causes of dosha aggravation or vitiation. These can be both external and internal. If the doshas become vitiated enough, the dh?tus and their agni will be abnormally affected, causing illness and disease (vy?dhi). The early stages of aggravation may be quite subtle and it may take further aggravation before it 'grabs the attention'. This can then lead to a progression that causes a change in cellular intelligence, abnormal changes in the quality of a dh?tu, and changes in organs and srotamsi.Ayurveda classifies this progression of disease in six steps, called the Satkriy?kala. Understanding these steps is vital for a doctor or practitioner of ?yurveda. It allows for a 'view of pathogenesis' and helps greatly in deciding how treatment is administered. A brief overview is presented here.

Sanchaya - Accumulation

In this stage the aggravated dosha begins to accumulate in its respective main site: Vata - Colon, Pitta - Small intestine, Kapha - Stomach. Symptoms are mild and/or irregular, but the disorder or condition can be detected and treated. It is easy to restore balance to the affected dosha(s) at this point. *Prakopa - Provocation:* When a dosha continues to be aggravated it will do so in its main site. During this second stage symptoms will be more significant, but the aggravated dosha can still be removed via the gastro-intestinal tract (GI tract) relatively easily. The doshas are still in their own sites during these first two stages food cravings will be healthy and appropriate.After those two stages, the disease is moving out of the GI tract, makes it harder to treat by yourself, and you should consult an Ayurvedic doctor or practitioner.

Prasara - Spread: If the dosha is still being aggravated it will leave its main site or 'home' in the GI tract and go to another site of that same dosha elsewhere in the body. P?rva Rupa, prodromal symptoms and signs, present themselves during this stage. Food and other cravings will begin to be abnormally affected. However, the condition is still curable.The doshas are in the GI tract at the first and second stages, the 'home' of Agni. As long as this is happening, there is the possibility of harm, with the Agni becoming impaired by further aggravation. Once impaired the dosha(s) will leave the GI tract and the disease or disorder will manifest further, making it more difficult to alleviate and harder to cure.

Samprāpti Symptoms and the Doshas

Stage	VĀTA	PITTA	KAPHA
Sañchaya	Bloating, gas Constipation Dryness, cramps Coldness Anxiety and insomnia	Acid in the stomach Yellowing of eyes, urine, and stool Sensations of heat Irritability Bitter taste in the mouth Loose and smelly stools	Sluggish digestion Lethargy Paleness Heavy limbs / head
Prakopa	*Intensified Sañchaya signs plus:* Stiffness in the body Tingling in hands / feet Talking excessively / fast Facial tension Sensitivity to sound Aversion to cold food Increased peristalsis Fleeting muscle pain	*Intensified Sañchaya signs plus:* Sour taste in the mouth Sweat smells sour Increased thirst Critical or angry speech Burning during urination Yellow eyes and/or skin Increased desire for alcoholic beverages/cold beverages	*Intensified Sañchaya signs plus:* Noticeable loss of appetite Increased secretions Sticky oral cavity and skin Mental lethargy Greediness Eating and sleeping more Whitish coating the tongue Feeling 'heavy'
Prasara	Vāta can spread to the skin, to the ears, air passages, intestines, bone, thighs, and pelvic cavity.	Pitta can spread to the skin, eyes, liver, brain (grey matter), plasma, blood, heart, and spleen.	Kapha can spread to the lungs, joints, brain (white matter, plasma, sinuses, pancreas, and tongue.
Sthāna Samshraya	During this stage, the aggravated dosha will tend to move into a khāvaigunya (defective space) in a dhātu. If the dhātu agni is weak, the dosha will change the qualities of the dhātu, affecting cellular intelligence. If dhātu agni is strong the dosha will return to the GI tract. If not, purva rupa (prodromal signs and symtoms) will become clear and the dosha becomes localized in the dhātu.		
Vyakti	In this stage the dosha manifests in the dhātu, overwhelms it, and changes its qualities. Cardinal signs and symptoms will be observed in this stage and one may see exactly which gunas (attributes) of the dosha are the most prevalent in the disease. In both the 4th and 5th stage the qualities of the doshas affect the functions of the dhātus as well as the srotamsi and organs. This is normally the point at which people realize something is wrong and seek medical attention.		
Bheda	In this stage, structural changes manifest. Complications in other organs, dhātus or systems become evident. It's the final expression of the disease. In this stage the tissue is affected or destroyed as well as its surrounding areas and their functions. It is always easier to treat the aggravated doshas while they are still in their original sites (Stages 1 and 2). Stage 3 is the transitional stage and when the doshas enter Stage 4 treatment can still be effective. In stages 5 and 6 treatment becomes very difficult but some alleviation and palliation is still possible.		

Disease Proneness

The current healthcare system is focused on disease management. Our current approach to treatment begins only after the diagnosis, and then attempts to treat the symptoms and prevent the progression. Despite increased global healthcare spending, there has been an increasing incidence, and severity of diseases pointing to impaired health of the populace.

This progressive deterioration in general health has created an unsustainable increase in healthcare costs that has hampered the economy. Much of the rising costs in healthcare are secondary to treating the progression of preventable diseases and focus on creating new treatments. There has been an ongoing discussion of incorporating a "defense" or prevention as part of our health system. However, there are few established guidelines beyond tactical use of vaccination in known infectious diseases and screening for chronic diseases and cancers. Ayurveda has the core competency and strategy for prevention of disease. Sushruta has propounded the laws of health, which are unknown to the current healthcare system.

In this day and age when the world has become a global village, people from one socio-demographic location can be found across the world, with a lot of cross mingling of relationships that stretch the barriers of place and time. In this scenario, the need of the hour is to develop a theory of personality that transcends this problem of cultural and racial bias to propound one that is valid across the world. For this, the basic requirement is that it should be universally acceptable, be of an elemental nature, and be valid to people across all genres. To understand this, the first source of knowledge that comes to mind to tackle the problem at hand is that of the Indian philosophical systems that have withstood the test of time to be applicable across millennia without losing their relevance and applicability to people from ages to the present day. The first discipline that comes to mind which is capable of identifying people is that of Ayurveda with its exact science of medicine and which is capable of giving answers to questions that are posed at a biological and physical level as to the constituents of man and the reasons for his biological behaviour.

All Diseases and our proneness toward them is determined by our Individual constitution. In other words, people with a kappa constitution have a tendency to be afflicted with disease and Illness associated with kappa.

During Their Lifetime They May Well Experience Repetitive Incidents Of Bronchitis, Congested Lungs, Sinusitis Or Tonsillitis. People With A Pitta Constitution Are Known To Be Susceptible To Disorders That Affect The Skin, Like Rashes, Psoriasis And Hives. They Also Suffer From Gallbladder And Liver Disorders, Peptic Ulcers, Inflammatory Diseases And Hyperacidity.

Vata Types Are Highly Susceptible To Sciatica, Paralysis And Neuralgia. They Are Also Often Affected By Excessive Gas, Pain In The Lower Back And Arthritis. Most Vata Disease And Illness Originate Within The Large Intestine, Pittas Are Most Often Affected By Illnesses Or Diseases In The Small Intestine And Kappas Are Prone To Disorders That Affect Their Stomach. The Imbalance Of Humors In These Specific Areas Will Manifest In Certain Symptoms And Signs Within The Body.

An Imbalance Which Causes Disease Or Illness May Originate In The Consciousness Of The Mind As A Negative Awareness, Planting The Seed Of The Affliction In The Form Of Fear, Attachments Or Unresolved Anger Issues. In Turn, These Negative Emotions Can Then Manifest Into The Body Through The Mind, Resulting In Disease And Illness. The Derangement Of Vata Can Be Caused By Repressed Fear, Excessive Quantities Of Pitta Can Be Caused By Anger And Unbalanced Kappa By Attachments, Greed And Envy.

These Imbalances Within The Tridohsa Can Have A Serious Effect On The Bodies Natural Resistance And Immune System And The Agni (Digestive Fire) Of The Body. As Such The Body Can Become Disease Prone And Susceptible To Illness And Poor Health. There Are Occasions And Times Where The Imbalance Which Causes The Disease Or Illness First Occurs In The Body And Then Passes Or Manifests In The Consciousness And Mind. Environments, Food Consumption And Living Conditions Similar To Those Of The Dosha Will Be Inimical To The Bodily Tissues.

They Will First Manifest An Imbalance On A Physical Level, Which Will Later, Through A Disturbance In The Tridosha, Affect The Mind. For Example, Unbalanced Vata Leads To The Creation Of Fears, Nervousness And Depression, An Excessive Buildup Of Pitta Will Create Anger, Hate And Jealousy Within A Person's Psyche. Aggravated Kappa Will Lead To Greed, Unhealthy Or Obsessive Attachments And Possessiveness. Because Of This We Know That There Is A Direct Connection Between Habits, Diet, Environment And Emotionally Manifested Disorders Samsargaja roga Samsargaja roga are those diseases which spread through contact in the form of frequent physical contact, through exhaled air, by dining, sleeping or sitting together and sharing objects that has been handled by the patient. Skin diseases, fever, TB & conjunctivitis etc are examples of such diseases.

- Frequent physical contact with the affected person (including sexual contact)
- Through the exhaled air of patient (Airborne infection)
- Dining, Sleeping and/or Sitting together
- Sharing dress, ornaments and unguents (lotions, soaps,creams, oils and/or any other cosmetics)

Concept of skin diseases and its Etiology

Skin is given due importance since time immemorial owing to the aesthetic value conferred upon skin, complexion and beauty by the society. Ayurveda has given prime importance to ahara and vihara in the maintenance of health and prevention of diseases. In the recent past the relation between diet and skin ailments is well established in contemporary medicine. Ayurvedic literature has described skin diseases mainly under the spectrum of kushta, the literary meaning of which is that which cause disfiguration.

Ayurvedic system of medicine describes a wide range of etiological factors for dermatological disorders. The etiological factors include physical, physiological, psychological, psychosocial, hereditary and Papakarma (sinful activities), based on the proximity of causes which are reclassified into sannikrishta (proximal cause) and viprakrishta (remote cause) nidana

Sannikrista Nidana (real causative factor) - Three Doshas viz. Vata, Pitta and Kapha and four Dushyas viz. Tvak (Rasa), Rakta, Mansa and Ambu or Lasika involved in the pathogenesis of skin diseases. These seven can be considered as sannikrishta nidana in kushta.

Viprakrista Nidana - These etiological factors are not involved directly in the pathogenesis, but they increase the disease proneness sensitize the body to the actual causative factors (Sannikrishta Nidana), Viprakusta nidana which include kulaja factors and janmottara kalaja (ahara, vihara and manasika factors).

Janmottarakalaja: The etiological factors in present life can be categorizes into three groups, Aharaja (diet & dietetic patterns), Viharaja (lifestyle related) and Manasika (psychological).

Kulaja Nidana: kushta is an adibalapravrtta roga which is said to arise from the day of conception by conjugation of sukra and artava with bijabhaga avayava dushti10. Ill effect is thought to be transmigrated from past lives (Poorva Janmakrata)

According to Sushruta if the person suffered from Kushtha in his previous life and if he takes rebirth then he develops Kushtha in his present life also Papakarma (sinful activities) has also been implicated in the etiology of kushta and is also said as a samsargja vyadhi (communicable disease). The Kushtha is generally described as Tridoshaja Vyadhi but type of the Kushtha ascertained upon the predominance of particular Dosha and is generally classified into mahakushta and ksudra kushta.

Nidana or the etiological factors closely linked with the manifestation, transmission and progression of the disease are broadly classified in the classical Ayurveda texts in the following categories:

1. Aharaja nidana- food related causes
2. Viharaja Nidana- regimen related causes
3. Manasika Nidana- psychological causes.
4. Visesha Nidana- an etiology that is not common in all diseases, but specifically act as hetu in this disease.
5. Sahaja Nidana - those factors which causes disease due to beeja bhaga avayava dushti.

Thus the etiological factors of skin disorders may be related to food, life style and psychological factors.

Key To Health Or Disease: Agni

Agni is the invariable agent in the process of Paka (digestion, transformation). Ingested food is to be digested, absorbed and assimilated, which is unavoidable for the maintenance of life, and is performed by the Agni. Different examples are available in our classics to indicate that Pitta is the same as Agni, but some doubt arises behind this concept, that Pitta is Agni. Agni is innumerable because of its presence in each and every paramanu of the body. But, the enumeration of the number of Agni varies in various classical Ayurvedic texts. According to the functions and site of action, Agni has been divided into 13 types, i.e. one Jatharagni, five Bhutagni and seven Dhatvagni. Jatharagni is the most important one, which digests four types of food and transforms it into Rasa and Mala. The five Bhutagnis act on the respective bhutika portion of the food and thereby nourish the Bhutas in the body. The seven Dhatvagni act on the respective dhatus by which each Dhatu is broken into three parts. In this way, the entire process of transformation consists of two types of products - PRasad (essence) and Kitta (excrete). The former is taken for nourishment while the latter one is thrown out, which otherwise defiles the body if it stays longer.

Ayurveda has described an important factor of digestion and metabolism in our body as Agni. Ingested food is to be digested, absorbed and assimilated, which is unavoidable for the maintenance of life, and is performed by Agni. In Ayurveda, the term "Agni" is used in the sense of digestion of food and metabolic products.

Agni converts food in the form of energy, which is responsible for all the vital functions of our body. Therefore, Ayurveda considers that Dehagni is the cause of life, complexion, strength, health, nourishment, lusture, oja, teja (energy) and prana (life energy). (Cha. Chi. 15/ 3.)About the importance of Agni, Acharya Charak has mentioned that after stoppage of the function of Agni, the individual dies, and when the Agni of an individual is sama, then that person would be absolutely healthy and would lead a long, happy, healthy life.

But, if the Agni of a person is vitiated, the whole metabolism in his body would be disturbed, resulting in ill health and disease. Hence, Agni is said to be the base (mool) of life. (Cha.Chi.15/4.)

According to modern medicine, metabolic processes, division and multiplication are going on in all cells (dhatu paramanu) of our body from birth till death. The cell is the functional unit of the body. According to Charak, the constituent parts of the body, if further divided into the atoms, are sure to become innumerable, as such cells or atoms are exceedingly numerous, very minute and ultrasensory. In the conjunction and disjunction of cells, the activating factors are Vata and the nature of action (Cha. sha.7/17).

In Shushrut, we can see how the "Avayavaas" are formed from "various dhatus" (Su.Sha.4/25-30). Thus, based on Charak and Shushrut, the above cells can be considered as "dhatu paramanus." For these constant processes in all cells, a biological energy is constantly essential, without which the survival of our body will be quite impossible. The same biological energy is provided by Agni in Ayurveda. This Agni-provided biological energy in the cells (dhatu paramanu) of our body is of two types: potential and kinetic.

Repressed Emotions

Repressed emotions refer to emotions that you unconsciously avoid. These differ from suppressed emotions, which are feelings you purposely avoid because you don't know exactly how to deal with them. Say you and your partner have a fight and decide to break up one evening. You still have to meet with an important client at work the next day, so you decide to suppress, or push aside, your feelings until you get home from that meeting.

Suppression can sometimes be a good short-term solution, as long as you make sure to address those emotions sooner rather than later. Repressed emotions, on the other hand, don't get a chance to be processed. But that doesn't mean they simply disappear. Instead, they might show up as a range of psychological or physical symptoms.

Why Does it Happen

Emotional repression often relates to childhood experiences.

Much of what children learn about behaviour and communication comes from their primary caregivers.

So, you'll probably feel pretty comfortable expressing your emotions if your caregivers:

- frequently talked about their feelings
- encouraged you to share how experiences made you feel
- normalized your positive and negative emotional experiences
- didn't judge or criticize your emotional expressions

Adults with repressed emotions often feel out of touch or disconnected from their feelings because they had a different childhood experience.

For example, you might be more likely to repress emotions if your caregivers:

- rarely showed emotion or talked about their feelings
- shamed or punished you for expressing your emotions
- told you your emotions were wrong or denied your experience

If showing your feelings in childhood led to distressing or painful outcomes, you probably learned it was much safer to avoid this entirely. As an adult, you might continue to bury strong emotions without realizing what you're doing. You might also notice you tend to push even the emotions you do notice aside.

What Kinds of Emotions Get Repressed?

For the most part, people tend to repress strong emotions, especially those associated with discomfort or other unpleasant experiences.

This includes emotions like:

- anger
- frustration
- sadness
- fear
- disappointment

Notice a pattern? These emotions are often described as negative. It's common to repress emotions you consider "bad" or believe other people might judge you for expressing.

Again, this stems back to your childhood. Maybe you grew up hearing things like:

- "You don't have any reason to be sad."
- "Calm down."
- "You should be grateful."

Even if your caregivers didn't specifically invalidate your emotional experience, they still might've discouraged you from expressing intense emotions freely by telling you to stop crying or shouting. As a result, you began to think of sadness, anger, and disappointment as emotions you shouldn't have, or at the very least, shouldn't acknowledge to anyone.You could feel more in touch with positive emotions, or those considered "normal" and generally accepted by others. It might seem easier to express them if you know they won't draw criticism, though this isn't the case for everyone dealing with emotional repression.

Can it Really Lead to Physical Symptoms?

"Hold on," you might think. "My emotions don't make me sick... do they?"

They actually can, in a way.

There's no evidence to suggest emotions directly cause illness, of course. Sadness can't give you the flu, and anger doesn't cause cancer.

But research has linked emotional repression to decreased immune system function. If your immune system doesn't work properly, you might get sick more frequently and recover slowly.

Repressed emotions can also factor into mental health conditions, such as stress, anxiety, and depression.

These issues often cause physical symptoms, including:

- muscle tension and pain
- nausea and digestive problems
- appetite changes
- fatigue and sleep problems

Childhood trauma, one possible cause of repressed emotions, may also play a part in chronic illness.

Unresolved anger can have some significant health consequences, too. If you struggle with expressing anger in productive ways, you may face a higher risk of developing:

- high blood pressure
- digestive problems
- cardiovascular disease

How Do I know if I Have Repressed Emotions?

It's not always easy to recognize when you're dealing with emotional repression, and there's no definitive test you can take. If you do have repressed emotions, however, you might notice a few key signs. These signs might show up in your feelings or your behaviour - both toward yourself and other people.

Recognizing emotional repression in your feelings: People with repressed emotions often have trouble naming and understanding their emotional experience. This can make it tough to describe how you feel to others, of course, but it also makes it difficult for you to recognize when certain aspects of your life aren't serving your needs.

You might:

- regularly feel numb or blank
- feel nervous, low, or stressed a lot of the time, even if you aren't sure why
- have a tendency to forget things
- experience unease or discomfort when other people tell you about their feelings
- feel cheerful and calm most of the time because you never let your thoughts linger on anything significant or upsetting

- feel distressed or irritated when someone asks you about your feelings

Recognizing emotional repression in your behaviour

Repressed emotions commonly show up in behaviour and can affect how you respond to others.

If you have a hard time expressing feelings as you experience them in healthy ways, your emotions can build up until they eventually explode, sometimes in response to very small triggers. This can contribute to problems in your interpersonal relationships.

Emotional repression can affect your ability to:

- talk about things that matter to you
- build intimate relationships
- understand how other people feel
- encourage or praise yourself

You might also notice that you:

- go along with situations instead of expressing what you really want and need
- use substances, TV, social media, or other activities to help you numb and avoid feelings you don't want to explore
- spend most of your time with other people to avoid being alone
- exhibit passive-aggressive behaviours to deal with situations that upset you

Still another sign: Others often describe you as "chill," "calm," or "relaxed"

Is it possible to Release Them

If you have trouble expressing or regulating your emotions, talking to a mental health professional is a good first step.

A therapist can help you explore potential causes of repressed emotions and offer guidance and support as you begin to address these reasons.

Therapy also provides a safe space to:

- work on naming and understanding your feelings
- increase your comfort level around talking about emotions
- learn more helpful methods of emotional regulation

Emotionally focused therapy (EFT) is one approach that may have particular benefit for emotional repression. EFT emphasizes emotional expression as one of the most important components of your personal experience and your ability to relate to others.

According to EFT theory, people who have a hard time accessing and understanding their feelings typically also struggle to enjoy meaningful relationships with others. This approach is often used in couples counseling, but it can also help you work through childhood trauma, depression, anxiety, and other mental health symptoms.

Things you can try right now

You can also get started practicing emotional expression on your own by trying these steps:

- Check in. Ask yourself how you feel right now. If you have a hard time speaking your emotions at first, trying using words or colours in a journal or piece of art. You can even find a song that matches your mood.
- Use "I" statements. Practice expressing your feelings with phrases like "I feel confused. I feel nervous. I feel terrified."
- Focus on the positive. It might seem easier to name and embrace positive emotions at first, and that's OK. The goal is to get more comfortable with all of your emotions, and small steps help.
- Let go of judgement. No matter what emotion you're feeling, avoid judging yourself or telling yourself you shouldn't feel a certain way. Instead, try finding a reason for the feeling: "I feel nervous because I'm about to have my yearly performance review."
- Make it a habit. Practice naming and sharing your emotions with the people you feel closest to. Encourage them to share their feelings, too.

The Three Malas

As per Ayurveda, waste matters of the body are as important as body tissues for maintenance of good health and longevity.

Malas are vital clues to human pathology as they are the by-products of bodily functions. The three important Malas are - Purisha (Faeces), Mutra (Urine) and Sveda (Sweat) - and these are generated from food. Other Malas are cellular wastes such as excretions from nose, eyes and ears. Hair is also a Mala where the body expels waste in the form of hair.

Malas must be discarded by the body regularly for it to function properly. Malas can transform and affect Dhatus, which will in turn impact the balance of Doshas. This can cause a series of ailments. Hence, wastes formed after the energy burning processes in the body have to be expelled. Mala-related problems include hair loss, abdominal pain, urinary tract infection, fungal infections, dehydration and body odour.

The Seven Dhatus

Ayurveda, the ancient Indian system of medicine, holds a holistic approach to health and well-being. According to Ayurvedic principles, the human body is composed of seven distinct tissue layers known as Dhatus. These Dhatus play a vital role in maintaining overall health and are interconnected to create a harmonious balance within the body. In this article, we will delve deeper into the concept of Dhatus, their functions, imbalances, and how to nurture them for optimal health. In common terms, the seven types of Dhatus are plasma, blood, muscle, fat, bone, bone marrow and reproductive fluid. In Ayurveda, they are called Sapta Dhatus - Rasa, Rakta, Mamsa, Meda, Asthi, Majja and Sukhra respectively. Rasa Dhatu's dominant element is Jala (Water).

The Concept of Dhatus in Ayurveda: Dhatus are the seven tissue layers in Ayurveda, and they are responsible for nourishing and maintaining the body. The term "Dhatu" translates to "support" or "that which holds," indicating their fundamental role in providing strength and structure to different organs and systems.

The Seven Dhatus and Their Functions

1. Rasa Dhatu (Plasma)

In Ayurveda, Rasa Dhatu refers to the plasma or fluid component of the blood. It is a vital element in the body that nourishes tissues, and supports the immune system. And serves as the primary source of nutrition for all other Dhatus (tissues). Let's explore the functions of Rasa Dhatu, the consequences of its imbalance, and how to maintain its health.

The function of Rasa Dhatu: Rasa Dhatu plays a crucial role in maintaining overall health and well-being. It is responsible for transporting nutrients, hormones, and other essential substances throughout the body. As the fluid component of the blood, Rasa Dhatu carries nutrients derived from the digestive process to all the cells and tissues, providing them with the necessary nourishment for optimal functioning. It also aids in flushing out waste products and toxins from the body, supporting detoxification and promoting a healthy internal environment. Furthermore, Rasa Dhatu contributes to the body's immune system, as it carries immune cells and antibodies, helping to defend against infections and diseases.

Imbalance and Symptoms: An imbalance in Rasa Dhatu can lead to various health issues, particularly concerning digestion, immunity, and energy levels. Digestive issues such as indigestion, bloating, or irregular bowel movements may arise when Rasa Dhatu is impaired, leading to inadequate nutrient absorption and assimilation.

Weak immunity is another common consequence, making individuals more susceptible to infections and illnesses. Moreover, imbalanced Rasa Dhatu can result in fatigue and reduced energy levels, as the body may not receive the essential nutrition required for optimal functioning.

How to Maintain Rasa Dhatu

Ayurveda offers valuable insights into maintaining the health of Rasa Dhatu and promoting overall well-being. Here are some essential tips:

1. Balanced Diet: Consume a balanced diet that includes fresh and nutritious foods, such as fruits, vegetables, whole grains, lean proteins, and healthy fats. Proper digestion and nutrient absorption are crucial for the health of Rasa Dhatu.
2. Hydration: Stay well-hydrated by drinking an adequate amount of water throughout the day. Hydration supports the fluidity and functionality of Rasa Dhatu.
3. Proper Digestion: Eat mindfully and avoid overeating. Include digestive spices like ginger, cumin, and fennel in your meals to support healthy digestion.
4. Stress Management: Chronic stress can impact digestion and the immune system. Practice relaxation techniques like meditation, yoga, or deep breathing to manage stress effectively.
5. Adequate Rest: Ensure you get sufficient restful sleep as it is essential for the body's rejuvenation and the health of Rasa Dhatu.

6. Herbal Support: Ayurvedic herbs like Amla and Tulsi are known for their immune-boosting properties and can be included in your routine after consulting an Ayurvedic practitioner.

2. Rakta Dhatu (Blood)

In the ancient healing system of Ayurveda, Rakta Dhatu represents the vital fluid known as the blood that circulates throughout the body.

Blood plays a crucial role in sustaining life by carrying oxygen, nutrients, and hormones to various tissues and organs while removing waste products and carbon dioxide. Let's explore the functions of Rakta Dhatu, the consequences of its imbalance, and how to maintain its health.

The Function of Rakta Dhatu: Rakta Dhatu is responsible for several essential functions in the body. One of its primary roles is to transport oxygen from the lungs to all the cells, enabling cellular respiration and energy production.

It also delivers vital nutrients, hormones, and immune cells to different parts of the body, supporting overall health and well-being. Moreover, Rakta Dhatu aids in maintaining body temperature by distributing heat evenly throughout the body. Additionally, it plays a significant role in regulating the body's pH balance, ensuring that the blood remains within the optimal pH range for proper cellular function.

Imbalance and Symptoms: An imbalance in Rakta Dhatu can lead to various health issues, particularly concerning the circulatory system and skin. Skin disorders, such as rashes, eczema, or psoriasis, may arise due to impurities or toxins in the blood. Inflammation is another common consequence of imbalanced Rakta Dhatu, as it can result in various inflammatory conditions in the body. Impaired circulation may lead to conditions like cold hands and feet, dizziness, or even cardiovascular problems. Additionally, blood disorders like anemia or excessive blood clotting can occur due to Rakta Dhatu imbalance.

How to Maintain Rakta Dhatu: Ayurveda offers valuable insights into maintaining the health of Rakta Dhatu and promoting a healthy circulatory system. Here are some essential tips:

1. Healthy Diet: Consume a balanced diet that includes fresh fruits, vegetables, whole grains, lean proteins, and healthy fats to provide essential nutrients to the blood.

2. Hydration: Stay well-hydrated to maintain blood volume and support overall circulatory function.
3. Regular Exercise: Engage in regular physical activity to promote cardiovascular health, improve blood circulation, and maintain a healthy weight.
4. Herbal Support: Ayurvedic herbs like Manjistha and Neem are known for their blood-purifying properties and can be used under expert guidance.
5. Stress Management: Chronic stress can impact blood circulation and overall health. Practice relaxation techniques like meditation, yoga, or deep breathing to manage stress effectively.
6. Avoid Smoking and Alcohol: Smoking and excessive alcohol consumption can negatively affect blood vessels and circulation.
7. Adequate Rest: Ensure you get sufficient restful sleep as it supports overall healing and rejuvenation.

3. Mamsa Dhatu (Muscle)

In Ayurveda, Mamsa Dhatu refers to the muscle tissues that play a vital role in supporting the body and facilitating movement.

Muscles are essential for various bodily functions, and their health is crucial for overall strength and well-being. Let's explore the functions of Mamsa Dhatu, the consequences of its imbalance, and how to maintain its health.

The Function of Mamsa Dhatu: amsa Dhatu is responsible for providing support and movement to the skeletal system. Muscles are attached to bones and work together to allow the body to move, maintain posture, and carry out various activities. Apart from enabling movement, Mamsa Dhatu also provides stability to the joints and helps protect internal organs.Additionally, it contributes to overall body strength, allowing individuals to perform daily tasks and physical activities effectively.

Imbalance and Symptoms: An imbalance in Mamsa Dhatu can lead to various muscular issues and impact mobility. Muscle cramps or spasms are common symptoms of imbalanced Mamsa Dhatu. These painful contractions can occur due to dehydration, nutrient deficiencies, or overuse of muscles. Muscle weakness is another consequence, making it challenging to perform routine tasks or engage in physical activities.

In severe cases, muscle wasting, known as muscle atrophy, can occur, where muscles start to shrink and lose mass, leading to a significant loss of strength and functionality.

How to Maintain Mamsa Dhatu: Ayurveda emphasizes the significance of maintaining the health of Mamsa Dhatu to promote overall physical strength and mobility. Here are some essential tips:

1. Protein-Rich Diet: Consume an adequate amount of protein from sources like lean meats, fish, legumes, nuts, and dairy products. Protein is essential for muscle repair and growth.
2. Hydration: Stay well-hydrated as water is necessary for proper muscle function and to prevent cramps and spasms.
3. Regular Exercise: Engage in regular physical activity that includes a combination of cardiovascular exercises, strength training, and flexibility exercises to promote muscle health and overall fitness.
4. Rest and Recovery: Allow sufficient rest between exercise sessions to give muscles time to recover and repair.
5. Avoid Overuse: Avoid excessive strain or overuse of muscles to prevent muscle fatigue and potential injuries.
6. Warm-up and Cool-down: Always warm up before exercising and cool down afterward to reduce the risk of muscle strain and improve flexibility.
7. Herbal Support: Ayurvedic herbs like Ashwagandha and Shatavari are known for their muscle-nourishing properties and can be included in your routine after consulting an Ayurvedic practitioner.

4. Meda Dhatu (Fat)

In the ancient healing system of Ayurveda, Meda Dhatu refers to adipose tissue or fat present in the body. It plays a vital role in maintaining overall health and well-being. Meda Dhatu acts as a reservoir of energy, providing insulation and cushioning to vital organs, and contributing to various physiological functions. Let's explore its functions, the consequences of its imbalance, and how to maintain its health.

The Function of Meda Dhatu: Meda Dhatu serves several essential functions in the body. One of its primary roles is to act as a storage site for energy. The body stores excess calories in the form of fat, and when needed, it can be converted back into energy to fuel various activities. Moreover, Meda Dhatu provides cushioning and protection to organs, helping to maintain their structural integrity and prevent damage from external impacts. Additionally, Meda Dhatu plays a role in supporting the nervous system and enhancing brain function, as some fatty acids are essential for cognitive health.

Imbalance and Symptoms: An imbalance in Meda Dhatu can lead to various health issues, particularly related to weight and metabolism. Excessive accumulation of fat can result in obesity, which is a risk factor for numerous health conditions such as cardiovascular diseases, diabetes, and joint problems. Moreover, imbalanced Meda Dhatu can lead to cholesterol issues, where there is an abnormal buildup of cholesterol in the blood, increasing the risk of heart-related problems.

Additionally, a sluggish metabolism can be a consequence of impaired Meda Dhatu, making it difficult for the body to efficiently convert and utilize energy.

How to Maintain Meda Dhatu: Ayurveda offers valuable insights into maintaining the health of Meda Dhatu and achieving a balanced body weight. Here are some essential tips:

1. Balanced Diet: Consume a balanced diet that includes a variety of nutrient-dense foods, such as whole grains, fruits, vegetables, lean proteins, and healthy fats. Avoid excessive consumption of unhealthy fats and processed foods.
2. Portion Control: Pay attention to portion sizes and avoid overeating. Eating mindfully and stopping when you feel full can help manage calorie intake.
3. Regular Exercise: Engage in regular physical activity to burn calories, improve metabolism, and maintain a healthy body weight.
4. Stress Management: Chronic stress can contribute to weight gain and imbalanced Meda Dhatu. Practice relaxation techniques like meditation, yoga, or deep breathing to manage stress effectively.
5. Herbal Support: Ayurvedic herbs like Triphala and Guggulu are known to support healthy fat metabolism and can be incorporated into your routine after consulting an Ayurvedic practitioner.
6. Adequate Sleep: Ensure you get sufficient and restful sleep as it is crucial for overall metabolic health.
7. Hydration: Stay adequately hydrated as it supports various bodily functions, including metabolism.

5. Asthi Dhatu (Bone)

Asthi Dhatu is a fundamental concept in Ayurveda, the ancient Indian system of medicine. It refers to the bones and teeth, which are integral components of the body's structural framework. Asthi Dhatu provides essential support, giving shape and stability to the body while also safeguarding vital organs. Let's delve into its functions, the consequences of its imbalance, and how to maintain its health.

The Function of Asthi Dhatu: The primary function of Asthi Dhatu is to facilitate bone formation and maintain mineral storage in the body. Bones serve as the scaffolding that holds our body upright, and they play a crucial role in protecting vital organs like the brain, heart, and lungs. Asthi Dhatu supports the body's overall structure, allowing us to move, perform daily activities, and maintain our posture.

Moreover, it acts as a reservoir for essential minerals like calcium and phosphorus, which are released into the bloodstream when needed to maintain mineral balance and support various bodily functions.

Imbalance and Symptoms: An imbalance in Asthi Dhatu can lead to several health issues related to bone and joint health. Weak bones, a condition known as osteoporosis, can result from an inadequate supply of minerals, particularly calcium, to the bones.

This makes the bones brittle and prone to fractures. Joint pain and stiffness may also arise due to poor bone health and reduced lubrication in the joints.

Additionally, imbalanced Asthi Dhatu can contribute to skeletal disorders like arthritis, which affects the joints' integrity and causes discomfort and reduced mobility.

How to Maintain Asthi Dhatu: Ayurveda offers valuable insights into maintaining the health of Asthi Dhatu and supporting bone strength. Here are some essential tips:

1. Calcium-Rich Diet: Consume foods rich in calcium, such as dairy products, leafy greens, almonds, and sesame seeds, to promote bone health and mineral storage.
2. Vitamin D: Ensure adequate intake of vitamin D through sunlight exposure or supplements, as it is crucial for calcium absorption and bone formation.
3. Regular Exercise: Engage in weight-bearing exercises, such as walking, running, or dancing, to promote bone density and strength.

4. Herbal Support: Certain Ayurvedic herbs like Shatavari and Guggulu are known for their bone-strengthening properties and can be used under expert guidance.
5. Maintain Healthy Digestion: Good digestion is essential for proper nutrient absorption, including minerals required for bone health. Incorporate fibre-rich foods and consider mindful eating habits to support digestion.
6. Avoid Excessive Caffeine and Alcohol: High caffeine and alcohol consumption can interfere with calcium absorption and affect bone health negatively.
7. Adequate Rest: Get sufficient rest and sleep, as it supports bone repair and rejuvenation.

6. Majja Dhatu (Marrow)

In the ancient healing system of Ayurveda, Majja Dhatu holds significant importance. It refers to the essential components of bone marrow, spinal cord, and nerve tissues. Majja Dhatu plays a pivotal role in nourishing and supporting the nervous system, which is vital for overall well-being and optimal bodily functions. Let's explore its functions, the consequences of its imbalance, and how to maintain its health.

The Function of Majja Dhatu: Majja Dhatu is responsible for maintaining bone health and supporting nerve function. It plays a crucial role in producing bone marrow, the soft, fatty substance found within bones, which is essential for blood cell formation. Furthermore, Majja Dhatu is intricately linked to the health of the nervous system, including the spinal cord and nerve tissues. It nourishes and protects these vital components, ensuring smooth communication between the brain and the rest of the body. Proper Majja Dhatu functioning is necessary for maintaining strong bones, supporting nerve impulses, and promoting overall neurological health.

Imbalance and Symptoms: An imbalance in Majja Dhatu can lead to various health issues, particularly concerning the nervous system. This imbalance may manifest as nerve disorders, causing sensations like tingling, numbness, or even weakness in the limbs.

Memory issues and difficulty in cognitive functions may also arise due to compromised nerve health. Moreover, imbalanced Majja Dhatu can lead to bone-related problems, such as weak or brittle bones, making individuals more susceptible to fractures and joint issues.

How to Maintain Majja Dhatu: Ayurveda emphasizes the significance of maintaining the balance of Majja Dhatu to ensure optimal bone health and nerve function. Here are some essential tips:

1. Nutritious Diet: Consume a well-balanced diet rich in calcium, vitamin D, and other essential nutrients that promote bone health. Dairy products, leafy greens, nuts, and seeds are excellent sources of these nutrients.
2. Adequate Sunlight: Exposure to sunlight helps the body synthesize vitamin D, which is crucial for calcium absorption and bone health.
3. Regular Exercise: Engage in weight-bearing exercises, such as walking, jogging, or resistance training, to strengthen bones and improve overall bone density.
4. Nervine Tonics: Ayurvedic herbs like Ashwagandha and Brahmi are known as nervine tonics and can be beneficial for nerve health when used under proper guidance.
5. Stress Management: Chronic stress can impact nerve health. Practicing relaxation techniques like meditation, yoga, or mindfulness can help alleviate stress and support nervous system function.
6. Adequate Rest: Ensure you get enough restful sleep as it is essential for overall nervous system repair and rejuvenation.
7. Herbal Supplements: Ayurvedic practitioners may recommend specific herbal supplements to support Majja Dhatu health based on individual needs.

7. Shukra Dhatu (Reproductive Tissue)

Shukra Dhatu is a fundamental concept in Ayurveda, the ancient Indian system of medicine. It is considered to be the essential reproductive tissue responsible for fertility and sexual function.

According to Ayurvedic principles, Shukra Dhatu is crucial for the overall well-being and procreative abilities of an individual. Let's delve deeper into its functions, the consequences of its imbalance, and how to maintain its health.

The Function of Shukra Dhatu: Shukra Dhatu plays a vital role in healthy reproduction and the overall vitality of the body. It is believed to be the essence of all bodily tissues, and its proper functioning is essential for the conception and development of a healthy offspring. Shukra Dhatu is responsible for the production of healthy ova in women and sperm in men. Additionally, it influences the quality and quantity of reproductive fluids involved in the process of fertilization. Moreover, Shukra Dhatu contributes to sexual vigor and vitality, promoting a satisfying and fulfilling sexual life.

Imbalance and Symptoms: An imbalance in Shukra Dhatu can lead to various reproductive problems and hormonal imbalances. In women, this may manifest as irregular menstrual cycles, difficulty in conceiving, or recurrent miscarriages. Men may experience reduced sperm count, poor sperm motility, erectile dysfunction, or decreased libido. Hormonal imbalances associated with Shukra Dhatu disruption can also lead to emotional disturbances, mood swings, and even affect overall energy levels.

How to Maintain Shukra Dhatu: To maintain the health of Shukra Dhatu and support its proper functioning, Ayurveda emphasizes the importance of a balanced lifestyle and dietary habits. Here are some essential tips:

1. Nutritious Diet: Consume a nourishing diet that includes a variety of fresh fruits, vegetables, whole grains, lean proteins, and healthy fats. Specific foods like almonds, ghee (clarified butter), dates, and saffron are believed to be beneficial for Shukra Dhatu health.
2. Adequate Hydration: Drink plenty of water throughout the day to support overall body functions, including reproductive health.
3. Stress Management: Chronic stress can negatively impact Shukra Dhatu. Engage in relaxation techniques like meditation, yoga, or deep breathing exercises to reduce stress levels.
4. Regular Exercise: Incorporate moderate physical activity into your routine as it enhances circulation, metabolism, and hormonal balance, all of which are essential for Shukra Dhatu health.
5. Avoid Harmful Habits: Minimize or avoid alcohol consumption, smoking, and drug use, as they can have detrimental effects on reproductive health.
6. Adequate Rest: Ensure you get enough sleep and maintain a regular sleep schedule to promote overall well-being and hormonal balance.
7. Herbal Support: Ayurvedic herbs such as Ashwagandha, Shatavari, and Gokshura are known to support reproductive

health and can be included in your daily regimen after consulting an Ayurvedic practitioner.

Benefits of Balancing Dhatus

Balancing Dhatus in the body offers numerous benefits that contribute to overall health and well-being. Ayurveda, with its holistic approach, emphasizes the significance of maintaining the equilibrium of these tissue layers. Here are some of the key benefits of balancing Dhatus:

1. Enhanced Immunity: When Dhatus are in balance, particularly Rasa Dhatu (plasma), the body's immune system functions optimally. It helps defend against infections, viruses, and diseases, keeping the body strong and resilient.
2. Improved Digestion: A balanced Rasa Dhatu supports proper digestion and assimilation of nutrients, ensuring that the body receives essential elements for nourishment.
3. Healthy Blood Circulation: Balanced Rakta Dhatu (blood) promotes smooth circulation, delivering oxygen and nutrients to all cells and tissues, and eliminating waste efficiently.
4. Strengthened Muscles: Balanced Mamsa Dhatu (muscle tissue) provides strength and support to the skeletal system, enabling better movement and posture.
5. Optimal Brain Function: Meda Dhatu (fat) in balance nourishes the nervous system and supports cognitive abilities, including memory and concentration.
6. Healthy Bones and Teeth: A well-maintained Asthi Dhatu (bone) contributes to strong bones and teeth, protecting the body's vital organs and providing structural integrity.
7. Nervous System Support: Majja Dhatu (marrow) in balance nourishes the nerves and spinal cord, ensuring smooth communication between the brain and body.
8. Reproductive Health: A balanced Shukra Dhatu (reproductive tissue) supports fertility and enhances sexual health and vitality.
9. Emotional Well-Being: Balancing Dhatus positively influences mental and emotional states, promoting a sense of contentment, joy, and overall emotional balance.
10. Vitality and Energy: Harmonious Dhatus result in increased vitality and sustained energy levels throughout the day.

11. Prevention of Health Disorders: By nurturing Dhatus, Ayurveda helps prevent various health issues before they arise, fostering long-term well-being.
12. Anti-Aging Benefits: Balanced Dhatus offer remarkable anti-aging benefits, as they contribute to slowing down the aging process. This balance helps reduce premature aging signs and fosters a state of healthy and graceful aging.
13. Resilience to Stress: A well-balanced body with harmonious Dhatus copes better with stress and adapts more effectively to challenging situations.
14. Restful Sleep: Restful sleep becomes attainable when the Dhatus are in harmony. This state of balance improves the quality of sleep, enabling the body to undergo rejuvenation and healing during the night.
15. Holistic Health: Holistic health is achieved through the balance of Dhatus, which brings a profound sense of harmony and equilibrium to the entire body-mind system. This process promotes overall well-being and a state of well-rounded and complete wellness.

Chapter 7

Diet

Introduction

Diet is one aspect of Ayurvedic medicine. Ayurvedic diets personalize a person's nutrition based on their tastes, the time of year, and specific health concerns. The Ayurvedic diet is not a diet in the traditional sense. Its aim is not weight loss, and there are no specific nutritional plans to follow. Instead, it focuses on healthy, unprocessed foods; overall wellness; and eating for one's individual health needs.

Ayurvedic practitioners believe that each person has a unique combination of energies, 2021 researchTrusted Source reports. These energies are called doshas. According to Ayurveda, illness occurs when a person's energies are imbalanced - and diet is important for balancing these energies. Ayurvedic medicine emphasizes the role of five elements: air, fire, water, space, and earth.

These elements make up Ayurveda's three energies, or doshas:

- Vata: This is a combination of space and air. People with the vata dosha are creative and active, but tire easily.
- Pitta: This is a combination of fire and water. People of this type are intelligent and temperamental, with a big appetite and healthy digestion.
- Kapha: This is a combination of earth and water. People of this type tend to have immense stamina and high intelligence.

The Ayurvedic diet emphasizes eating the right food for a person's dosha.

In addition to diet, Ayurveda also says a person should take other steps to balance their dosha. For example, people with pitta dosha should avoid activities that increase the element of fire. The Ayurvedic diet is just one aspect of Ayurvedic medicine. Practitioners believe in embracing an entire Ayurvedic lifestyle to realize Ayurveda's full benefits.

Eating for Your Dosha

The Ayurvedic diet is not a strict or specific diet plan. People trying this eating plan seek input from an experienced Ayurvedic practitioner before making nutritional decisions. It is also a good idea to consult a registered dietitian, if possible, especially if an individual has preexisting health conditions. In general, Ayurveda recommends the following foods for each dosha. It is important to note that these are general guidelines, and people should eat what feels right for them.

Vata dosha: People can try eating warming spices such as pepper, ginger, and cardamom. They should avoid combining too many different types of foods and drink plenty of water. Additionally, they should avoid foods that increase vata, which include very sweet or pungent foods, such as sour fruits, lettuce, tomatoes, buckwheat, millet, white sugar, and honey. Oily, warm, hot, soft, and liquid foods, such as stews and soups, are considered ideal for this type.

Pitta dosha: People who are high in pitta should avoid most spices, especially chili and pepper. They should also avoid acidic foods like salad dressing, tomatoes, and plain yogurt. Instead, include foods such as milk, cheese, sweetened yogurt, green vegetables, and grains.

Kapha dosha: Ayurveda says that people who are high in kapha should balance their water element with pungent and bitter foods such as garlic, ginger, peaches, and pears. They should use a variety of spices in their food. It is important for kapha people to avoid excessively oily and high fat foods, root vegetables, and frozen foods.

Benefits

Some benefits of Ayurvedic eating include:

- It encourages a person to think about what they eat, carefully weigh their needs, and make food decisions based on those needs.
- It may offer similar benefits to other healthy, nutrient-dense diets. For example, a 2021 randomized controlled trial found that an Ayurvedic intervention for irritable bowel syndrome significantly reduced symptoms.

- It is not a restrictive diet. The focus is not on reducing calories or losing weight, but instead on attaining good overall health.
- It may help reduce obesity. A 2019 studyTrusted Source looked at an Ayurvedic diet and yoga as a tool for weight loss. Six months after the 3-month-long study ended, participants had lost an average of 13 pounds. Importantly, the intervention used not just an Ayurvedic diet, but a holistic Ayurvedic approach.
- A person may use Ayurvedic eating as part of their spiritual or cultural practices. The diet may be personally meaningful, incentivizing a person to stick with it.

Research into Ayurvedic medicine is limited, and many studies have been small and poorly controlled.However, people have practiced Ayurveda for centuries, and it is a meaningful cultural practice. It is possible that science has not yet measured Ayurveda's benefits - or that the benefits are spiritual or cultural, not medical.

Risks and downsides: Researchers have not documented any specific risks with Ayurvedic nutrition. The dietary options for each energy group include a wide variety of foods. Plus, the emphasis is on nutritious whole foods rather than processed foods.

Some potential risks include:

- Using Ayurvedic medicine as a substitute for medical treatment could delay care.
- Rigid adherence to any specific diet may be triggering for people with a history of eating disorders.
- Avoiding certain foods can feel difficult, and there is no scientific evidence that avoiding groups of foods based on energetic type offers any specific benefit.
- Using only some elements of Ayurvedic medicine may be a type of cultural appropriation that ignores the rich spiritual and cultural history of Ayurveda.

Fasting

To fast or to feast, that is the question. Food sustains us, yet it is important that we practice fasting every once in a while. There are multiple traditional records, scientific research, and independent studies on the practice of fasting and how it is an effective way of healing and regenerating the body. Modern-day research has highlighted that regular practice of fasting can offer potential benefits, including delayed aging, a healthier gut, and enhanced immunity. Different cultures have evolved different methods of fasting, and here we are going to talk about it in the Ayurvedic way.

What is fasting as per Ayurveda: Ayurveda sees fasting as a remedy for multiple illnesses and as a way to promote good health and well-being. In traditional records, the Sanskrit word that describes fasting is upavasa where 'Upa' means "near" and 'Vasa' means "to stay". So, fasting means "to sit or stay near (the Lord)" or to keep the Lord close to our hearts/minds. Thus the very word fasting highlights an inbuilt orientation toward the divine in the form of therapy. In Ayurveda, upavasa (fasting) is one of multiple daivavyapashraya (divine therapies).

Fasting in Ayurveda refers to abstinence from chewing, licking, and swallowing food but also refraining from all pleasures that kindle the senses. According to Charak Samhita, fasting is a complete dissociation from sinful acts and an association of virtuousness. It must not be regarded as the emaciation of the body. According to Ayurveda, the digestive system and the digestive fire (agni) impact an individual's health. The digestive organs act as a furnace that burns the digestive fire. Any waste accumulation can weaken the digestive system and sabotage the digestive fire. With weak digestion, metabolic toxins, and waste accumulate in our digestive tract, disrupt cellular metabolism, and lead to illnesses.

Upavasa (fasting) leads to the removal of these accumulated toxins and fats, clears the blocked channels, and restores and maintains digestive power. According to Ayurveda, ama is a result of poor digestion, which is the root cause of all diseases. If we continue to indulge in poor dietary habits, we are creating more ama, which will eventually enter the bloodstream and circulate throughout the body. In addition to this, disruption of the doshas can also result in different toxicities. Therefore, we need to make our digestive fire and boost our digestive process. This can be achieved through fasting, which adds a vital halt to the digestive process, strengthens agni, and helps eliminate ama before it causes more profound problems. Fasting allows rest to the digestive system, and the system gets an opportunity to heal naturally. Research has also highlighted that fasting helps enhance the production and activity of certain enzymes involved in detoxification.

Comparison between detox and fasting: What really fasting and detoxing do, Are they interchangeable, and do they perform the same job. Fasting can be seen as voluntary abstinence from some or all foods, drinks, or both for a specific period. It can be of different types. An absolute fast is defined as abstinence from all food and liquid for a defined period. In contrast, other fasts may be partially restrictive. A person can be assumed to have been fasting once a period of 8-12 hours has passed since their last meal.

Detoxing, on the other hand, is generally considered a short-term dietary change to eliminate toxins from your body. A common detox diet may typically involve regulated fasting followed by a strict diet. Sometimes detox may also include consuming only herbs and teas. Detox therapies are most commonly used to treat potential exposure to toxic chemicals in the environment or diet. Thus, even though fasting and detoxing help with various health problems, they are not the same.

Benefits of Fasting

As discussed above, in Ayurveda, upavasa is one of the daivavyapashraya therapies. In Ayurveda, upavasa (fasting) is regarded as a treatment therapy for various diseases, including vamana (vomiting), atisara (diarrhea), hridroga (cardiac disorders), visuchika (cholera), alasaka (paresis of the bowel), jwara (fever), etc. According to Charaka Samhita Sutrasthana, if these ailments of less severity are experienced by someone, then they should be treated by fasting. In addition to these, fasting has been shown to have many other additional health benefits:

Better digestion and a cleansed digestive system: The digestive organs form an integral part of our body. They require a tremendous amount of energy to perform their functions and may also need rest from time to time. Fasting allows for the resting of the digestive tract and frees up energy to be used for healing. This freed-up energy is also potentially used by the body to improve agni (digestive fire), burn away toxins, and support a strong digestive system.

Rejuvenation of the body and mind: Fasting is believed to play a vital role in removing toxins from our bodies. As our bodies clear out unwanted toxins, we can connect with our minds more easily. With fasting, our body feels lighter, there is an increase in energy, and the mind becomes clearer and more focused. Some studies have shown that alternate-day fasting can enhance brain function and improve learning and memory, as indicated by improvements in performance on behavioural tests of sensory and motor function due to increased production of new neurons from neural stem cells.

Reduces inflammation: According to Ayurvedic wisdom, upavasa is an integral part of treatment for santarpanajanya vikara (diseases due to over-satiation including over-nutrition). Since over-satiation can cause disorders like inflammation, autoimmune diseases, metabolic disorders, hypertension, joints, skeletal problems, etc., fasting may offer potential relief. Modern-day research has highlighted some potential benefits of fasting in this regard.

Acute inflammation is a normal immune process to help fight off infections. However, prolonged chronic inflammation can have serious impacts on our health. Research shows that inflammation may be involved in leading to chronic conditions like heart disease, cancer, and rheumatoid arthritis. A review of 18 studies highlighted that fasting could significantly reduce levels of C-reactive protein, which is a marker of inflammation. Therefore, with a reduction in inflammation, a person is less likely to develop the serious health complications mentioned above.

According to research, alternate-day fasting has also resulted in significant reductions in serum TNF? and ceramides in asthma patients. Furthermore, one study highlighted that following a very low-calorie diet to mimic the effects of fasting could potentially reduce levels of inflammation and could be beneficial in the treatment of multiple sclerosis (a chronic inflammatory condition).

Mindful eating habits and weight loss: Many people experiment with fasting to try to lose weight. Abstaining from certain foods and beverages does decrease the overall calorie intake, which could lead to weight loss over time. Some research has also found that short-term fasting may potentially boost metabolism by increasing levels of the neurotransmitter norepinephrine, which could improve weight loss. One review showed that whole-day fasting could reduce body weight by up to 9%. Research has also highlighted that alternate-day fasting was more effective in inducing weight loss compared to continuous calorie restriction.

Improves blood sugar control: There is a large area of research that connects fasting with improved blood sugar control. Several scientific studies have found that fasting may improve blood sugar control, which can be critical for those at risk of diabetes. In fact, a study highlighted that people with type 2 diabetes showed significantly decreased blood sugar levels with short-term intermittent fasting. Later, another 2014 review found that fasting was as effective as limiting calorie intake at reducing insulin resistance. Reduced insulin resistance coupled with the potential blood sugar-lowering could potentially help keep blood sugar steady and prevent spikes and crashes in blood sugar levels.

Dosha-specific information: Individuals with a Vata-dominant constitution or imbalanced Vata are recommended to limit themselves to an overnight fast. These individuals should consume a regular breakfast, healthy lunch, and light well-cooked dinner followed by a 14-hour fast until breakfast the next morning. Longer fasts are not recommended as they can make an individual experience dizziness, ungroundedness, pain, and degenerative changes due to excessive dryness triggered by fasting.

Individuals with a Pitta-dominant constitution or Pitta-imbalance have sharp and intense agni. Therefore, often they cannot tolerate fast very well. However, fasting can be done sparingly to help with the removal of toxins from the body. Just like Vata, these individuals should consume a regular breakfast, healthy lunch, and light well-cooked dinner followed by a 14-hour fast until breakfast the next morning. Longer fasts are not recommended as they may lead to acidity, burning pain in the stomach, reflux, loose stools, burning sensation in the lower abdomen, etc.

The individual with a Kapha-dominant constitution can try fasting due to damp agni. These individuals can tolerate fasting for up to 18 hours. However, this should only be done for a limited period of time to strengthen the agni. People with Kapha dominant constitutions can make the most from the regular practice of fasting. The lightness, dryness, and warming effect of fasting can help balance the heaviness, density, cloudiness, and sluggishness associated with Kapha. While fasting, individuals can consume herbs like black pepper, ginger, long pepper, etc., to impart warming qualities to balance the cold/dampness of Kapha dosha.

Best time to fast, tips & how to do it the right way: According to Ayurveda, spring is the best season for upavasa (fasting). Ayurvedic wisdom suggests that self-cleansing forces heighten in our body when the power of the sun begins to set in to boost our metabolism. That said, this does not mean that one cannot fast during other seasons. If you wake up in the morning feeling tired and dull and have a coating on your tongue, notice any type of indigestion, it is your body sending you signals that something is off. These are times when a person should fast and allow the body to clear up any ama. However, it is important to choose the length of your fast conservatively, and if you choose to fast one day a week, it is better to choose the same day every week as it helps build a routine and manage your schedule. Moreover, some people fast for astrological reasons; therefore, fasting on fixed days to support their charts, therefore fasting on fixed days can be beneficial for all.Once you finish your fast, it is important not to jump back into a regular diet as you may stress your digestive fire causing more harm than good. Therefore, it is better to eat fruits or lighter meals.

According to Ayurveda, the functioning of the digestive system impacts the health of an individual. So, if you plan on adding fasting to your routine, remember to honor and understand your own unique doshas and bodily requirements. Fasting is a practice that has been associated with many potential health benefits, and there are many different types of fasting that fit nearly every lifestyle. Thus, coupled with a healthy diet and good lifestyle, incorporating fasting into our routine could benefit our health and potentially bring us near the Lord!

Vitamins

There is no mention of vitamins in Ayurveda. The Ayurvedic diet is based on the principle of six tastes. Rather than looking at nutritional labels for x amount of vitamin A and y amount of vitamin B, the six tastes naturally guide us toward proper nutrition.

Ayurvedic Treatment for Vitamin Deficiency: Food consumption is mainly categorized based on its constitution like proteins, vitamins, minerals etc. However, in Ayurveda, the food is classified on the basis of taste -sweet, sour and pungent.

Ayurveda offers a holistic approach to treating vitamin deficiency, emphasizing the importance of a balanced diet, lifestyle practices, and natural remedies. Unlike conventional medicine, which often relies on synthetic supplements, Ayurveda encourages natural sources of vitamins and minerals. It also recognizes the interconnectedness of mind, body, and spirit in maintaining optimal health, offering a comprehensive solution to vitamin deficiency.

Understanding Vitamin Deficiency: A balanced diet consisting of proteins, vitamins, and minerals is essential for a healthy life. A deficiency in deficiency can lead to fatigue, dry skin and hair, depression, poor wound healing, and other symptoms. Typically, obvious impacts do not appear until you have had low levels for several months. Vitamin D deficiency can cause weak bones and fractures, while a lack of folate can cause anemia, which causes weariness and weakness.

A deficiency can arise as a result of inadequate vitamin intake or certain medical conditions. Let's take look at some of the common symptoms and causes of vitamin deficiency

- Weakness and Fatigue
- Dry Skin and Hair
- Bruising and Bleeding
- Depression
- Slow wound healing
- Skin colour changes
- Bone fracture

Vitamin deficiency is often related to your diet. They are complex compounds found in foods such as fruits and vegetables, cereals, meat, poultry, and shellfish. Each vitamin can be found in more than one type of food, and certain foods are vitamin-fortified. Milk, for example, includes calcium (a mineral, not a vitamin), yet it is fortified with vitamin D.

Ayurvedic Approach towards Vitamin Deficiency: The Ayurvedic approach to treating vitamin deficiency involves a holistic view of health, emphasizing the importance of a balanced diet, lifestyle practices, and natural remedies. Ayurvedic practitioners believe that a balanced and nutrient-rich diet is the foundation of good health and that vitamin deficiencies are often caused by poor digestion or lifestyle habits.

Ayurveda also encourages the use of natural sources of vitamins and minerals, such as herbs, spices, and plant-based supplements. In addition, Ayurvedic lifestyle practices, such as meditation and yoga, can help to reduce stress and promote overall health and well-being.

Ayurvedic Diet for Vitamin Deficiency: The Ayurvedic diet is a central aspect of Ayurvedic treatment for vitamin deficiency. It emphasizes the importance of consuming nutrient-dense foods that are easy to digest and assimilate. Ayurvedic principles suggest that the body is better able to absorb nutrients from whole foods rather than synthetic supplements.

Therefore, an Ayurvedic diet for vitamin deficiency typically includes a wide variety of whole foods, such as fruits, vegetables, grains, legumes, nuts, and seeds. Ayurvedic practitioners also recommend cooking with specific herbs and spices that are known for their vitamin-rich properties, such as turmeric and cumin. Following are some of the ayurvedic herbs that can be added to your diet recommended by the experts:

- Amla

Amla, an excellent source of Vitamin C or Ascorbic Acid, boosts your immune response. It is also high in Vitamin A, flavonoids, tannins, antioxidants, and phytochemicals, all of which aid in detoxification.

- Triphala

It contains a high concentration of tannins, flavonoids, vitamin C, and phytochemicals. Triphala also has anti-bacterial and antioxidant capabilities and is known for its ability to eliminate free radicals from your body's cells.

- Krishna Tila

Krishna Tila or black sesame seeds, which are high in vitamins B and E, magnesium, iron, and copper, are a nutritious powerhouse that enhances your immune system. Due to its high efficiency, it is a main component of Ayurveda Rasayanam.

- Turmeric

Turmeric is an excellent source of calcium, iron, zinc, flavonoids, vitamin C, and curcumin. They are responsible for their anti-inflammatory and antiseptic qualities. Consuming raw turmeric on a daily basis helps your body fight germs that cause colds, coughs, and congestion.

- Tulsi

Tulsi is rich in vitamins A, C, and B, Calcium, Zinc and Magnesium. It is known as an excellent source of immunity boosters. It is good for organs including the heart, liver and kidneys.

Also, the Ayurvedic diet emphasizes the importance of eating according to one's unique dosha or body type, as different body types have different nutritional needs.

Finally, Ayurveda recognizes the importance of mindful eating practices.

Overall, an Ayurvedic diet for vitamin deficiency can help to support overall health and wellness by providing the body with the nutrients it needs to function optimally.

Taste

For those with kapha dosha, sweet taste can lead to an increase in kapha dosha and qualities of heaviness, coolness, slowness and stickiness. On the other hand, sweet taste in those with vata dosha , when taken in moderate quantities, can prove to have a positive effect on the health and balance out disorders.

Svasthya, "to be established in one's self or own natural state" is optimal health according to Ayurveda. In order to achieve this, one has to have a balance of structural and physiological factors, metabolic and excretory processes, body tissues, senses, mind, and attain a state of self awareness and contented self (6).

Ten factors (dasa vidha pariksa) are used to determine the state of health of an individual per Ayurveda namely, body tissues (dusya), residing location (desa), physical strength (bala), seasons/time (kala), digestive and metabolic processes (agni or anala), genetic and phenetic constitution (prakriti), age (vaya), mental strength or temperament (sattva), habituation (satmya), and food (ahara) (7). It is interesting to note that sattva is said to influence health. While these are mainly used for diagnostic purposes, these can also be used to measure the wellbeing of an individual.

Ahara, a Pillar of Life: Ahara is one of the three pillars of life according to Ayurveda; the other two being sleep and regulated sexual life. The classical texts of Ayurveda of 300 BC-700 AD dedicate elaborate sections on foods (6). Unique aspects include detailed descriptions of food and beverage, food classification based on their taste, therapeutic qualities, etc., food safety and measures for the same, different incompatibilities of food based on their tastes, processing, dose, time, place, etc., prescriptions of consumption, food qualities and intake based on the digestive ability of an individual, and the nature of food that is being consumed (3). Primary classification of food is based on its appropriateness to body and mental constitution based on the five elements and the tridosa theories. Five elements combine and dissociate in the natural transformation of any material, living or non-living (8).

Taste (Rasa) as an Indicator of Health Effects: One of the ways of food classification in Ayurveda is based on rasa. There are six major tastes according to Ayurveda, viz., sweet, sour, salty, pungent, bitter, and astringent. There are primary and secondary qualities (guna) that increase the properties of a material. This is further augmented by potency (virya), post digestive effect (vipaka), and therapeutic action (karma). According to Ayurveda, the classification based on rasa, guna, virya, vipaka, and karma is not only applicable to foods but also for all materials, including medicines, and is dealt with under Dravya guna sastra (the science of materials' properties), the Ayurvedic pharmacology (8).

Food Can Alter Moods: Another interesting taxonomy of foods is based on their effect on psychological dispositions of individuals. According to Ayurveda, there is a subtle link between disease manifestation and the six psychological expressions, such as lust, anger, greed, desire, attachment, and ego. These psychological states are closely linked to foods. This connection is further discussed in terms of three states of being including sattva, rajas, and tamas. Sattva is the contented state, rajas an excited state whereas tamas relates to a lethargic disposition, i.e., foods can induce these states of mind (9, 10).

The Fundamentals of Taste

According to Ayurveda, it is incredibly important to taste our foods, our herbs-our lives. Rasa, the Sanskrit word for taste, has a number of potent meanings, among them: experience, enthusiasm, juice, plasma (as in rasa dhatu), and essence. These diverse meanings only hint at the significance of taste within the Ayurvedic tradition. Rasa is, in a very real way, the essence of life and quite literally affects every aspect of our being-from structure and physiology straight through to our overall state of mind and consciousness. Ayurveda sees rasa, or taste, as a tremendously powerful therapeutic tool that determines not only how we experience our food, but ultimately, the overall flavor of our existence.

Taste is assigned a much deeper significance in Ayurveda than we are accustomed to in the West; it is considered critically important in determining the effect that various foods, spices, therapeutic herbs, and experiences will have on our state of balance-body, mind, and spirit. Ayurveda recognizes six tastes, each of which has a vital role to play in our physiology, health, and well-being.

The sweet, sour, salty, pungent, bitter, and astringent tastes combine in countless ways to create the incredible diversity of flavors we encounter throughout our lives. Even the same substance can taste differently depending on where it is grown or raised, when it is harvested, whether it is stored or preserved, if and how it is cooked or processed, and how fresh or how old it is.

Thus, taste can tell us a great deal not only about what we're ingesting, but also about the physical and energetic qualities we're taking in as a result. In many ways, taste is a living representation of experience: that of the substances we take in, and our own, as we taste them. Ayurveda teaches us to fully acknowledge, appreciate-even relish-the variety of flavors we encounter throughout each day. Only then can we truly harness taste's potential to affect positive change in our minds and bodies.

Tending to the experience of taste also helps us better understand the six tastes, cultivate a deeper relationship with each of them, and begin to adapt our habits according to what we learn.

Breaking Down the Experience of Taste: One of the foundational teachings of the Ayurvedic tradition is that everything in the universe is composed of five elements-earth, water, fire, air, and ether (space). The tastes are no different; each of them contains all five elements. That said, each taste is predominantly composed of two elements.

The 6 Tastes and Their Predominant Elements

Sweet (Madhura)	Earth & Water
Sour (Amla)	Earth & Fire
Salty (Lavana)	Water & Fire
Pungent (Katu)	Fire & Air
Bitter (Tikta)	Air & Ether
Astringent (Kashaya)	Air & Earth

From these elementary beginnings, the experience of taste initiates a complex cascade of influences that touches every aspect of the mind-body organism. For each substance, that mosaic includes its:

- Rasa, or taste (a single taste or a combination of different tastes)

- Aggravating or pacifying effect on each of the doshas (vata, pitta, kapha)
- Virya, or temperature (whether the substance is heating or cooling in nature)
- Vipaka, or post-digestive effect (affects the excreta and nourishes individual cells)
- Prabhava, or an unpredictable action unique to a particular substance (i.e. ghee is cooling and yet it kindles the digestive fire)
- Gunas, or associated qualities
- Affinity for particular organs or tissues
- Direction of movement within the body
- Emotional influence

The combination of all of these factors can affect a wide range of responses in different individuals. While each substance is undoubtedly unique, each of the six tastes tends to exert a somewhat predictable influence on our physiology.

The Six Tastes and You

As with most things in Ayurveda, the combination of tastes that's right for you depends a lot on, well, you-your constitution, your imbalances, your age, your environment.

In other words, while each of the tastes is necessary for all of us, the specifics are determined by the context of each individual, and may change over time.

A balanced diet will include an appropriate quantity of each of the six tastes, according to one's constitution (prakriti), current state (vikriti), and season.

It doesn't matter whether this exploration of taste is a new endeavor for you, or one you're-refining with time and experience. The fact is that taste, rasa, is an inherently potent means of fine-tuning the flavor of your life-whether through diet, lifestyle, relationships, or through the types of experiences you pursue.

Evolving a deepened relationship with taste can shed light on your unique strengths, vulnerabilities, and needs. At the same time, you'll be implementing a powerful tool in support of your path toward perfect health. May your life taste rich and rewarding in every way.

Chapter 8

Medicinal Usage of Kitchen Herbs and Spices

Introduction

Spices and herbs have been in use for centuries both for culinary and medicinal purposes. Spices not only enhance the flavor, aroma, and colour of food and beverages, but they can also protect from acute and chronic diseases.

From older times, spices had played a vital role in the lifestyle of people from certain parts of the world. Herbs and spices have been used for generations by humans as food and to treat ailments. Bio-molecules in the plants play a crucial role in health maintenance and promotion. They have served numerous roles through history, including as colouring agents, flavoring agents, preservatives, food additives and medicine. The active photochemical derived from these spices have provided the molecular basis for these actions. There are several medicinal uses of spices in our daily life, many spices are used in kitchen and have certain medicinal activity like purgative, laxative, expectorant, carminative, diuretic etc. Since ancient time and till today spices are used for many purposes medicinally. Spices such as turmeric, fenugreek, mustard, ginger, onion and garlic have a wide variety of bio functions and their additive or synergistic actions are likely to protect the human body against a variety of insults. Traditionally spices, as part of the diets, have holistic effects on human health.

In whole world, India is the most recognized country for the spices and traditional medicine; these are having a wide range of physiological and pharmacological properties. A spice is a dried seed, fruit, root, bark or flower of a plant or a herb used in small quantities for flavor, colour or as a preservative. Moreover, for people of the world, spices stimulate appetite and create visual appeals to food. All types of spices were use from the ancient time in our kitchen for daily so they fulfill the body requirements on routine basis. Many of these substances are also used in traditional medicines. Globalization has made these spices easily available, and increasing their popularity.

This chapter reviews the traditional uses of selected spices. In addition to making food taste good, culinary spices have been used as food preservatives and for their health-enhancing properties for centuries. Spices are functional foods; those can be demonstrated to have a beneficial effect on certain target functions in the body beyond basic nutritional requirements.

More Americans are considering the use of spices and herbs for medicinal and therapeutic/remedy use, especially for various chronic conditions. There is now ample evidence that spices and herbs possess antioxidant, anti-inflammatory, antitumorigenic, anticarcinogenic, and glucose- and cholesterollowering activities as well as properties that affect cognition and mood. Research over the past decade has reported on the diverse range of health properties that they possess via their bioactive constituents, including sulfur-containing compounds, tannins, alkaloids, phenolic diterpenes, and vitamins, especially flavonoids and polyphenols. Spices and herbs such as clove, rosemary, sage, oregano, and cinnamon are excellent sources of antioxidants with their high content of phenolic compounds. It is evident that frequent consumption of spicy foods was also linked to a lower risk of death from cancer and ischemic heart and respiratory system diseases. However, the actual role of spices and herbs in the maintenance of health, specifically with regards to protecting against the development of chronic, noncommunicable diseases, is currently unclear. This review highlights potential health benefits of commonly used spices and herbs such as chili pepper, cinnamon, ginger, black pepper, turmeric, fenugreek, rosemary, and garlic.

Cloves

Its botanical name Syzygium aromaticum, or Eugenia aromaticum or Eugenia caryophyllata), It is a precious and valuable spice of the world, the part used is basically the dried aromatic buds of flower of a tree in the family of Myrtaceae. Cloves flower buds are mainly found in Indonesia and it's used as a spice in cuisine all around world. The name derives French "clou," (meaning "nail") as the buds vaguely similar small irregular nails in shape. This spice is used in Chinese medicine, Ayurveda, and Western herbalism and dentistry, where the essential oil is used as an anodyne (painkiller) for dental emergencies [3]. Cloves action also reported as analgesic property, anesthetic action, antibacterial property, antiparasitic action, antidotal property, antioxidant action, antiperspirant action, antiseptic property, carminative action, deodorant, digestive disorders, rubefacient action, stimulant property, stomachic action.

Cardamom

Cardamom (Zingiberaceae) is widely used spice and it is also used as flavouring agent. It contain two genera called Elettaria and Amomum. Green colour cardamom is well known as elaichi in Marathi, Hindi and Urdu in South Asia. In Telugu and Tamil it is well known as elakkaya and elam respectively. All species of cardamom are used as kitchen cooking spices. It also helpful in flatulent indigestion and to stimulate the appetite in people with anorexia. In Ayurveda it is well known for carminative property, diuretic action, cough relive, colds and cardiac stimulation. Traditionally it used against kidney and urinary disorders and also having gastrointestinal protective property. Cardamom oil having anti-inflammatory and antibacterial property. In India, green cardamom (A. subulatum) have widely used to treat infections against teeth and gums, to overcome treat throat trouble, congestion of the lungs and pulmonary tuberculosis, asthma, heart disease, inflammation of the eyelids and digestive disorders. Nasal preparation for cold is prepared by mixing cardamom with neem and camphor. Cardamom infusion used as a gargle to relieve sore throats. It is reported as an antidote for both snake and scorpion venom and also used for food poisoning. In Chinese it is also traditionally used to treat stomachache disorders, constipation problem, dysentery in children, and other digestion related problems. The pods of Cardamom, also effective when it is used as fried and mixed with mastic and milk, are effective against bladder problems. Cardamom seeds are well known to be an aphrodisiac property.

Coriander

Coriandrum sativum L. (Umbelliferae) is originated to region of southwestern Asia and North Africa and known as cilantro, cilantro, Chinese parsley, Mexican parsley, Arab parsley, Dhania and Yuen sai. Traditionally it is used in infection related to digestive problem, respiratory and urinary systems and having stimulant action. The coriander plant is highly recommended for anxiety and insomnia in Iranian folk medicine, very common in Mexican diet, usually consumed uncooked, the oil of coriander also having an antimicrobial property and as a natural fragrance in perfumery industry. Coriander also called as "Maadnouss" in Morocco and well recommended for urethritis, cystitis, urinary tract infection, urticaria, rash, burns, sore throat, vomiting, indigestion, nosebleed, cough, allergies, hay fever, dizziness and amebic dysentery.

Fenugreek

Fenugreek is a kind of seed, which are mainly used as kitchen spices in India, commonly known as maithray (Bangla, Gujarati), methi or mithi (Hindi, Nepali, Marathi, Urdu and Sanskrit). In Latin "fenugreek" or foenum-graecum is known for "Greek hay." In medicines it is used as an aphrodisiac property, astringent, demulcent action, carminative, stomachic, diuretic, emmenagogue, emollient, expectorant, lactogogue, restorative, and tonic. Fenugreek also used for a variety of health situations, including digestive disorders, bronchitis, tuberculosis infection, fevers, sore throats problem, wounds healing, arthritis, abscesses, swollen glands, skin irritations reaction, loss of appetite, ulcers and menopausal symptoms, diabetes, as well as in the treatment of cancerous infection.

Leaves infusion is used as a gargle for treatment of mouth ulcers. It also overcomes problem releated to reduce blood sugar level and to lower blood pressure. Kalonji Kalonji mainly found in India every kitchen and having so many medicinal property. Nigella sativa is an annual flowering plant, native to southwest Asia, derivative of Latin niger meaning "black" having carminative, diaphoretic, digestive, diuretic, emmenagogue, excitant, lactagogue, laxative, expectorant, antipyretic, antihelminthic, resolvent, stimulant, sudorific, parasiticide, stomachic, property. It is also known as kalonji(Hindi), kezah(Hebrew), chernushka (Russian), çörek otu(Turkish), habbat albarakah(Arabic "seed of blessing") or siyah daneh (Persian).

Kalonji also effective in dog bites which are mad. It also effective in paralysis, facial palsy, migraine, amnesiareleated problem. Its powder if taken with water is effective in treating haemorrhoids. Vinegar solution of boiled seed is very effective in inflammation and pain of gums and teeth. Its fine powder also effective in early stages of cataract problem. Black seed oil has also women's beauty secret since ancient times. Black cumin and its oil having anti-parasitic activity and very effective in abscesses, hemorrhoids, orchitis and has been used to remove lice from the hair.

Cinnamon

Cinnamon is very commonly used spices in kitchen. (Cinnamomum verum or C. zeylanicum) is mainly present in India, Sri Lanka, Bangladesh, and Nepal [18]. The "cinnamon" names arise from Greek kinnám ? mon, itself ultimately from Phoenician. The botanical name for the spice, Cinnamomum zeylanicum, is derived from Sri Lanka's former (colonial) name, Ceylon. In sinhala (Sri Lanka), it is also known as kurundu, Hindi as dalchini, and in Gujarati as taj. In Malayalam cinnamon is called karuva or elavarngam.

The (karuvappatta/elavarngappatta) karuva dried skin has an important part of spicy curries. This spice is regarded as antipyretic, lowering in body temperature, antiseptic, astringent, inflammatory problem, carminative, diaphoretic, fungicidal, stimulant, and stomachic. The powdered spice cinnamon bark in water is applied to overcome headaches and neuralgia. Cinnamon is combined with ginger to stimulate digestion & circulation. In addition it is also used by different people of Kashmiri origin, cinnamon is used for treat infectious diseases. It regarded as a folk remedy for indurations (of spleen, breast, uterus, liver and stomach) and tumors (especially of the abdomen, liver and sinews)

Garlic

Garlic is the oldest remedy used as early as 3000 BC for the treatment of intestinal disorders and is known for its fibrinolytic activity with lowering blood cholesterol. Garlic (Allium sativum L.) species mainly refer to the onion family, Alliaceae. This spice has also been used in folk medicine for diabetes and inflammation treatment. In Nepal, East Asia and the Middle East has been used to treat all manner of illnesses including fevers, diabetes, rheumatism, intestinal worms, colic, flatulence, dysentery, liver disorders, tuberculosis, facial paralysis, high blood pressure and bronchitis.

In Ayurvedic and Siddha medicine juice of garlic has been used to alleviate sinus problems. In Unani medicine, an prepared extract by the dried bulb is inhaled to promote abortion or taken to regulate menstruation. Unani physicians has also use garlic to treat paralysis, forgetfulness, tremor, colic pains, internal ulcers and fevers.

Ginger

It is also known as aadu (gujarati), shunti (Kannada), allam (Telugu), zanjabil (Arabic), inji (Tamil and Malayalam) and adrak (Hindi and Urdu). Ginger (Zingiber officinale) is common used as a spice in cooking throughout the world and spicially used in kitchen. The ginger rhizome mainly diversify l used in Ayurvedic and traditional Chinese medicine to overcome a vast varaity of gastrointestinal disorders, mainly nausea and vomiting associated with motion sickness and pregnancy, abdominal spasm, as well as respiratory and rheumatic disorders [23]. As a home, ginger is widely used for dyspepsia, flatulence, abdominal discomfort and nausea. It also used as astringent (an agent that causes shrinkage of mucous membranes or exposed tissues and that is often used internally to check discharge of blood serum or mucous secretions).

Mint

The "mint" word generated from Greek word minthe, catargerised in Greek mythology as Minthe, a nymph who was appearing into a mint plant. Mentha (mint) has been a popular used spice and have a genus of about 25 species (and many hundreds of varieties) of flowering plants in the family Lamiaceae (mint family). The different types of mint including Mentha aquatic, water mint or marsh mint; Mentha arvensis corn mint, wild mint, Japanese peppermint, field mint or pudina; Mint leaves are also used in teas, beverages, jellies, syrups, candies, and ice creams. In Middle Eastern cuisine mint are used in lamb dishes.

In British cuisine, mint sauce is popular with lamb. Mint is a necessary ingredient in Touareg tea, a popular tea in northern African and Arab countries. This plant is mainly used as a herbal agent in the treatment of loss of appetite, bronchitis, sinusitis, common cold fever, nausea and vomiting, and indigestion related problem.

Red chilli

Red chilli is the commonly used spice bins our daily life. Red chilli, plant specify genus Capsicum, which among the most popular consumed spices all around the worldwide. This name, chile, or chilli, arises from Nahuatl ch?lli via the Spanish word chile. Red chili has one another application used as an alternative medicine for the inflammation treatment, diabetes problem, and low back pain and also uses in to treat acute tonsillitis. capsicum plaster, that contains finely divided powdered capsicum and capsicum tincture solution, has been used in Korean hand acupuncture to reduce postoperative nausea, sore throat problem, vomiting.

Turmeric

Turmeric cultivation in India occupies 60% of the total area intended for spices and condiments. It is also named as kunyit (Indonesian and Malay), besar (Nepali) and haldi or pasupu in some Asian countries. Turmeric has appearence yellow coloured spice arises from the rhizome of Curcuma longa plant. Turmeric also used as traditional medicine from ancient times in China and India. It is called halodhi in Assanese. In medieval Europe, turmeric also known as Indian saffron, so this widely used for alternative far more costly saffron spice. The yellow powder which is obtained from rhizome of turmeric has been used in Asian cookery, different medicine, cosmetics products, and textile and fabric colouring for the last 2000 years. As a traditional remedy, turmeric has also been quite extensively used for centuries to treat various disorders such as rheumatism, body ache, skin diseases, intestinal worms, diarrhea, intermittent fevers, hepatic diseases, urinary discharges, dyspepsia, inflammations, constipation, leukoderma, amenorrhea, dental diseases, digestive problem such as dyspepsia and acidity, indigestion, flatulence, ulcers, and colic inflammatory disorders such as arthritis, colitis and hepatitis.

Caper

The caper bush, are also called Flinders rose that is a perennial herb plant wich bears spiral, fleshy leaves and large white to pinkish flowers. This plant mainly best known for the edible buds of flower, often used as a seasoning, and the fruit (caper berries), both of which are usually consumed pickled. Other varaities of Capparis are also picked along with C. spinosa for their buds or fruits. Other parts of Capparis plants are used in the manufacture of medicines and cosmetics. Capparis spinosa is found in the wild in the Mediterranean, East Africa, Madagascar, South-Western and Central Asia, the Himalayas, the Pacific Islands, Indomalaya, and Australia. It is present in almost all the circum-Mediterranean countries. When ready to pick,the bud are a dark olive green colour and size about of a fresh kernel of corn (Zea mays). These are picked and then pickled in salt, or a salt and vinegar solution, and drained. A high Intense flavor, described as being similar to black pepper or mustard, is appear as mustard oil (glucocapparin) is released from each caper bud. This type of enzymatic reaction emphasis for the formation of rutin, also seen as crystallized white spots on the surfaces of any individual caper buds.

Alkanet

Alkanet is the common name of several related plants in the borage family Boraginaceae Alkanet, Alkanna tinctoria, the source of a red dye; this is the plant most commonly called simply "alkanet". Alkanet is traditionally used in Indian food under the name "Ratan Jot", and lends its red colour to some versions of the curry dish Rogan Josh. In Australia alkanet is approved for use as a food colouring, but in the European Union it is not. It has been used as colourant for lipstick and rouge (cosmetics). The colouring agent in Alkanna tinctoria root has been chemically isolated and named alkannin. In folklore medicine Alkanna tinctoria is also used to treat abscesses and inflammations.

Ajwain

Family Apiaceae or Umbelliferae, It originated in India. Both the leaves and the seed-like fruit (often mistakenly called seeds) of the plant are consumed by humans. The name "bishop's weed" also is a common name for other plants. The "seed" (i.e., the fruit) is often confused with lovage "seed". Ajwain's small, oval-shaped, seed-like fruits are pale brown schizocarps, which resemble the seeds of other plants in the Apiaceae family such as caraway, cumin and fennel. They have a bitter and pungent taste, with a flavor similar to anise and oregano.

They smell almost exactly like thyme because they also contain thymol, but they are more aromatic and less subtle in taste, as well as being somewhat bitter and pungent. Even a small number of fruits tend to dominate the flavor of a dish. Ajwain is used in traditional Ayurvedic medicine primarily for stomach disorders such as indigestion, flatulence diarrhea and colic. In Siddha medicine, it is used as a cleanser, detox, and antacid. In general, the crushed fruits are applied externally as a poultice.

Tamarind

Tamarindus indica is a leguminous tree in the family Fabaceae indigenous to tropical Africa. The genus Tamarindus is a monotypic taxon, having only a single species. The tamarind tree produces pod-like fruit, which contain an edible pulp that is used in cuisines around the world. Other uses of the pulp include traditional medicine and metal polish. The wood can be used for woodworking, and tamarind seed oil can be extracted from the seeds. Because of the tamarind's many uses, cultivation has spread around the world in tropical and subtropical zones. The fruit has a fleshy, juicy, acidulous pulp. It is mature when the flesh is coloured brown or reddish brown. The tamarinds of Asia have longer pods (containing six to 12 seeds), whereas African and West Indian varieties have shorter pods (containing one to six seeds). The seeds are somewhat flattened, and a glossy brown. The fruit is best described as sweet and sour in taste, and is high in tartaric acid, sugar, B vitamins, and, unusually for a fruit, calcium.

Licium verum

Licium verum is a medium-sized evergreen tree native to northeast Vietnam and southwest China. A spice commonly called star anise, star anise seed, Chinese star anise, or badiam that closely resembles anise in flavor is obtained from the star-shaped pericarps of the fruit of I. verum which are harvested just before ripening. Star anise oil is a highly fragrant oil used in cooking, perfumery, soaps, toothpastes, mouthwashes, and skin creams. About 90% of the world's star anise crop is used for extraction of shikimic acid, a chemical intermediate used in the synthesis of oseltamivir (Tamiflu). It is used as a spice in preparation of biryani and masala chai all over the Indian subcontinent. It is widely used in Chinese cuisine, and in Malay and Indonesian cuisines. It is widely grown for commercial use in China, India, and most other countries in Asia. Star anise is an ingredient of the traditional five-spice powder of Chinese cooking. It is also a major ingredient in the making of, a Vietnamese noodle soup.

Star anise is the major source of the chemical compound shikimic acid, a primary precursor in the pharmaceutical synthesis of antiinfluenza drug oseltamivir (Tamiflu). Shikimic acid is produced by most autotrophic organisms, and while it can be obtained in commercial quantities elsewhere, star anise remains the usual industrial source. In 2005, a temporary shortage of star anise was caused by its use in the production of Tamiflu. Later that year, a method for the production of shikimic acid using bacteria was discovered.

Poppy seed

Poppy seed is an oilseed obtained from the poppy (Papaver somniferum). The tiny kidney-shaped seeds have been harvested from dried seed pods by various civilizations for thousands of years. It is still widely used in many countries, especially in Central Europe, where it is legally grown and sold in shops. The seeds are used, whole or ground, as an ingredient in many foods-especially in pastry and bread, and they are pressed to yield poppy seed oil. In a 100 gram amount, poppy seeds provide 525 Calories and are a rich source of thiamin, folate, and several essential minerals, including calcium, iron, magnesium, manganese, phosphorus and zinc (table). Poppy seeds are composed of 6% water, 28% carbohydrates, 42% fat, and 21% protein (table). In Indian cuisine white poppy seeds are added for thickness, texture and also give added flavor to the recipe. Commonly used in the preparation of korma, ground poppy seeds, along with coconut and other spices, are combined as a paste, to be added at the last stage of cooking. It is quite hard to grind them when raw, so they are normally toasted/broiled and water added when grinding to get the right consistency In Indian traditional medicine Ayurveda soaked poppy seeds are ground into a fine paste with milk and applied on the skin as a moisturizer. Poppy seeds are pressed to form poppy seed oil, valuable commercial oil that has multiple culinary, industrial, and medicinal uses.

Pomegranates

The pomegranate (Punica granatum) is a fruitbearing deciduous shrub or small tree in the family Lythraceae that grows between 5 and 8 m (16 and 26 ft) tall. The fruit is typically in season in the Northern Hemisphere from September to February and in the Southern Hemisphere from March to May. As intact arils or juice, pomegranates are used in baking, cooking, juice blends, meal garnishes, smoothies and alcoholic beverages, such as cocktails and wine. Pomegranate juice can be sweet or sour, but most fruits are moderate in taste, with sour notes from the acidic ellagitannins contained in the juice. It is well known popular drink in whole world. In India's ancient Ayurveda system of traditional medicine, the pomegranate is frequently described as an ingredient in remedies.

Nigella sativa

An annual flowering plant in the family Ranunculaceae, native to south and southwest Asia. The seeds of N. sativa are used as a spice in Indian and Middle Eastern cuisines. The black seeds taste like a combination of onions, black pepper, and oregano. They have a pungent, bitter taste and smell. The dry-roasted seeds flavor curries, vegetables, and pulses. They can be used as a "pepper" in recipes with pod fruit, vegetables, salads, and poultry. In some cultures, the black seeds are used to flavor bread products, and are used as part of the spice mixture panch phoron (meaning a mixture of five spices) and alone in many recipes in Bengali cuisine and most recognizably in naan. Nigella is also used in Armenian string cheese, a braided string cheese called majdouleh or majdouli in the Middle East.

Liquorice

Liquorice is the root of Glycyrrhiza glabra from which a sweet flavour can be extracted. The liquorice plant is an herbaceous perennial legume native to southern Europe and parts of Asia, such as India. It is not botanically related to anise, star anise, or fennel, which are sources of similar flavouring compounds. Liquorice flavours are used as candies or sweeteners, particularly in some European and Middle Eastern countries. Liquorice extracts have been used in herbalism and traditional medicine. Excessive consumption of liquorice (more than 2 mg/kg/day of pure glycyrrhizinic acid, a liquorice component) may result in adverse effects such as hypokalemia, increased blood pressure, and muscle weakness. Liquorice flavour is found in a wide variety of candies or sweets.

In most of these candies, the taste is reinforced by aniseed oil so the actual content of liquorice is very low. Liquorice confections are primarily purchased by consumers in the European Union. In the Netherlands, liquorice confectionery (drop) is one of the most popular forms of sweets. It is sold in many forms. Mixing it with mint, menthol, aniseed, or laurel is quite popular. Mixing it with ammonium chloride (salmiak) is also popular. A popular liquorice in the Netherlands is known as zoute drop (salty liquorice), but contains very little salt, i.e., sodium chloride. The salty taste is due to ammonium chloride. Strong, salty sweets are also popular in Nordic countries. In traditional Chinese medicine, liquorice (G. uralensis) is believed to "harmonize" the ingredients in a formula. Liquorice has been used in Ayurveda for rejuvenation and in the belief it may aid jaundice or other diseases. It is used as an expectorant in traditional medicine in Egypt.

All the spices have a wide variety of bio-functions and their additive and synergistic actions that protect the human body. Traditionally, spices are the part of diet, having holistic approach. Because they tend to have strong flavors and are used in small quantities, spices tend to add few calories to food, even though many spices, especially those made from seeds, contain high portions of fat, protein and carbohydrate by weight. However, when used in larger quantity, spices can also contribute a substantial amount of minerals and other micronutrients, including iron, magnesium, calcium and many others, to the diet.

Most Used Ayurvedic Herbs And Their Benefits

As we can not scrub, rub or cleanse our inner body as our outer, we must maintain a healthy nutrition intake. Ayurvedic herbs make one simple yet effective mode of nutrition for optimum health in humans. Whether one aims at increasing their Ayurvedic antioxidants intake or is trying to tackle concerns such as inflammation of joints, certain Ayurvedic herbs can have a relieving effect against certain health concerns.

In this blog, we will discuss many Ayurvedic herbs that are widely popular, used, and appreciated for their health benefits. Perhaps our readers may find a natural route to a healthier life.

A Brief History Of Ayurvedic Herbs And Their Significance

Ayurvedic healingis one of the oldest modes of medication and healing. For over 5,000 years, Ayurveda has been helping individuals build and maintain good mental and positive health through various methods such as Yoga, meditation, and a wide range of herbs, offering a wide range of health benefits. Herbs and other plants, including oils and common spices, are used extensively in Ayurvedic treatment. Apart from medicinal use, Ayurvedic herbs can also be used for purposes like pest control, natural dyes, and formulation of food items, teas and perfumes among others. If we look at various researches from across the world, a sudden spurt in cases of people turning to natural herbs for treatments and usage in everyday life has gone up significantly. Going back to the basics, people have realized the threat chemically treated products pose to their life and are rightly so adopting healthier ways of life by including Ayurveda and its principals as the mainstay of their life. Nearly all the herbal recipes and Ayurvedic remedies we use in the present day are an evolution or a revision of the ancient authentic Ayurvedic recipes. For thousands of years, this knowledge of herbs and Ayurveda has enabled Ayurvedic practitioners and doctors (Vaidyas) to help individuals dealing with health concerns.

Benefits & Importance of Medicinal Plants: Ayurvedic herbs are time tested for their health and other benefits. The nutritive value that they pack are highly recommended for their healing powers. Known to induce no side effects, they have a unique aroma and flavor and when consumed regularly, they act as a perfect mechanism to bring about a balanced harmony between mind and body. They rejuvenate the whole system instead of focusing on one specific organ or body part.

- They have a holistic approach and aid in proper absorption and digestion
- They are not disease specific but act as a preventive medicine that positively effects the overall health and well-being by boosting the immune system
- They are at par with allopathic medicines and are at times known to be effective in treating diseases like cancer and autoimmune diseases
- They are self-contained and nutritive holistic in nature, therefore, are non-toxic and harmless
- It deals with the overall well-being and aims to bring harmony between mind, body and soul
- Several metabolic and chronic conditions can be treated without any side effects using Ayurvedic medicines and treatments

Ayurvedic Herbs/Spices & Their Medicinal Values

- Ayurvedic Herbs and spices such as black pepper, cinnamon, aloe, sandalwood, ginseng, red clover, burdock, bayberry, and safflower are used to heal wounds, sores and boils.
- To reduce fever and the production of heat caused by the condition, certain antipyretic herbs such as Chirayta, black pepper and sandal wood are recommended
- Sandalwood and Cinnamon are great astringents apart from being aromatic. Sandalwood is especially used in arresting the discharge of blood, mucus etc.
- Ajwain, Amalaki, Aswatha etc., serve as antacids and are recommended for healthy gastric acid flow and proper digestion
- Herbs like Cardamom and Coriander are renowned for their appetizing qualities. Other aromatic herbs such as peppermint, cloves and turmeric add a pleasant aroma to the food, thereby increasing the taste of the meal
- Herbs like Aloe, Sandalwood, Turmeric, Sheetraj and Khare Khaskhas are commonly used as antiseptic and have very high medicinal values

- Camomile, Basil, Cardamom, Ginger, Peppermint and Coriander are known to promote blood circulation in the body and keep the heart healthy

Most Powerful Ayurvedic Herbs And Their Benefits

Ashwagandha

Figure: *If you were raised in the Indian subcontinent, or if your family is Indian, you might have grown up hearing from your grandparents how Ashwagandha can help lead a healthier life.*

From improving digestion to boosting energy and helping maintain healthy blood sugar levels, Ashwagandha can do it all.

Kerala Ayurveda offers several Ashwagandha based products that can help reap the following benefits of Ashwagandha easily:

- Can help enhance memory and cognition.
- Eases stress.
- Supports healthy digestion and metabolism.
- It helps to maintain a healthy immune system and promotes muscle strength to support the comfortable joint movement.
- It is considered as the best herb for calming Vata.

Triphala

Figure: *Triphala is another one of the immensely popular herbs in the Indian subcontinent. For thousands of years, people have been using it for easing constipation, improving gut health and for a bunch of other benefits.*

Here's a list of benefits that one can reap by consuming Triphala, in its bitter natural form, or as an easier and more pleasant Triphala Sparkles or tablets:

- Triphala can help improve the digestion process and improve gut health.
- It is a natural laxative that can help reduce constipation, while improving the consistency of bowel movements
- As Triphala improves metabolism, it can be good for weight management.
- Triphala is a rich source of antioxidants that help fight free radicals and oxidative stress
- It preserves the health and beauty of hair and skin.

Brahmi

Figure: *Brahmi is often known for its benefits on brain health. However, that doesn't explain everything about how it can be helpful. Here's a more comprehensive list of benefits:*

- Brahmi can help enhance memory, increase intelligence, and boost concentration.
- Brahmi can decrease the cortisol levels in the body and reduces stress and anxiety
- Brahmi supplements are cooling and relaxing and can make excellent supplements for optimising Pitta.
- It can help calm the Vata in the mind and can help eliminate excess Kapha in the body.
- It is one of the top Ayurvedic herbs to help reduce stress.

Manjistha

- It can help purify the blood.
- It is a natural detox agent that can help cleanse the body by eliminating toxins and waste.

Figure: *Manjistha is one of the perennial climber Ayurvedic plants offering several health benefits such as purification of the blood, elimination of wastes from the body, regulating the immune system, and more. For a clearer understanding, here's a comprehensive list of Manjistha's sought after benefits:*

- Manjistha can act as an active lymph mover, which can also help reduce excessive Pitta levels and break up the congested Kapha.
- Manjistha can be one of the best Ayurvedic herbs that can cleanse the liver, ensure healthy kidney function, and clear acne.

Precautions: While Ayurvedic herbs are naturally grown and maintained through organic means, they are safe to consume in prescribed quantities. Most herbal products you may use or consume may never counter good health. However, excessive consumption/ usage is not advised.

For optimum results, and a healthy body, prescribed quantities should not be exceeded, and a professional Ayurvedic doctor's prescription is advisable before starting dosage.

Also, all herbal skincare products and massage oils are composed of various herbs, a few (or more) of which may have an allergic reaction to specific skin types. To rule out the risk of allergy, always start with a patch test, and continue using only if there's no reaction.

Chapter 9

First Aid

Introduction

First aid is the first and immediate assistance given to any person with either a minor or serious illness or injury, with care provided to preserve life, prevent the condition from worsening, or to promote recovery until medical services arrive. First aid is generally performed by someone with basic medical training. Mental health first aid is an extension of the concept of first aid to cover mental health, while psychological first aid is used as early treatment of people who are at risk for developing PTSD.

There are many situations that may require first aid, and many countries have legislation, regulation, or guidance, which specifies a minimum level of first aid provision in certain circumstances. This can include specific training or equipment to be available in the workplace (such as an automated external defibrillator), the provision of specialist first aid cover at public gatherings, or mandatory first aid training within schools. Generally, five steps are associated with first aid:

1. Assess the surrounding areas.
2. Move to a safe surrounding (if not already; for example, road accidents are unsafe to be dealt with on roads).
3. Call for help: both professional medical help and people nearby who might help in first aid such as the compressions of cardiopulmonary resuscitation (CPR).
4. Perform suitable first aid depending on the injury suffered by the casualty.
5. Evaluate the casualty for any fatal signs of danger, or possibility of performing the first aid again.

Aims

The primary goal of first aid is to prevent death or serious injury from worsening. The key aims of first aid can be summarized with the acronym of 'the three Ps':

- Preserve life: The overriding aim of all medical care which includes first aid, is to save lives and minimize the threat of death. First aid done correctly should help reduce the patient's level of pain and calm them down during the evaluation and treatment process.
- Prevent further harm: Prevention of further harm includes addressing both external factors, such as moving a patient away from any cause of harm, and applying first aid techniques to prevent worsening of the condition, such as applying pressure to stop a bleed from becoming dangerous.
- Promote recovery: First aid also involves trying to start the recovery process from the illness or injury, and in some cases might involve completing a treatment, such as in the case of applying a plaster to a small wound.

It is important to note that first aid is not medical treatment and cannot be compared with what a trained medical professional provides. First aid involves making common sense decisions in the best interest of an injured person.

Setting the Priorities

Protocols such as ATLS, BATLS, SAFE-POINT are based on the principle of defining the priorities and the procedure where the correct execution of the individual steps achieves the required objective of saving human life.

Basic points of these protocols include the mnemonic ABCDE or cABCDE:

- catastrophic bleeding (massive external bleeding, added in some protocols)
- Airway (clearing airways)
- Breathing (ensuring respiration)
- Circulation (ensuring effective cardiac output)
- Disability (neurological condition), and/or Defibrillation (cardio-respiratory failure, which can be also included as 'Breathing' or 'Circulation')
- Exposure (overall examination, environment)

A major benefit of these protocols is that they require minimum resources, time and skills with a great degree of success in saving lives under conditions unfavourable for applying first aid.

ABCDE Method

Source:

- Airway (clearing airways): If the patient responds in a normal voice, then the airway is patent. Airway obstruction can be partial or complete. Signs of a partially obstructed airway include a changed voice, noisy breathing (e.g., stridor), and an increased breathing effort. With a completely obstructed airway, there is no respiration despite great effort (i.e., paradox respiration, or "see-saw" sign). A reduced level of consciousness is a common cause of airway obstruction, partial or complete. A common sign of partial airway obstruction in the unconscious state is snoring. Untreated airway obstruction can rapidly lead to cardiac arrest. All health care professionals, regardless of the setting, can assess the airway as described and use a head-tilt and chin-lift maneuver to open the airway. With the proper equipment, suction of the airways to remove obstructions, for example, blood or vomit, is recommended. If possible, foreign bodies causing airway obstruction should be removed. In the event of a complete airway obstruction, treatment should be given according to current guidelines. In brief, first aid for conscious patients of choking uses anti-choking procedures (usually five back blows, alternating with five abdominal thrusts, or alternating with five chest thrusts in the case of the pregnant and the very obese victims, until the obstruction is relieved). If the victim becomes unconscious, it is required, according to guidelines, to call for help to emergency medical services and to any useful people that is near and to start cardiopulmonary resuscitation for unconscious victims of choking (attempting to extract the object, with extreme care, from time to time). In modern times, some commercial anti-choking devices have been invented to simplify the solution of choking. Importantly, high-flow oxygen should be provided to all critically ill persons as soon as possible.
- Breathing (ensuring respiration): In all settings, it is possible to determine the respiratory rate, inspect movements of the thoracic wall for symmetry and use of auxiliary respiratory

muscles, and percuss the chest for unilateral dullness or resonance. Cyanosis, distended neck veins, and lateralization of the trachea can be identified. If a stethoscope is available, lung auscultation should be performed and, if possible, a pulse oximeter should be applied. Tension pneumothorax must be relieved immediately by inserting a cannula where the second intercostal space crosses the midclavicular line (needle thoracocentesis). Bronchospasm should be treated with inhalations. If breathing is insufficient, assisted ventilation must be performed by giving rescue breaths with or without a barrier device. Trained personnel should use a bag mask if available.

- Circulation (internal bleeding): The capillary refill time and pulse rate can be assessed in any setting. Inspection of the skin gives clues to circulatory problems. Colour changes, sweating, and a decreased level of consciousness are signs of decreased perfusion. If a stethoscope is available, heart auscultation should be performed. Electrocardiography monitoring and blood pressure measurements should also be performed as soon as possible. Hypotension is an important adverse clinical sign. The effects of hypovolemia can be alleviated by placing the patient in the supine position and elevating the patient's legs. An intravenous access should be obtained as soon as possible and saline should be infused.
- Disability (neurological condition): The level of consciousness can be rapidly assessed using the AVPU method, where the patient is graded as alert (A), voice responsive (V), pain responsive (P), or unresponsive (U). Alternatively, the Glasgow Coma Score can be used.16 Limb movements should be inspected to evaluate potential signs of lateralization. The best immediate treatment for patients with a primary cerebral condition is stabilization of the airway, breathing, and circulation. In particular, when the patient is only pain responsive or unresponsive, airway patency must be ensured, by placing the patient in the recovery position, and summoning personnel qualified to secure the airway. Ultimately, intubation may be required. Pupillary light reflexes should be evaluated and blood glucose measured. A decreased level of consciousness due to low blood glucose can be corrected quickly with oral or infused glucose.

- Exposure (overall examination, environment): Signs of trauma, bleeding, skin reactions (rashes), needle marks, etc., must be observed. Bearing the dignity of the patient in mind, clothing should be removed to allow a thorough physical examination to be performed. Body temperature can be estimated by feeling the skin or using a thermometer when available.

Ayurvedic First Aid

Ayurveda is a holistic system of medicine that emphasizes the connection between the mind, body, and spirit. It recognizes that each person has a unique body constitution or dosha, which determines their physical and emotional traits. The goal of Ayurvedic medicine is to balance the doshas and promote overall well-being. Ayurvedic remedies use herbs, spices, and other natural ingredients to restore balance and treat common ailments. Ayurvedic remedies have been used for centuries and have a rich history of success in managing various health conditions. From herbal teas to natural oils, these remedies are designed to promote overall health and wellness by treating the root cause of an ailment. Incorporating Ayurvedic remedies into your daily routine can not only help you feel better but can also prevent illnesses from occurring in the first place. By taking a holistic approach to health, Ayurveda aims to balance the mind, body, and spirit to support a healthy and fulfilling life.

Here are Some Easy-to-Follow Remedies for Common Conditions

Asthma	Ginger and licorice powder boiled in water and taken with honey or salt is a good Ayurvedic remedy for asthma. This drink can help alleviate symptoms and promote respiratory health.
Backache	A paste of ginger applied to the affected area or massaging with eucalyptus oil can provide relief. Furthermore, you can also make your own massaging oil by boiling garlic in sesame or mustard oil.
Bleeding (External)	Applying a paste of sandalwood powder can help stop external bleeding and promote wound healing. Drinking warm milk with turmeric powder and saffron or alum can also help alleviate pain.
Burns	A paste of fresh aloe vera gel with turmeric powder and ghee or coconut oil can soothe burnt skin and promote healing.
Cold	Boiling grated ginger, cinnamon powder, and licorice powder in water and drinking the resulting tea with honey can help alleviate symptoms of a cold.
Diarrhea	A mixture of fresh grated ginger and nutmeg powder blended in water can help stop diarrhea.
Earache	Firstly, boiling garlic in sesame or mustard oil and using the cooled oil to drop in the aching ear can provide relief. Additionally, a mixture of onion juice and honey can also be used to alleviate earache.
Eye Burn	Putting pure rose water in the affected eye can reduce redness and itching.
Boils	Applying cooked onion as a poultice or a mixture of ginger powder and turmeric powder on the boil can help reduce inflammation and promote drainage.
Exhaustion	Drinking coconut water or grape juice, or cooking dates in milk or water can provide instant energy and help combat heat exhaustion.
Gum Bleeding	Drinking lemon juice and honey in water can help alleviate gum bleeding. Massaging gums with coconut oil can also be beneficial.
Menstrual Cramps	Mixing aloe vera gel and black pepper powder and taking it 2-3 times a day can help alleviate menstrual cramps.

Ayurveda has been used for centuries as a natural and holistic approach to healthcare. Its remedies can be easily incorporated into our daily routines and can help us maintain our health and prevent common ailments. Ayurveda aims to balance the body, mind, and spirit by using natural remedies, such as herbs, spices, and oils. Hence we have provided in this article Ayurvedic remedies in the form of Ayurvedic First Aid.

These Ayurvedic remedies (Ayurvedic First Aid) can help with a variety of conditions, including digestion problems, stress, anxiety, skin issues, and more. They can also help promote healthy sleep and boost immunity.

However, it is important to remember that while Ayurvedic remedies are generally safe, they should be used with caution, and consulting with a qualified Ayurvedic practitioner is recommended. Additionally, those with chronic health conditions should not rely on Ayurvedic remedies as a substitute for professional medical advice and treatment.

10 Ayurvedic Medicines That You Should Have In Your Medicine Cabinet

Most of us have a first aid box at home that holds all the ingredients necessary to deal with the sudden scrapes and ills our family faces in everyday life. Some of us also stock a few over-the-counter medicines to deal with minor ailments such as a headache, body pain, indigestion or constipation.

Several effective herbal medicines are also available for these health problems and considering that these are free of side effects, it makes better sense to stock up on these natural products. Here are 10 Ayurvedic medicines that you should have in your medicine cabinet.The medicines mentioned here are the generic products and different manufacturers sell them under their own unique brand names.

Chyawanprash: One of the most well-known Ayurvedic medicines, Chyawanprash is a sweet and sour dark brown, viscous paste with a jam-like consistency. It is made up of honey, ghee, sugar and a combination of different herbs that work together to improve immunity. Taking one tablespoon of this medicine twice daily with some warm water or milk helps to improve your resistance and stay healthy. Apart from improving your immunity it has various other health benefits and also keeps your respiratory system healthy.

Triphalachurna: Triphalachurna is a medicine that is made up of three major herbs amalaki, bibhitaki and haritaki. Together, these herbs act to combat indigestion, relieve gas and ensure appropriate detoxification. As a result of consuming this medicine, not only does your digestive system stay in order, but you also acquire a glowing skin, brighter eyes and a stronger immune system. Apart from having various other health benefits it is also an excellent home remedy for constipation.

Ashtachurna: Ashthachurna, as the name indicates, is a combination of 8 different herbs of which the major ones are cumin, asafetida, ginger and black pepper. These herbs work in combination to improve digestion of food and hasten the expulsion of the gas generated during the digestive process.

AvipattikaraChurna: Hyperacidity is one of the common health complaints today because of our unhealthy lifestyle that includes untimely meals, junk food and stress. Avipattikarachurna is an Ayurvedic medicine that is made up of 14 herbs including amla, cardamom, and triphala that help to relieve the distress of hyperacidity. This must be taken in the prescribed doses along with milk or honey as directed by your physician.

Ajwain Ark: Ajwain is a staple in every Indian household and is used for its various health benefits including getting rid of flatulence. Ajwain ark is an aqueous extract of ajwain which has strong carminative properties. Ajwain contains a volatile oil that helps to expel the gas from the stomach and intestine and therefore, this product is very effective against flatulence. People who suffer from flatulence and bloating often have loss of appetite or dyspepsia; so Ajwain ark can help get rid of these problems, too.

Lasunadivati/gutika: With garlic as one of the major ingredients, Lasunadivati is one of the best Ayurvedic remedies for indigestion, stomach pain and diarrhea. This preparation also contains other herbs such as cumin, rock salt and asafetida, which makes it effective against gas, too.

NeemGhrita: Skin irritation or itchy skin is something most of us encounter and the best way to find relief is to use an Ayurvedic cream with soothing and antibacterial properties. Neemghrita is such a cream made up of neem oil, gotu kola, manjishta and turmeric. Applying this cream to the affected area helps reduce skin irritation and also gives relief from itching.

NarayanaTaila: One of the most popular Ayurvedic oils, Narayanataila works well on musculo-skeletal and neuro-muscular conditions such as pain in the joints, pulling pain in the limbs, osteoarthritis and cervical spondylosis. This oil is made up of herbs such as bilva, ashwagandha, kantakari, bala and atibala which make it effective against joint and muscular pain when massaged on the affected area.

Panchatulsi Drops: Tulsi is one of the most effective natural antibacterial, anti-allergic and expectorant herbs. As the name indicates, Panchatulsi drops is a product made from five different species of tulsi. Rich in antioxidants, this product has preventive properties against allergy, flu, asthma, cough and cold. It also helps improve immunity and ensures good health when consumed on a regular basis. The drops must be mixed in the prescribed quantity with water or milk and taken twice a day regularly to see best results.

BhringarajAsava: Bhringaraj is a strong expectorant and helps to reduce the viscosity of the thick phlegm that is commonly seen in upper respiratory tract infections. Bhringarajasava is a combination of bhringaraj with other herbs such as pepper and cardamom, and provides relief from cough and cold.

Most of these Ayurvedic medicines have been used since ages and have been proven to be safe and effective. However, some of these may interact with other medication and enhance or reduce their efficacy. Especially if you are on prescription medication such as anti-diabetics, anti-hypertensives or blood thinners, it is vital you speak to your physician before using these Ayurvedic medicines.

15 Necessary Items For Your Herbal First Aid Kit

Do you need a natural first response for health problems Have you heard about the use of herbs as first aid? Knowing about the potency of herbs is not complete. You can further harness this potency with the knowledge of herb use as first aid. Lots of minor and major injuries occur at home.

These injuries, including cuts, blisters, and burns, often require urgent attention. The first response is usually first aid, especially if you are not lucky enough to have a medical center around. We often focus on having medications in our first aid box. But it is almost impossible to have all medicines for various injuries. Besides the fact that they might be too expensive, the administration is not easy. So, the use of herbs as first aid kits comes in handy. Several herbs can serve as the first response to various health challenges. These herbs are not rare; they are regular plants and oils.

Making herbal first aid kits is easy and not expensive. In this guide, you will find some of the essential elements for assembling herbal first aid kits. You will also get necessary clues on how to use these elements. So, keep reading to find out!

Benefits of Herbal First Aid Kit

Before we dive into herbal first aid kits and their elements, it is essential to understand their benefits. Here are some advantages of having herbal components in your first aid kit;

- It induces speedy recovery and mitigates vulnerability to infections.
- It is easy to administer.
- There is only a negligible risk of overdose or side effects.
- It is less expensive and safe to use.
- The components are 100% natural and do not contain any artificial elements like colours, fillers, and flavors.
- It is environmentally friendly because it uses all-natural ingredients.

Elements to Include in Your Herbal First Aid Kit

1. Aloe Vera Aloe vera is one of the versatile first responses to injuries. It is a succulent plant that can grow indoors and outdoors. This green plant has a mucilaginous gel that contains medicinal and healing properties. This gel has anti-inflammatory properties, and it is beneficial for other conditions. You can use it as the first response for acne, eczema, and psoriasis. It is also useful for burns and sunburns. You can cut the plant and get the gel immediately if you want to use it. Alternatively, you can cut the gel and store it in the fridge for future use.
2. Comfrey Comfrey is another useful plant for treating various conditions. This plant is easy to grow and store. It is both functional as a green plant and in a dried form. You can infuse the dry state with olive oil to enhance its performance. This plant's potency is due to its high allantoin level. This element

makes it useful for enhancing tissue growth. So, comfrey is helpful in the treatment of tissue scars. It helps treat deep wounds and cuts. And it combats growing infection in cuts.

3. Chamomile Chamomile is a popular herb useful for both internal and external health. You can make chamomile into tea and soups. You can also use it for an eye bath. Taking chamomile tea or soups can help children and adults soothe stomach upset. This tea provides body relaxation. So, it is useful for women suffering from menstrual cramps. Chamomile tea has mild antiseptic properties that can provide a soothing effect on irritated skin. You can use this herb to treat eye strain, mild conjunctivitis, and blepharitis. It is also helpful for soothing sore eyes.
4. Ginger Ginger is another common plant with many uses. Ginger is famous for its dietary value and ability to serve as a spice. But its use is beyond that. It also has a place as one of the most potent herbs for first aid kits. It is useful for providing relief for stomach issues and morning sickness. Ginger can also serve as your first response for flu, cold, and motion sickness.
5. Lavender Lavender is famous as one of the best essential oils. This oil has lots of medicinal and healing properties. Lavender has antiviral and antimicrobial properties. Also, it has elements that make it an active insect repellant. This herb can also help you handle and treat insect bites, grazes, and cuts. Lavender, like most other essential oils, has a relaxing effect. So, it is useful for mitigating shock, depression, nervous tension, and stress. The herb's relaxing properties help it promote sleep and reduce migraine symptoms.
6. Thyme Thyme is another plant famous for its spicing properties. But it is also a valuable addition to your first aid kit. The leaves of this plant can be used fresh or dried. Either way, thyme can serve as the first response for cold and flu. It is useful for throat clearing and cough. Some manufacturers make thyme into a medicinal tea. Thyme is a valuable herbal first aid kit element regardless of how you use it.
7. Tea Tree Tea tree is one of the purest forms of essential oil with loads of health benefits. It has antifungal and antiseptic properties. It is one of the best treatment options for body parts

with tough skin. These parts include palm and feet soles. So, you can use tea tree oil for wound dressing, wound care, insect bites, and fungal skin rashes. It is not ideal to use concentrated tea tree oil on sensitive skin parts. It is best to dilute it to a slightly neutral concentration.

8. Witch Hazel The name of the plant is primarily due to its explosive healing ability. This plant has antiseptic and anti-inflammatory properties. This potency is mainly due to the presence of tannins in the plant. It can stop bleeding and prevent infections from developing on wounds. So, witch hazel is an ideal response to cuts or other injuries that causes bleeding. You can trust it to address your shaving burns and scraps. It also mitigates inflammation and swelling. Witch hazel is useful for treating various insect bites and stings. Also, it is helpful for other conditions like hemorrhoids and blisters.
9. Turmeric Do you need to add a valuable pain reliever to your herbal first aid kit? Turmeric is one of your best shots! This plant provides significant pain relief for severe conditions like rheumatoid arthritis and osteoarthritis. Besides, turmeric can help you tackle various digestive and body discomforts. It mitigates inflammation after operations and offers digestive supports. So, turmeric can be your healer in times of indigestions, colitis, and other GIT problems. You can use turmeric in various forms, and they are all effective. You can use it in powdery form, tablets, or herbal tea.
10. Eucalyptus Eucalyptus is another essential oil with substantial health benefits. Although it is only ideal for external use, it still offers solutions to many internal health problems. Eucalyptus is generally not suitable for ingestion except for some modified commercial forms. Eucalyptus is one of the best herbal pain relievers to add to your first aid kit. A few drops of eucalyptus oil are enough to treat conditions like headaches and muscle aches. It is also a good response for ailments like colds, flu, asthma, sinus problems, and respiratory issues. There are several ways to harness eucalyptus oil for external use. You can add a few drops to a steamy shower to clear your airways. It will also help you deal with cold and flu, which are primary causes of blocked airways. You can add eucalyptus to a carrier oil to improve its performance. You can rub the

mixture on your hands, legs, and other body parts to relieve muscle strain and ache. It will also help you accelerate the cold sore's healing process.

11. Arnica Have you heard about the potency of the arnica plant? Arnica might not be one of the most common herbs, but it is one of the most potent options. It is suitable for first aid kits because it provides quick relief to bruising, strains, and sprains. Arnica is commonly available in gel, cream, and ointment. Unlike eucalyptus oil, you can safely use Arnica internally without any fear. It is useful for the treatment of external tissue damage. It can also aid your speedy recovery after rigorous processes like childbirth, dental work, and surgery. But it is best to avoid the topical application of this herb during special conditions like pregnancy. Breastfeeding mothers and people with broken skin should also stay away from the herb.
12. FeverFew Do you need a fast action response to chronic conditions like a migraine? FeverFew might be the simple solution you've been seeking for a long time. This herb has an optimal magnesium level, which is the herb's healing power. Using FeverFew in suitable doses will help you treat migraines from slight headaches. It is also useful for treating visual disturbance, nausea, and other similar conditions. Note that fresh FeverFew is not advisable because of its side effects. It is best to use only standardized doses for safe use. Also, stay away from this herb if you are sensitive to chrysanthemums and ragweed.
13. Slippery Elm Here is another herb that can perform super wonders. Slippery elm's effect is slightly different from other herbs on this list. It helps draw out foreign agents, boil, and splinters from the body. It can also help you to deal with inflamed guts membrane conditions. It is best to use it with hot water for the right consistency and result. You can hold it on the affected site until you experience significant relief. And the herb is suitable for both internal and external use.
14. Calendula It is common to get wounds and cuts at home. Aside from preventing bleeding and ensuring pain relief, it is also vital to prevent infections. Calendula is one of the best herbs that can help you to protect your wound and injuries from external infections. You can add the herb's powdery form to

hot water before using it to compress the wound. So, it prevents infection and aids speedy healing of wounds. You can even repeat its application a few times after the injury.

15. Gotu Kola Collagen is a vital element in wound healing. Gotu kola works by inducing collagen synthesis in wound areas. The herb has been in use for many centuries, particularly in India and other parts of Asia. This herb is available and useful in liquid extract, tea, or compress tincture. Also, the herb is available in shops, and getting it is hassle-free.

The Ayurvedic First Aid Tips

We all have a first aid tin at home packed with plasters, antiseptic cream & wipes, antacids, anti-inflammatory, pain killing drugs, etc. But what if you wanted to achieve a quick first aid fix naturally?

With just a little know how and patience you can easily find a remedy from within your own kitchen cupboards for so many common conditions.

Here are 8 of my favourite first aid natural remedies. Sore throat: A classic combination is honey and turmeric, mix a dessert spoon of both of these ingredients and suck on the spoon. Also gargle with warm water, turmeric and rock salt. Just watch the results.

Cuts & grazes: apply a paste of honey and turmeric, this is both anti-septic and will help the wound heal super fast. Burn - immediately run through cold water, then apply a paste of fresh aloe vera gel with a pinch of turmeric powder. Once the initial sting subsides you can continue with aloe or apply a little ghee or coconut oil with rose and sandal wood to enhance the cooling effect.

Headache - for a temporal headache, apply a paste of dry ginger to the forehead and lie down for about 5-6 minutes, remove the paste and take some rest. Headaches are often a sign of dehydration, so increase your water intake. A local massage to the forehead, temples, neck and shoulders can help loosen up tightness that can contribute to headaches.

A downward dog yoga pose can help increase the blood supply the head. Acid reflux - Often caused by an increase in the pitta dosha; a pitta pacifying diet would be advised. Correct diet will play a very important role in managing this condition. As a quick home remedy try chewing on fennel seeds after food or drinking aloe vera juice.

Drink a small glass of buttermilk with a pinch of asafoetida, turmeric and fenugreek with or directly after the meal.

Indigestion - Simple, avoid overeating! Since we live in an indulgent society and want a quick fix and you can have pomegranate juice or seeds or drink hot water infused with lemon juice.

Fasting is also a favourable option to allow the digestive system to recover. Drink buttermilk after the meal to improves digestion with cumin seeds and a little salt. Cough - For dry cough take a decoction of liquorice root.

For a cough with mucous take a decoction of turmeric, ginger, lemon, pinch of black pepper and a squeeze of honey once cool. You can also chew on ginger root and eat a little paste of garlic.

Diarrhoea - drink a glass of buttermilk with a pinch of salt and cumin as a general remedy. A great remedy is powdered mango seed taken with honey twice a day. A mix of dry ginger, rock salt and jaggery is very effective in cases of loose motions cause by indigestion.

Food Antidotes

Most people are under the impression that Ayurveda takes a longer time to heal the damaged tissue parts and restore health and hence, it may not be effective for managing acute illnesses such as allergies, food sensitivities, or poisoning. However, this is not true. Ayurvedic treatments also involve the use of antidotes that could neutralize the toxins in the body. Here is a brief discussion about the use of ayurvedic herbs as food antidotes.

An antidote is a substance that counteracts or neutralizes a particular medicine, food, or an unpleasant sensation. Sometimes, the food we eat causes problems like nausea, vomiting, skin rashes, diarrhea, gastric trouble, and asthma.

While it is ideal to avoid overindulgence, it is hard to not give way to the temptation at all times. Other than food items, there are several other factors like excessive exposure to the sun and traveling that can also affect our well-being.

Ayurveda allows you to counter the negative effects of such factors by using natural herbs. I've listed below some of the powerful, natural antidotes that you can use to offset the 'not-so-healthy' effects of certain things.

Overindulgences & Their Antidotes

Alcohol

The worst effect of excessive alcohol consumption is on the liver cells. Alcohol can produce an adverse effect on the liver functions resulting in hepatitis, alcoholic liver disease, ascites, and finally, liver cancer.

Though the effects cannot be reversed completely, a remarkable reduction in liver damage could be achieved through the use of turmeric. It is advisable to take 1 or 2 pinches of this herb in a glass of water or add it to normal cooking as a part of your general routine.

Drinking hot water with a pinch of turmeric can also provide relief from a hangover. The stimulant and depressing effects of alcohol could be avoided by eating 1 or 2 cardamom seeds or chewing a pinch of cumin seeds.

Other herbs that can help to treat the hangover include those that can restore high energy levels and promote Ojas. Ojas refers to your vigor or vitality that forms the essence of life. Improved Ojas would enhance your digestion. It is believed to be the primary link between the consciousness and our body. It is considered the material equivalent of bliss and gives us mental clarity and resistance to disease. Natural remedies that promote Ojas and work as an antidote include honey, amla and dates.

Chocolate: In Ayurveda, chocolate is considered a classic example of 'Srota Blocker'. Srotas are the 'channels' in the body that must be kept clear in order to ensure good health and vitality. When these channels are obstructed or blocked, unpleasant symptoms appear resulting in the development of diseases.

The main culprits in chocolates are the high level of carbohydrates as well as milk solids. You can counter the bad effect of chocolates by drinking hot water with cardamom pods. The hot water would 'melt' the improperly digested foods and cardamom pods re-open the Srotas or the channels.

Seafood: Seafood is 'hot' by nature and is known to cause problems related to the digestive fire such as heartburn, acid reflux, gastritis, and indigestion. The best antidote to offset the effect of seafood is Peppermint Tea. It reduces the stomach heat and prevents unpleasant symptoms.

Red eyes: Soreness, itching, or redness of the eyes occur due to a number of reasons including infections, overuse, and sun exposure. An effective and time-tested antidote for the sore eyes caused due to the exposure to the sun is rose water eye spray.

Add 2 to 3 spoons of rose water in a glass of water and splash it on your eyes or take eye bath with cold milk. Putting sliced cucumbers on both the eyelids can also counter the effect of harsh sun rays on the eyes.

Sunburn: The best antidote to relieve the symptoms of sunburn is Aloe vera. Aloe vera gel is considered highly therapeutic for the sun-damaged skin. You may apply it regularly to prevent skin damage and hasten repair.

Motion sickness: Ayurveda recommends freshly squeezed ginger juice for reducing motion sickness. Take a 1/4 teaspoon of the ginger juice and add a little lemon juice and a pinch of salt to it. Simply lick the spoon dipped in this mixture to get rid of the sensation.

Coffee: Most people will be surprised to know that the excessive intake of coffee can cause unpleasant symptoms. Coffee contains caffeine, which over-stimulates the nervous system resulting in insomnia. Drinking a glass of warm milk or 2 to 3 glasses of warm water will counter the effect of excess caffeine in your body and will help you get an undisturbed sleep. The ill-effects of coffee can also be kept at bay by using nutmeg powder.

Besides these, there are several other substances like cheese, eggs, meat, curd, and fish that can cause a negative effect on our body. Since the adverse effects of these foods are known, it is advisable to make them wholesome by combining them with the proper antidotal foods given below:

- Eggs, in their raw forms, can increase kapha and in cooked form, can worsen pitta dosha. Counter this by adding turmeric or by eating raw onions with them.
- Cheese promotes the mucous production and congestion in the respiratory passages resulting in nose block and breathlessness. It also aggravates pitta and Kapha. You may counteract this effect by adding black pepper to it.
- Curd is also known to increase the mucus production and cause nasal congestion. Using cumin and ginger can help you take care of the ill-effects of curd.

- Ice-cream can cause severe breathing problems and nasal congestion. If taking ice-cream is inevitable, top it with cardamom and clove.
- Fish can increase pitta. Lime, coconut, and lemon are the best remedial measures to antidote the bad effects of fish.
- Legumes are known to produce gaseous distention of the abdomen. Garlic, black pepper, cloves, ginger, and chilli powder are the best antidotes for this.

The use of these antidotes can protect your health against the harmful effects of these substances and restore health.

Bibliography

Apte, V. M.: *Social and Religious Life in the Grihya Sutras*, Rawat Press, Bombay, 1954.

Baba, Pagal : *Temple of the Phallic King: The Mind of India*, Simon and Schuster, New York, 1973.

Beyer, Stephen : *The Cult of Tara: Magic and Ritual in Tibet*, University of California Press, Berkeley, 1973.

Chattopadhyaya, Sudhakar: *Reflections on the Tantras*, Motilal Banarsidass, New Delhi, 1978.

Comfort, Alex: *The Koka Shastra: and other Medieval Indian Writings on Love*, George Allen and Unwin, London, 1964.

Cozort, Daniel : *Highest Yoga Tantra,* Snow Lion Publications, New York, 1986.

De Ropp, S. R. : *Sex Energy: The Sexual Force in Man and Animals*, Corgi Books, London, 1972.

Douglas, Nik and Slinger, Penny: *Sexual Secrets: The Alchemy of Ecstasy*, Destiny Books, New York, 1979.

Eliade, Mircea: *Rites and Symbols of Initiation*, Harper Torchbook, New York, 1965.

Farrow, G. W. and Menon, I. : *The Concealed Essence of the Hevajra Tantra,* Motilal Banarsidass, Delhi, 1992.

Gambhirananda, Swami: *Brahma Sutra Shamkar Bhasya,* Adavita Ashrama, Calcutta, 1977.

Hopkins, W. E.: *Ethics of India,* Yale University Press, New Haven, 1924.

Jacobs, Hans : *Western Psychotherapy and Hindu Sadhana*, George Allen and Unwin, London, 1961.

Kaushalayan, Bhadant Anand: *Swami Vivekananda and the Great Buddha*, Buddha Bhoomi Prakashan, Nagpur 1994.

Kramrisch, Stella: *Manifestations of Shiva*, Philadelphia Museum of Art, Philadelphia, 1981.

Lessing, Ferdinand : *Introduction to the Buddhist Tantric Systems*, Motilal Banarsidass, Delhi, 1993.

Majumdar, A. K.: *Caitanya: His Life and Doctrine*, MacMillan, Bombay, 1969.

Mulin, G. H. : *Meditation on the Lower Tantras*, Library of Tibetan Works and Archives, Dharamsala, 1983.

Narayanananda, Swami : *The Kundalini Shakti*, Rishikesh, 1950.

Panikkar, K. M.: *Himdnism and the West*, Panjab University Publication, Chandigarh, 1964.

Payne, E. : *The Shaktas: An Introduction and Comparative Study*, Calcutta, 1933.

Rajneesh, Bhagwan : *Tantra: The Supreme Understanding,* Chidvilas, Boulder, 1993.

Ranade, R. D.: *Mysticism in Maharashtra*, MacMillan, Delhi, 1933.

Ranganathananda, Swami: *Science and Religion*, Advaita Ashram, Calcutta, 1978.

Rastogi, Navjivan : *The Krama Tantricism of Kashmir*, Motilal Banarsidass, Delhi, 1979.

Schmidt, Toni : *The Eighty-Five Siddhas*, Stat Etnografiska Museum, Stockholm, 1958.

Singer, June : *Androgyny: Toward a New Theory of Sexuality,* Anchor Press/ Doubleday, New York, 1976.

Singh, Kirpal: *Jap Ji: The Message of Guru Nanak*, MacMillan, Delhi, 1964.

Sircar, D. C. : *The Sakta Pithas*, Indological Publishers and Booksellers, Delhi, 1973.

Taylor, A. E.: *Elements Metaphysics*, Methnen & Co., London, 1924.

Trevor Leggett: *Realization of the Supreme Self: the Bhagavad Gita Yogas*, Kegan Paul International, London, 1995.

Van Kooij, K. R. : *Worship of the Goddess According to the Kalikapurana*, E. J. Brill, Leiden, 1972.

Vidhushekhara Bhattacharya: *The Agamasastra of Gaudapada*, Motilal Banarsidass, Delhi, 1989.

Wayman, Alex : *Yoga of the Guhyasamaja Tantra*, Motilal Banarsidass, Delhi, 1977.

Wheeler, Robert Eric Mortimer: *Civilization of the Indus Valley and Beyond*, McGraw-Hill, New York, 1966.

Winternitz, M. : *Notes on the Guhyasamaja Tantra and the Age of the Tantras*, IHQ, Calcutta, 1933.

Woodroffe, Sir John : *The World as Power*, Ganesh and Co., Madras, 1966.

Yogananda, Paramahansa, *Autobiography of a Yogi,* Self-Realization Fellowship, Los Angeles, 1946.

Yogananda, Swami : *Autobiography of a Yogi,* Fellowship, Los Angeles, 1946.

Zimmer, Heinrich: *Myths and Symbols in Indian Art and Civilization*, Joseph Campbell, Delhi, 1946.

Zvelebil, Kamil. V. : *The Poets of the Powers*, Rider and Co., London, 1973.

Index